DESTINED TO LIVE
ONE WOMAN'S WAR, LIFE, LOVES REMEMBERED

Editors' note

The Foundation Memorial to the Murdered Jews of Europe would like to thank HarperCollinsPublishers Australia for granting permission to publish this English language edition in Germany. Extracts from the German version have been translated into English for this edition by Caroline Pearce.

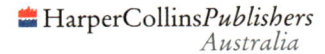

HarperCollins*Publishers*
Australia

The Foundation Memorial to the
Murdered Jews of Europe is funded by the

Federal Government Commissioner
for Culture and the Media

upon a decision of the German Bundestag

Credits

Edited by Ulrich Baumann and Uwe Neumärker
Foundation Memorial to the Murdered Jews of Europe

2nd edition, 2018
Chief editor: Uwe Neumärker

Cover photo: Borysław, 20 January 1943: Sabina Haberman (centre), her brother Josef (first from right) and their friends Imek Eisenstein (second from right), Ducek Egit (second from left) and Rolek Harmelin (first from left), all wearing armbands with the Star of David on them.
© Sabina van der Linden-Wolanski
Typesetting, formatting and lithography:
buschfeld.com – graphic and interface design, Berlin
Printing and binding: Bonifatius GmbH, Paderborn

All rights reserved.

ISBN: 978-3-942240-21-5

This publication is listed in the catalogue of the German National Library. Bibliographical details are available at http://dnb.ddb.de.

www.stiftung-denkmal.de

Sabina van der Linden-Wolanski with Diana Bagnall

DESTINED TO LIVE
ONE WOMAN'S WAR, LIFE, LOVES REMEMBERED

Foundation Memorial to the Murdered Jews of Europe
Edited by Ulrich Baumann and Uwe Neumärker

Stiftung
Denkmal für die
ermordeten Juden
Europas

In loving memory of my parents, Sala and Fischel Haberman, my brother, Josek, and grandparents, Chana and Joel Kulawicz.

And for my children, Josephine and Phillip: having you made sense of my life.

CONTENTS

Preface by the former Federal President Prof. Dr. Horst Köhler 7
Foreword by the former Australian Prime Minister Kevin Rudd 9
Prologue 12
I. Growing up 15
II. The Russian occupation 25
III. Pogrom 31
IV. Belzec 40
V. Imek 48
VI. August *Aktion* 56
VII. Ghetto 60
VIII. Hiding 66
IX. Discovery 71
X. The camp 74
XI. The forest 81
XII. The end of the war 88
XIII. Liberation 93
XIV. Desperate times 106
XV. Marriage 115
XVI. Róża 121
XVII. Janek 127
XVIII. Zdenek 131
XIX. Bondi 140
XX. Divorce 147
XXI. Hildebrand´s trial 152
XXII. Adrian 158
XXIII. Queen Street 164
XXIV. Kjeld 169
XXV. Remembering 180
XXVI. Berlin 186
XXVII. Sabina´s speech on 10 May 2005 193

Living and Surviving in Central Europe from 1939 to 1948:
A Historical Afterword 196

Acknowledgments 209
Acknowledgments for the German Edition 210
Bibliography 212
Permissions' acknowledgments 213
Picture Credits 214
Photos .... 215 – 245
Map 246

1: Berlin, 10 May 2005: Federal President Prof Dr Horst Köhler and Sabina following the inauguration of the Memorial to the Murdered Jews of Europe

Der Bundespräsident

Berlin, den 26. August 2009

Sehr geehrte Frau Wolanski,

mir ist gut die bewegende Stunde in Erinnerung, als im Mai 2005 das Denkmal für die ermordeten Juden Europas feierlich eingeweiht wurde. Sie haben damals stellvertretend für alle Überlebenden der Shoah ein Grußwort gesprochen, das alle Zuhörer und auch mich tief berührt hat. Ihre Worte haben damals nicht nur das unermessliche Leid in Erinnerung gerufen – Sie haben auch zur Versöhnung aufgerufen. Ihr Grußwort selber war ein Ausdruck von Mut zur Vergebung und Versöhnung. Dafür bin ich Ihnen bis heute dankbar.

Jetzt erscheinen Ihre Erinnerungen in deutscher Übersetzung. Sie sind aus dem gleichen Geist und aus der gleichen Gesinnung geschrieben wie Ihr Grußwort. Ich wünsche Ihrem Buch Erfolg und aufmerksame Leser. Möge es ein Beitrag dazu sein, dass das Schreckliche, von dem Sie schreiben, sich nie mehr wiederholt. Möge es gerade auch den nachwachsenden Generationen ihre Verantwortung für ein friedliches und gerechtes Zusammenleben aller Menschen zeigen.

Mit freundlichen Grüßen

Ihr Horst Köhler

The Federal President – Berlin, 26 August 2009

Dear Ms. Wolanski,

I clearly remember the touching moment, when the Memorial to the Murdered Jews of Europe was opened in May 2005. At that time you – representative for all survivors of the Shoah – spoke a greeting, which moved all listeners and me very much. Your words not only commemorated the immeasurable suffering – you also appealed for conciliation. Your greeting was an expression of bravery for forgiveness and conciliation. Therefore I am very grateful.
Now a German translation of your commemorations will be released. They are written in the same esprit and with the same attitude as your greeting. I wish your book success and alert readers. May it be a contribution so that the terrible things you write about will never every happen again. May it especially point to the younger generation their responsibility for a peaceful and fair life together with all human beings.

With best regards – Yours Horst Köhler

2: Berlin, 7 July 2009: The Australian Prime Minister Kevin Rudd at the Holocaust Memorial in Berlin

PRIME MINISTER
CANBERRA

FOREWORD FOR 'DESTINED TO LIVE'

Sabina Wolanski's incredible story is an inspiration to us all. Faced with unimaginable horror, Sabina's courage and determination to survive is a testament to the power of humanity. The power to overcome the worst of adversity, but also the power to reconcile, to love and to heal.

In her profoundly moving speech at the opening of the Memorial to the Murdered Jews of Europe in Berlin in 2005, Sabina spoke about the ultimate triumph of the human spirit against brute force. I visited the same memorial in Berlin in 2009, and Sabina's message of bravery and hope remains undiminished. It is a reminder to us all that we must never let this happen again.

But Sabina's story is about more than just survival. It is also about her courage to rebuild her life after everything she had endured. Sabina came to Australia in 1950, like many survivors who left behind unspeakable atrocities in Europe to begin a new life on our shores. Sabina has lived a full, rich and adventurous life in Australia, raising a family and running successful businesses. She has made a great contribution to the vitality and vibrancy of our great nation.

I offer my warmest congratulations to Sabina on the German translation of her book, and I thank her for sharing her life and experiences with us.

The Honourable Kevin Rudd MP
Prime Minister of Australia

Alas for those who cannot sing, but die with all their music in them. Let us treasure the time we have, and resolve to use it well, counting each moment precious – a chance to apprehend some truth, to experience some beauty, to conquer some evil, to relieve some suffering, to love and be loved, to achieve something of lasting worth.

Sha´arei Teshuva – Gates of Repentance

PROLOGUE

I grew up in the foothills of the Carpathian Mountains with the smell of oil in my nostrils, dreaming of Paris. My mother was a romantic. Her own exuberant nature was channelled into running the wholesale business that she and my father owned and into caring for her children. We lived in Borysław, a hard-living oilfields town in eastern Poland, and to my knowledge she never travelled beyond our backwater province. But she found it utterly natural to suppose that her saucy little daughter, Binka, would one day take the French capital by storm.

I did get to Paris, and as my mother had promised, found it was my kind of town. That was in 1948, and the doors of the world were just beginning to open for me. I was young and in love. I was intoxicated by the air. I could breathe without fear. It wasn't the smell of oil I wanted out of my nostrils when I left Poland, but the paralysing stench of fear and death. Yet even as I was joyfully diving into a swimming pool on the banks of the Seine, wearing that season's sensation, the bikini, I would have given anything to be able to go home to Mama. Mama was dead, as were my brother and my father, and any possibility of life for me in Poland. Hitler's Third Reich had seen to that.

As the decades rolled over I returned to Paris from my new home in Australia many many times. It still is my kind of town. How strange then, how surreal, that now, at this end of my life, when I look at what it all adds up to, it is Berlin, not Paris nor Sydney, to which I must give the starring role.

My mother never spoke to me much of Berlin, though German was her second language and German culture almost as familiar to her as our own Polish culture. Her favourite brother, Adolf, lived in Berlin between the two wars. I remember him coming to Borysław to say goodbye when he emigrated to America in 1936. By the time my parents were ready to follow him, it was too late. Our family stayed in Borysław, and what came next is, as they say, history.

My mother, my father and my brother were murdered by Hitler's brutes. I, Sabina, daughter of Sala and Fischel Haberman, and younger sister of Josek, survived. More than survived. I›ve lived, and lived well. And though I never took Paris by storm, I did take Berlin. I took it not as a pianist, nor as a writer, as Mama and I had dreamed, but as a Holocaust survivor. It wasn't something I expected to happen. When the war was over, I wanted to forget that I had ever shared the Jewish fate. Who didn't? I was never much interested in Judaism as a religion and even now I can't be sure what it means to be a Jew. But I was born to Jewish parents in 1927 in Poland, which made it my lot, as an adolescent girl, to confront the worst manifestation of evil in human history, and now that I am growing old I feel an urgent need to remember my and my family's part in that history. Remembering is painful, but not as painful as forgetting, and being forgotten.

So it was that on 10 May 2005, I stepped up to a podium to speak at the opening of Germany's Memorial to the Murdered Jews of Europe in the heart of Berlin. After much hand-wringing, the Germans chose to build their memorial, an open and permanent display of their shame and guilt, a stone's throw away from where Hitler had his bunker. Beneath the memorial's vast undulating field of stone pillars there's an information centre that documents the history of the Holocaust and, within it, our story, the story of the Haberman family of Borysław, together with the stories of 14 other families of European Jews.

Mama, can you imagine? I, little Binka, spoke for the Nazis' six million Jewish victims and for those of us who survived their systematic torture and slaughter. If you could have seen me that day ... Graciously smiling and shaking hands, making small talk – in English to the German foreign minister and the Israeli ambassador, in German to the German chancellor and the president of the parliament, the Bundestag – before taking my place in the front row. I don't know if you'd call it double vision, but while I was waiting my turn to speak, I could see what was happening in our town during the war. But Mama, I was in Berlin, in the lion's den. I wasn't frightened, not any more. Nervous, yes, and apprehensive, but not frightened. I knew why I was there and what I had come to do.

My given name on the programme was Sabina van der Linden, a name which belonged to the man I call my third husband (but that's a story for later). My two adult children, who carry the name Wolanski, the name of my second husband, their father, were there in Berlin with me, with their children, my grandchildren. My fourth husband, a gentle Dane whose name I have never taken, was there too. I would have liked to call myself Sabina Haberman, but the time for that was long past. During the years when I hid my Jewish identity I was Sabina Kulawicz, the name of my maternal grandparents. I clung to it for many years after the Russians liberated our town. For years afterwards I didn't admit to being Jewish. When I rose to speak in Berlin that day it was as a longtime exponent of the art of disguise.

I began my speech with these words: »Not even in my wildest dreams could I have dreamed of this extraordinary day.« What I didn't say was that for many years the only dreams I had were nightmares, and that as a rule, I like to leave the past where it belongs. There is a Polish proverb ›Co było a nie jest nie pisze się w rejestr‹ [whatever was is not now]. I have a talent for living in the present for which I am deeply grateful. But this was a time for looking back.

The media reported my words around the world, highlighting where I said that I did not believe in collective guilt. I borrowed the thoughts of the great writer and Nobel Peace Prize winner Elie Wiesel: The children of the killers are not killers, he wrote. His notion that the children of killers should not take the blame for their elders' crimes, but are responsible for what they do with the memory of those crimes was not just a vague idea to me. My deep friendship with the daughter of an SS officer over four decades had helped to bring me to this understanding.

As a girl, I was always writing. I kept a succession of diaries during the war, mostly in the cheap notebooks we used for schoolwork. Miraculously, I still have a few of these diaries, or fragments of them, as well as precious photographs of my family, and letters written to me by my brother while I was living under a false identity. I don't know to this day how that is possible. If anybody had found these documents which identified me as Jewish, I would have been killed instantly, no questions asked. I didn't look back at my diaries until very recently. I couldn't bring myself to. But as I have allowed myself to read, I remember how, even as our world closed in around us, my brother and I and his friends, who were my friends too, would talk about what we'd do if we survived. We wanted to study. We made plans for our lives. We understood the hopelessness of our situation, but still we tried to think and behave like normal young people. I'm a bit embarrassed re-reading a letter which Josek sent to me when I was hiding with a Christian family in May 1943.

He tells me of progress on the bunker he and his friends were clandestinely preparing and writes of what was happening around us — an impending Aktion (that dreadful word which strikes fear into me even now), the approaching Russian front, and of four Gestapo officers having been killed in our provincial capital, Lwów.

Then, he writes: I have ordered gloves for you, and also eau de cologne. In the middle of everything, I was asking for gloves and eau de cologne! I was something. I haven't changed. I still need my comforts.

My mother once told me that while I was not beautiful, I had salt and pepper. I didn't know what she meant. She told me I would find out one day. Today she might say that I had sex appeal. I liked being around boys, and as a woman I have always enjoyed the company of men. But I think she was talking about my joie de vivre which could never be completely extinguished, even on that terrifying night when I was flushed out of the hiding place my brother and his friends built and thrown into a filthy police cell to await execution at dawn.

My longtime friend Róża, whose cool intelligence has drawn me like a magnet all my life, once sharply admonished me for »not understanding the difference between living life and having a good time«. I have tried to do both. My mother too was a woman with a zest for life. She was murdered, while I survived in order to live, and to live well, as she dreamed I would.

I. GROWING UP

Borysław nestles into the rounded hills of the lower Carpathians amongst beautiful, deep forests that were once considered its best asset (Borysław literally means famous forests). For all I know, the Ukrainians who live there now may still enjoy the region's natural beauty, as we once did. As children, we holidayed in summer in nearby mountain villages with cool rushing rivers, and in winter we skied close to town on powdery slopes (Borysław sits at around 900 m above sea level). But there's not much left of the town itself as I knew it, except for its wide streets that straggle on kilometre after kilometre, as they always did. Western Ukraine, for all the fecundity of its soil and its much-vaunted democratic spirit, is these days a dirt-poor corner of

Europe, and the vital juices of Borysław, once synonymous with Poland's oil industry, have long been sucked dry.

In 1939, Borysław had a population of around 45,000. Roughly speaking, about one-third was Jewish, with the balance shared between Poles and Ukrainians. The borders in this trauma zone of Europe have been rubbed out and redrawn so many times and old enmities are stained deep in its soil. But I can honestly say that until war broke out I was blissfully unaware of the volatile ethnic mix in our town, and its potential for bloody mayhem. If I had been older, I might have been better prepared. I might have known that at the end of the 18th century, when Poland was partitioned between three great powers, Borysław became part of Galicia, the Austro-Hungarian province, which linked ethnically Ukrainian towns and cities in the east with purely Polish towns and cities in the west. Galicia had a rich Jewish heritage (important towns like Crakow, Przemyśl and Lwów had been settled by Jews in the 14th century), but enduring ethnic conflict came with the territory. At the end of World War I, the Soviet Red Army, Ukrainian nationalists and Polish troops fought terrible battles over this corner of Eastern Europe and tens of thousands of Jews caught in the battle zone were massacred. A 1921 treaty – the Treaty of Riga – gave most of Ukraine to the Soviet Union, while the newborn Polish state took the territory of Galicia, essentially western Ukraine. This left the Ukrainian nationalists out in the cold, a ticking political time bomb of which I was largely ignorant.

In my defence, I was young, and oblivious to much beyond my immediate circle of family and friends. I knew that our family was relatively prosperous, and that my father was a prominent figure in town. He was the director of a bank, and a wholesale merchant trading in flour, rice and sugar. My mother worked as hard as my father in the business, and we had a maid and, later, a cook to help with the household. Of course I knew that we were Jewish, but at that time, prewar, it was hardly central to my identity. We weren't a religious family. I don't remember our family going to the synagogue except on special holy days, though my parents never worked on the Sabbath. That was the custom. All Jewish businesses in Borysław were closed on Saturday. In a small town, everybody knew each other, and it was prudent to keep up appearances even if one were not, strictly speaking, a believer. If, for example, a woman bought non-kosher meat, within five minutes everyone would know and people who were religious would stop doing business with her husband. I suppose my parents must have kept a kosher home, probably in deference to my mother's parents who were observant. I have a studio photograph of my maternal grandparents, given to me by a cousin in Argentina, where they're dressed in their Sabbath best; she wearing a wig as was the custom for Orthodox Jewish women, he a yarmulke. For me, Saturday was special because I loved having my mother at home. Every morning when I was very young, before I learned to count the passing of the days, I would get up and ask, »Mama, is today Saturday?« She would say, »Not today, darling. I will tell you when Saturday comes.«

When I was older I went to school on Saturday. Observant Jews don't even write on the Sabbath, but my brother and I went to Polish state schools. At home we spoke Polish, the language of the poetry I most treasure. For a short time, when I was about 10 or 11, I had Hebrew lessons, but all that sticks in my memory is a rhyming verse which, translated, means, »Bina, Bina, go to the corner.« I never learned to speak Yiddish. If my parents didn't want my brother and me to understand what they were saying, they would speak to each other in German. For my parents, as for other educated Poles of their generation who had grown up under Vienna's influence, Germanic culture epitomised civilisation as they knew it. For me, it was different. I was born on Polish territory, in the Polish republic. I was a patriot. I remember the day that our Polish hero, the soldier-statesman Marshal Józef Piłsudski, died in May 1935. I wore a black armband and cried along with everyone else.

Borysław wasn't just any Polish town. It had its own raison d'etre. Its currency was oil and its derivatives, profit and jobs. People came to Borysław to make their fortunes out of the black goo that seeped out of the ground and floated on the river Tyśmienica, which ran through the centre of town. (I say river, but it was normally only about 15 cm deep.) I remember seeing poor people mixing sticky oily muck in their hands with sawdust. They hawked the lumps as fuel. There was oil in the pores of our town.

The oil rush started slowly in the 1840s with the discovery of ozokerite, a waxlike fossil paraffin. At first, small landholders dug deep pits and shafts by hand and laboriously extracted and processed the soil wax from the rocks. It was used for making candles and soap. But no-one got rich doing this. It was the discovery of crude oil at the moment when the world was developing its insatiable appetite for the stuff that transformed what was a little mountain hamlet into a busy, dirty boom town. From the mid 1850s people started to pour into Borysław. One of the first oil rigs in the world was built in Borysław in 1861, based on the work of pioneer oil researcher Ignacy Lukasiewicz, after whom the street we lived on was named. As oil drilling became more mechanised, large banks and foreign companies bought up land in expectation of huge profits.

Borysław's geographical spread made it the third largest town in Poland in terms of territory after Warszawa and Lodz, but unlike those great cities, it wasn't built to last. It was a jerry-built frontier town known for its wooden footpaths and muddy streets. When it rained or when snow melted in spring, the gutters would overflow and an oily sludge covered the footpaths, staining shoes and making it difficult to walk.

Borysław wasn't laid out like a traditional medieval town with a town square and a town hall and streets radiating outwards from the centre. It had a long main street leading south towards the mountains, crossing the Ty mienica, and another street which crossed it at right angles. At the centre of town there was a bridge where young people met and men leaned against railings waiting to be hired for odd jobs.

Outsiders sneered at Borysław. It was a dump, a hovel, they said. There was a saying that people lived in Drohobycz (the neighbouring town, about 11 kilometres away, and our region's administrative centre), made their money in Borysław, but spent it in Vienna – a train ran once a week between Borysław and Vienna. Still, those of us who lived there, townspeople like my parents and their families who also profited from the oil money (though not so much as to be able to go shopping in Vienna), were fond of our home town. It was rough around the edges, but it had certain charms. When London was still lit by smudgy gas lamps, Borysław's hundreds of oil well towers were strung with electric light bulbs, and at night our small town sparkled like a city of skyscrapers.

By the time I was born in 1927, the Romanian oilfields had stolen Poland's thunder as Europe's main centre of crude oil exploration, production and refining. But the Drohobycz-Borysław area was still vital to Poland, supplying the bulk of the country's oil and oil products. For those who came to conquer, it was a valuable prize, a town marked out for special consideration. Not so special though that the Nazis and their collaborators refrained from ripping out its Jewish heart. They simply did so more slowly, so as to keep oil pumping into the war machine for as long as possible. Then, when the spoils of war delivered the town into the hands of Soviet ›liberators‹, they crushed what was left of its soul. Tadeusz Wróbel, an engineering professor from Warszawa who has devoted his retirement to chronicling the fortunes of the home town he left in 1945, called his first book *Borysław Doesn't Laugh Any More*.

My childhood was full of laughter. I was the baby of the family, born three years after my brother, Josek. I was very spoilt. I was also high-spirited and liked to do things my way. »No, no, no. I'll do it myself«, I'd tell my mother firmly if she offered to help me. There's a lovely Polish poem about a little girl called Zosia, whose name rhymes with samosia, which means myself. This little girl, like me, was very willful and the poet calls her *Zosia, samosia,* which is what my mother called me.

My parents were not from Borysław, though my father, Fischel Haberman, was born not far away in Drohobycz. His younger brother, Joshua, lived in our town and ran a small delicatessen. This uncle had a wife and a son, Benjamin (known as Benio), but our two families were never close and I knew nothing else about my father's wider family. I wasn't interested in him at all as a child. I found him stern, and remote, though with hindsight I expect he was a typical middle-class European man of his time. After our main meal at midday we children had to be quiet so he could sleep. I always thought of him as elderly, though of course he wasn't — he was 29 when I was born. I certainly never thought of him as handsome. I know this, because I remember thinking that my friend Ilka's father was extremely handsome. I think my father probably adored me, and even preferred me to my brother, who sometimes got the rough end of his discipline. When he went away on buying trips he would often bring me back little treats, and nothing for my brother. But I had eyes only for Mama. Mama, whose soft dark grey cardigan I always kept close to me when she herself could not be, its fine wool holding in its fibres the comfort of her scent, a light floral fragrance of the kind I myself have always preferred. My mother, Sala, and my brother, Josek, were my ground and my sky.

When I was born, our family lived in a modest little house beside the Borysław police station. I found the house when I briefly visited the town in 2006. Nothing much had changed.

Red foxgloves and the last of summer's tall yellow flowers were in bloom against peeling pink walls. Around the back was a chicken run, and a garden planted with corn, potatoes and beans. The wooden fence against which Mama, Josek and I are standing in a very early photograph I have is still there, or at least a fence just like it. I am four or five in this photograph, and have a cheeky grin on my face. In the background you can just see our friend and neighbour, Jurek Staniszewski, who was the same age as Josek, peeking through his hands and his little hat into our garden. We were close friends. Josek and I used to celebrate Christmas with Jurek and his parents. I loved Christmas trees and I loved going to midnight mass when you could see snow floating in the night sky, beautiful lazy flakes, and hear your steps in the crispness of the fresh fall. And of course I loved presents. The Staniszewskis always had gifts for my brother and me.

Jurek and his family lived on top of the police station. We children used to play together in the yard at the back of the station, where there was a swing. I remember playing a game where we were on a ship. Josek and Jurek were both captains, and I was the cabin boy. I wasn't happy about this. Why couldn't I be a captain? I remember another game probably a few years later because I was in possession of a bit of pocket money, where my brother persuaded me to hand over my money to him. He told me that he would bury it next to his money, and that together his money and mine would make children. I gave him my money, and then I waited, and waited, and waited. Finally I asked him, »Well, what happened? Where are the children?« He said, »I don't know.« I said we should go and find out. So we went to where he'd buried the money, and there was nothing. No money. »Well?« I said. He shrugged. »Maybe they died or something.«

Maybe they did. If my brother said so, I was willing to believe it. He was my god. Anything he did, I wanted to be doing too. I usually got what I wanted. When I decided it was time to go to school, because my friend Ilka, who lived across the road and was a year older than me, was already at school, I carried on so much that my mother relented and walked me down there. The headmistress explained that I was too young to enrol, but my mother pleaded with her to let me sit in the classroom. So I went to school for a year before I was officially enrolled. I was very happy to be learning.

If I was a little nuisance, I was also a much-loved one. I remember going to visit my grandparents in the country. We didn't go often because they lived several hours west by train in Hureczko, a tiny village near Przemyśl, a trading city on the river San, southeast of Crakow. My grandparents kept cows and horses, and employed a few people in the fields. At midday, they sat down to eat with their workers. My grandmother Chana sat at one end of a long table and I sat on my grandfather Joel's knee at the other end. I considered myself a very important person. I don't remember having a conversation with my grandfather, but I remember being mesmerised by his incredible blue eyes, just like my mother's. All my life I have had a weakness for light-coloured eyes like hers.

My grandparents lived in a small country cottage, which had a certain rustic charm with its thatched roof and window frames painted white and decorated with potted colour. I remember when they first had electricity installed they put it in the barn for the animals. They shared the house with their eldest son, Bernard, and his family. My grandparents had two rooms. The first room was the kitchen, where they also ate, and the second room was the bedroom. If I loved the sweet little biscuits my grandmother made especially for me, I loved the bedroom even more. I slept with my grandmother in one of the two beds. I remember beautiful white starched pillowcases, the pillows stacked from large to small on top of each other. A traditional Polish ceramic tile oven stood in the corner and there were lovely carpets on the floor. The branches of an apple tree gently brushed the window pane. Underneath the window was an enormous trunk in which my grandmother kept her special things. Sometimes she allowed me to look inside.

When my grandmother came to visit us in Borysław she would bring fresh eggs and butter because she disapproved of the processed butter my mother bought. My mother was a country girl at heart. She had this wonderful habit of buying the most expensive butter, taking it out of the packet, putting it in water, adding salt and churning it as she had done as a girl. But there was nothing of the country girl in me. My mother accepted that, though my grandmother couldn't quite believe what she had on her hands. I showed no aptitude for riding, and unlike my brother, who wanted to study agronomy, I had no interest in things that grew in the fields or garden. I remember her pulling me out of the fresh hay in the barn, telling me it was dangerous, that if I fell asleep in its heavenly comfort I might die from breathing in its toxic gases. I was a city miss, raised in a large apartment with running water (although only cold, not hot), elegant custom-made furniture, and a maid to wash and braid my long thick hair and lace up my boots. (By the time I was five or six my parents' business was prospering. They had bought a building a little further down on the same road as our first home, and ran their shop on the ground floor, while we lived above it.) I had my own account at a coffee shop where I could take my friends for hot chocolate and cakes. I had new dresses made for me twice a year by a woman who came to the house to sew. I learned to play piano. I had books to read. One of my favourite places to read was in the back of the shop sitting on top of a big sack of sugar or rice (flour would have been too dirty) and leaning against another, with my feet dangling down. My mother always knew where to find me.

Even before I started school, she began to teach me the lessons that would stay with me all my life. The first was that people who had more than others had a responsibility to share what they had with those who had less. On Fridays, she and our cook would bake huge trays of bread to give away for the Sabbath to poor Jews, of whom there were many in Borysław. (She knew the pickpockets around town well enough to shame them into returning our maid Kasia's watch when they stole it.) Even under Nazi rule, when we Jews were non-people, stripped of all our valuables and more, she could find people much hungrier than us to help.

I aspired to be as kind and generous as my mother, but I wasn't like her at all. I was a selfish little girl. I remember getting a new dress, a very ornate dress in the latest style, which I disliked intensely. There was a girl at school called Klara whom I knew was poor, and I saw an excellent opportunity to impress my mother. I decided to give this dress to Klara. I wrapped it carefully and took it around to her home. She was astonished. I told her I hadn't wanted to hurt her feelings by giving it to her at school, and delicately explained to her, as I thought my mother would want me to, that I had another dress and that I thought she would like this one.

There was some occasion soon after when my mother looked for the dress and, not being able to find it, asked me where it was. I told her, »I've given it away to Klara. She didn't have a nice dress, so I thought I'd give it to her.«

My mother paused. Then she said to me, »That's really very lovely of you. But one dress is not enough. You should give her another dress, so she can have a choice of what to wear.« She picked out from my wardrobe the dress that I loved more than any other. »I think you should give her this dress«, she said.

I knew exactly what I'd done wrong. I took the other dress, the one I loved, and gave it to Klara. When I came home, I cried and cried. When I was ready, my mother said to me, »I know that hurt you, but when you give something, you must give it from all your heart, not because you want to get rid of it.« Then she said something else which I've never forgotten: »What the right hand gives, the left hand must not know. You never talk about it.«

I realised when I came to bring up my own children how ahead of her time she was. She was always ready to talk, about anything and everything. Her progressive ideas nearly got me expelled from school, though she wasn't the confrontational or radical type. I began menstruating early, and to help me understand what was happening to my body she allowed me to read her copy of *Ideal Marriage*, a bestseller and, in its time, controversial sex manual written by Dutch gynaecologist Theodoor van de Velde. I read only the chapter on menstruation, as Mama had directed me, and eagerly shared what I'd learned with my friends at school. Word got around, and my mother was called in by the school principal, who wanted to know if she knew what her daughter was reading. She told him she'd given the book to me, and that she didn't see what all the fuss was about. Actually, she was proud that I was talking about sex to my friends.

Mama trusted me, and in doing so, taught me that human beings flourish when they are trusted. For instance, she never questioned me about what I put on the account at the coffee shop. I was forbidden to eat ice cream because I often had throat infections. I could have bought any ice cream I wanted, but I never did. Nor did I ever go over what I knew was my monthly allowance, though the account had no stated limit. When she was no longer with me, I knew intuitively what my mother would want me to do in any given situation. She had fixed my moral compass.

II. THE RUSSIAN OCCUPATION

I think I first heard the name Hitler in 1936 when my mother's brother, Adolf, who lived in Berlin, came to say goodbye. He was going to America. I remember the adults were speaking in German, so I didn't know what they were saying, but my mother was upset and crying. I understood that this was because Berlin was so close to Poland and that the reason my uncle and his family were leaving was because of Hitler, who was in Berlin. But I was a child, and to be honest, I was ignorant of the Jew-hatred fostered among Germans during the chaos of the post-First World War period.

About half the German-Jewish population (around 230,000 people) fled Nazi persecution in the years between 1933 and 1939. They emigrated mainly to the United States, Palestine and other European countries (where many would later be trapped as the Nazi invasion spread), Latin America and the open city of Shanghai, which required no visa or other documentation for entry.

News services weren't as efficient as they are now, but in the years after Hitler came to power in 1933, stories about the Nazi regime filtered through to Borysław, and made us fearful of war. The tragedy, however, was that nobody really believed the stories. Or believed them enough. I've since learned that people in our town did collect clothes and money for the thousands of Jewish refugees who faced exposure and starvation on the Polish-German border towards the end of 1938. (On 28 October, Germany expelled 17,000 Jews with Polish citizenship. The Polish police denied them entry, and Germany refused to allow them to return, leaving them stranded in makeshift pens in the frontier town of Zbąszyn, about 80 kilometres east of Frankfurt/Main.) But in general, because the tales were so horrific, it was much more comfortable to dismiss them and get on with life as usual.

Because I was young, I don't remember much at all from this time. I didn't know, for example, that in July 1938, a few months before this debacle with refugees on the Polish border, representatives of 30 governments convened in the French spa town of Evian, at the prompting of the United States, to discuss alternative havens for the hundreds of thousands of Jews who were trapped in the Greater Reich. Virtually none of these governments, though expressing their sympathy, wanted to open their doors to Europe's doomed Jews. The Australian delegate, a Colonel T. W. White, was particularly forthright in his assessment of the situation: »As we have no real racial problems, we are not desirous of importing one.« Shameful words that Australians have had plenty of time to regret, but which at the time accurately represented my adopted country's foundation principle of racial purity (the so-called White Australia Policy), and its failure to recognise its treatment of indigenous Australians as a 'racial problem'.

The thing was, that as Europe hurtled towards catastrophe, I had my own little crises to deal with. The few remnants of my diary that date from before 1939 are hopelessly innocent. I write, for example, about which of my friends I'm not talking to, and how I have defied my father and gone to school on a very windy, wintry day when he said I should stay at home.

My naivety came to an abrupt end shortly after I learned to swim in the Rybnik River in August 1939. I was 12.

Rybnik is a village at the foot of the Carpathians where year after year families from Borysław and Drohobycz, including my family, brought their children for summer holidays. The day I learned to swim, during the last normal summer of my childhood, I was playing by the river with children my own age. I was unaware that I had attracted the attention of an older girl, Róża. At 19, she wasn't someone I would have known through school. I didn't meet her until a couple of years later, when her cousin, Imek, and I became close. But I remember the incident which she describes in a brief digest of recollections she sent me when I asked for her help with this book (her daughter Joanna translated her Polish into English). I seem to have fascinated her.

»I know all the regular vacationers, but this pretty long-legged girl with exotic eyes I have never seen before. If she were just pretty, I would look once for pleasure, and take no more interest. But there is something in the way she comports herself that keeps my attention. Like all children, she naturally needs attention. But she is neither coaxing nor insistent. She treats adults like her equals, and they do not tell her to go. What is so special about the child? She is relaxed and natural as if the thought of rejection never crossed her mind.

I suddenly see that, no longer interested in the people on the beach, she is looking greedily at those moving in the water in a way unfamiliar to her. I know what's going to happen next. I can't swim, and I'll not be able to save her life when she drowns.

Luckily, an older boy, perhaps her brother, takes care of her.

Two days later I am on the beach again, and I am on the lookout for the girl. I can't find her. The crowded beach seems empty to me. Lunchtime is drawing near; the holidaymakers are leaving the river and the beach. There she is, swimming. She seems to be quite at home in the new environment. Perhaps she expects no harm here either.

The end of August 1939 is so nervous that people are cutting short their stay in Rybnik to get home as soon as possible. I lose sight of the girl and I do not even know which town she comes from.«

It wasn't my brother who hauled me out of the current. There was a group of boys swimming in the river, the Polish equivalent of a scout troop, and it was their leader who pulled me to the shore. He asked me if I wanted to learn to swim. I said I did, and that's why Róża saw me swimming like a little fish a few days later. I'm a fast learner.

The simple pleasures of my childhood, including my new-found joy in swimming, disappeared when Germany invaded Poland on 1 September 1939 and World War II began.

The German army arrived in Borysław on 18 September 1939 after a prelude of air raids and bombings. I remember soldiers riding into town on enormous motorbikes, extremely well dressed. They didn't stay long, and during that first brief German occupation, the only physical disruption I remember to our lives was that we didn't go back to school as we should have. On 29 September the Nazis and Soviets divided up Poland under the terms of the non-aggression Nazi-Soviet pact, which had been signed on 23 August by the German foreign minister Joachim von Ribbentrop and the Soviet foreign minister Vyacheslav Molotov. The Germans retreated from our town, and we in Borysław found ourselves under Soviet occupation. But we saw and heard enough about the Nazis to be afraid. In a speech he gave in the city of Radom in central Poland on 25 November 1939, the governor general of occupied Poland,

Hans Frank, told German officials: »What a pleasure finally to be able to tackle the Jewish race physically. The more that die the better.« I didn't hear about such things until later, but I was aware that many Poles were escaping from the German-occupied western and central parts of Poland. My mother's sister, Nesia, and her husband and daughter, Sala, were among them. They fled their home in the prosperous city of Katowice, about 70 kilometres west of Crakow, and came to live with us in Borysław. Katowice was heavily bombed on the first day of the war, and then on 4 September, the Nazis burned down the city's Great Synagogue. British historian Martin Gilbert, in his *Atlas of the Holocaust*, says that after Poland was partitioned, and before the border was sealed two months later, more than a quarter of a million Jews fled from the German to the Soviet side.

When the Soviets arrived in Borysław in late September 1939 they seized control of the town's oil industry, needless to say, and began to organise what looked like normal life. The power station and the gas works were fired up, the workers were called back to extract crude oil, and eventually, after some delay, we students went back to school.

I started high school that year. Our gymnasium, as we called it, was a handsome, two-storeyed building built at the peak of the town's prosperity in 1911. It's still there, looking much the same, nearly 70 years on. I remember the day I enrolled. The registrar, taking down my name, quizzed me. »Haberman. Are you a sister of Josek?« I said I was. »Are you as good as Josek?« he continued. (Josek was clever, a top student in mathematics, science and languages.) I assured him I was much better, though actually I was hopeless at mathematics and science. But I loved languages and history, and I still do.

The Russians scrapped the Polish syllabus, and introduced their own. In history, we were told that everything we had learned before was wrong. That's when I understood that history belongs to whoever wins the war. I began questioning the truth of history.

We could choose to do our lessons in Polish or Russian, but we had to learn the Russian language and study the Soviet constitution. My friend Rita Harmelin, who also emigrated to Sydney after the war, says school was better after the Russians came. Rita's a little bit older than me, and had more years at high school than I did. She remembers there being quite a few anti-Semitic teachers who had hassled Jewish students before the Russians came, but under the Soviets, such discrimination was illegal. Still, I remember a teacher called Pani Borkowa, who spoke beautiful Polish, being annoyed that her best pupils were Jewish, not Polish. That said, I was one of her favourite students.

So, we were back at school, and the Germans had gone away. But not long after, I can't remember exactly when, we had the first indication of how the war would change our lives. My father was arrested, and taken to the police station at Drohobycz. Then we had a visit from the NKVD, Stalinist Russia's much-feared secret police service, the forerunner of the KGB. They asked for my parents. My Aunt Nesia said they were away (I think my mother may have been in Drohobycz trying to secure my father's release). They told us we should contact them immediately because they had orders to evict us from our house within 48 hours. My aunt begged them to give us an extra day, and my uncle sent a telegram to my mother who came home the next day. The Soviets, who were dispossessing us so as to provide accommodation for the administration which followed the army, gave us no other place to live. We couldn't take much with us, but I remember packing in a hurry, my mind struggling to absorb the shock and disbelief. Why was someone taking my home away from me? What had we done?

Among the fragments of my diary there's an entry in which I describe our eviction.

»They took so many things – wardrobes, bedside tables, day beds, all the lights, all the carpets, the chairs – and they left us only two beds. Plus the small day bed. All our belongings, dresses, clothing, everything was tossed out onto the floor, and they said categorically that we had to leave on the date they'd given us. It's terrible. We didn't know where to go, but we had to leave. I was sleeping at my cousin's house, and then a few days later, Mrs. Begleiter [a friend of my mother's] offered us one room. This is where we live now. We don't know what will happen. Only God knows.«

Our crime was being bourgeois capitalists. My father was a banker, and my parents owned their own business and some property. Both the business and our home were confiscated. At school we were told that capitalists were people who had too much of everything. For a while I had an identity document on which I was described as daughter of capitalists, or something to that effect. I thought it was unfair. We had plenty of everything, but I knew my parents had worked extremely hard for what they owned. And I knew that my mother was a good person.

Somehow my mother managed to have my father released but the condition of his release was that he was not allowed to live or work in Borysław. In the circumstances, that was a good result. Other people like him were being transported with their families to Siberia. But with hindsight, I wish we had been taken to Siberia because then my family would have survived.

My father found work as a waiter in a spa town called Truskawiec, about 8 kilometres east of Borysław through the hills. Truskawiec was famous for a smelly blackish mineral water called *naftusia*, derived from nafta, which in Polish means oil. People bathed in it to cure their ailments, and also drank it. During my father's time there, the town had a certain faded elegance, but these days it is a vulgar and overdeveloped Ukrainian resort town, visited mainly by Ukrainians, Russians and Poles.

Once my father had a job, the family was allocated accommodation in a very poor part of Borysław called Łoziny. We had one room and a kitchen. There was no space for my mother's sister and her family, so they went to live with my grandparents in Hureczko. I never saw them again. Our maid Kasia left us too. I had to learn to lace my own boots. My mother took over the job of washing and plaiting my long thick hair. Because the business was gone, she was at home every day, which I liked very much. We'd lost our home, but I still had my mother and brother.

I didn't miss my father while he was away in Truskawiec. I never had much to say to him anyway. In my childish eyes he was an aloof, cold man while my mother on the other hand was affectionate, gregarious, humorous, and our confidante. I thought they were a mismatch. They often fought, and my brother and I used to dream of taking Mama away from our father's tyranny as soon as we were old enough. However, my father changed after the Soviets stripped him of the props of his business and social status. In some senses they broke him, and after that it was my mother who held our family together.

I have a letter written by my mother to her brothers (for by then she had three brothers living in the United States) on 26 March 1940, in which she tells them that she has lodged application papers with the US consulate in Warsaw, but that the queue is years long. She talks of people she knows who have left, and says she hopes that my father can, if possible, go before her. »Ich kann es aushalten« [I can hold out], she writes. She knew she was the stronger of the two. By June 1940 the US Congress had shut the door on all further immigration from Europe, leaving us all to hold out.

As for Josek and me, once the fear of being transported to Siberia was over, we succumbed to a false sense of security. The war was far away, beyond our range of interest. We still went to school, saw the same friends, went skiing. We didn't have much to do with our new neighbours, but we adapted to our reduced circumstances. I don't remember the Russian occupation as an unhappy time.

It was not until 22 June 1941, when Hitler, intent on fulfilling his vision of ruling Slavic Europe, tore up the Molotov-Ribbentrop pact and launched his long-planned invasion of the Soviet Union that the war began for us.

No-one took their children on holiday to Rybnik when school ended for the summer of 1941. There was a sense of uneasiness and confusion in the air, a feeling that our life was about to unravel. My father, like many others, lost his job as the Russians began their retreat, and he returned to Borysław to live with us. By 1 July, the German army had marched back into Borysław. The next day the Nazi occupiers granted the locals leave to murder their Jewish neighbours in a 48-hour pogrom.

III. POGROM

Over the years I've tried to piece together for myself the order and magnitude of what happened after the Nazis arrived in our town, to construct a timeline, with dates of pogroms, mass shootings and deportations to death camps, the numbers of people killed and where and how. I've taken notes from historical accounts that mention Borysław, or other towns in our part of Poland. I've cross-referenced survivors' memories, even snippets of memories, where I've come across them in print, on the internet, and in correspondence. Then there is my own paper trail of diaries, or parts of them, letters and notes, extraordinary pieces of paper that make my heart stop when I think of the circumstances in which they were written, and by whom.

On the dates and numbers, I've done my best but there are many question marks still in my mind. Some dates are less contestable than others because the Nazis documented their killing schedules in such heartless detail. The numbers, too, were often clinically documented, but there's some variation between different accounts I've consulted. As I say, I've done my best.

I've tried to put some order into what follows. It's not been easy for me. I don't sleep at night after a day spent in the company of savagery and degradation and abandonment and fear. I know that my recollection will be different from, say, my friend Rita Harmelin's recollection of those horrendous years. It's not that one person is right and others are wrong. But as Rita says, it was different for all of us, even in a small town where it's easy to assume that everyone knows everything about each other. It was different if you lived half a street away from someone else, or were a different age, or came from a wealthy or poor, or religious or non-religious family. Everyone has a different view of what happened to them. It's hard enough for anyone to keep details in their mind for 60 years. Then you add in the fact that for so long we deliberately tried to excise from our memories what happened to us during the war. Rita says we have erased so much, and in particular we've erased the worst of what happened to us. We couldn't live otherwise. What we recall are the least painful things, she says. She is sceptical about the value of telling our stories. At this point in my life, I'm obviously not. I take her point, but I think the memories, however painful to retrieve, and however incomplete, should be mustered while it's still possible.

This first pogrom, which began on 3 July 1941, only two days after the German army entered our town, tore my world apart in a way that two years of Russian occupation hadn't achieved. I don't consciously remember having heard the ominous word pogrom as a child, but as soon as the pogrom started it was as though some buried collective fear kicked in. Somehow I knew that what was happening to us had happened before. This didn't lessen the shock, but I knew to be very afraid.

I don't remember many details of this first, and for me, most traumatic slaughter in our town. Maybe Rita is right. We erase the worst. But I remember the impact the pogrom had on me. Nothing in my life had prepared me for this, for the killing, the mutilation, the rape and torture which happened in the streets of our town over those 48 hours. I remember asking my mother, »Why? Why are they doing this to us?« My poor mother. What could she say to me?

We were caught unawares. Nothing was organised. No-one was prepared. We heard the sound of running and shouting in the street, and hid wherever we could; in a cellar, behind a cupboard, under a bed, anywhere, like mice scattering and darting into holes. I remember that we were hiding at home, my mother, my brother and me. Strangely, I don't remember where my father was hiding. I could hear people outside in the street, crazed mobs shouting, running from house to house and dragging terrified Jews from their hiding places in order to torment and slaughter them. Our attackers weren't German. They were people we knew, and people who knew us – Poles and Ukrainians. Mostly they were peasants who lived in the surrounding countryside, people who brought their produce to our marketplaces, and whose forested mountain hamlets, like Rybnik, we children from the towns knew as our summer playgrounds. My parents sold flour and sugar and rice to them. And there they were turning the steel blades of their sickles, ordinarily used to swish through swathes of grass and wheat, against human flesh and bone, the flesh and bone of Jewish men, women and children. Several decades later, television images from Rwanda of Hutus butchering Tutsis with machetes caused me to have flashbacks to Borysław, where Ukrainians sliced up their Jewish neighbours while German soldiers watched. In Lwów, the German soldiers filmed the pogrom they instigated and the Ukrainian masses carried out.

My mother tried to protect me, to prevent me from seeing too much. I, who had never seen a dead person before, probably peeped through the window and then didn't want to see any more. I saw men being pulled by their beards. I heard people running in the streets, being beaten, screaming. I was stunned, quite literally stunned into incomprehension. How could this be? What did we do? What did I do? I hadn't done anything wrong. I hadn't changed overnight, yet suddenly, in the eyes of our attackers, I was no longer a 14-year-old girl with great expectations but an elusive animal to be hunted down.

The body count was close to 200 when the Germans called a halt to the killing. People went into the streets to collect their dead for burial. My mother went with others to care for the injured. I don't think we personally knew any of the murdered, many of whom were Orthodox Jews, visible targets in their religious clothing. Later I was told that the Germans had lit the fuse of Ukrainian fury by letting it be known that when they had opened the cellar of the NKVD building they had found the bodies of about 50 Ukrainian nationalists. The local population accused the Jews of murder and of being Soviet sympathisers. But any excuse for a pogrom would have done.

This is when I first understood fear. Until then, I thought being afraid was what I felt when my mother was considering whether to deprive me of sweets, or when I imagined someone stealing something from us. I had never had any occasion to be afraid just because of who I was. But during those terrifying 48 hours, a different order of fear seeded itself deep in my being and I've never completely rid myself of it. I never adapted to living with fear. I survived, but I didn't adapt.

A couple of weeks after the pogrom, we Jews were ordered to wear an armband so the Germans could recognise us without having to rely on local informers. In Borysław the armband was white with a blue Star of David. Wearing one made you fair game. Jews weren't protected by the law. Anyone on the street could hit us, they could attack us, spit on us, shoot us if they felt like it. I didn't understand why I should be marked in this way, and often walked without my armband, playing silly games as a girl does. I wouldn't walk far, but my mother let me go out to see my friends. I had plenty of time on my hands because when school resumed after the summer in 1941 there was an immediate announcement that Jewish children were prohibited from attending. I was bewildered. Why weren't we allowed to go to school? I didn't know that there was no point in educating Jewish children because we Jews had no future in the Nazis' grand plan for the world. We were not considered human. Later, when I learned what the Nazis thought of us, I never gave in to thinking that way. It became even more important that I try to be a better than average human being – I desperately wanted to be cleaner, better dressed and better behaved than other people. I remember that feeling very well.

Initially, when Jews were banned from going to school, my mother organised for Josek and me to have private lessons, which was illegal. Someone came to the house. I continued to educate myself by reading. In one of my diary entries I mention a book called *Morgen ist alles besser* [Tomorrow Everything Will Be Better], published in a Polish translation. Its young author, an Austrian Jew called Annemarie Selinko, had escaped from the Nazis before the war and was living in Denmark. (She went on to write the hugely popular historical romance Désirée, about Napoleon's mistress, which was later made into a movie starring Marlon Brando and Jean Simmons.)

Every day, it seemed, there was a new notice displayed in the places where people circulated. Jews weren't allowed to own businesses, or to work for anyone else. Jews had to give away all their warm clothing, which of course included furs. Jews had to hand over their jewellery. Disobeying the decree, or holding back or hiding what was asked for, was punishable by death. I remember sticking close to my mother when an SS man came to take her jewellery. I didn't want to lose sight of her.

My mother was our lifeline. Food was becoming scarce, and while the peasants still brought in some produce to sell, there was more on offer in the countryside. Mama, who was renowned for her robustness (a Cossack is how Rita describes her), took big risks to keep our family fed, walking long distances into the surrounding villages, carrying everything on her back. Non-Jews did that too. It wasn't just Jews who starved under the Germans. There were going rates of exchange on the black market, an understanding of equivalences. I wrote in one of my diaries that I sold »a shirt for one kilogram of wheat and two kilograms of potatoes«. I remember a period when we exchanged quite a lot of clothing for food – shoes, jackets, dresses, shirts. My mother tried to stock up as much food as possible in reserve.

At the end of November 1941, there was an even bloodier pogrom, only this time it wasn't called a pogrom. It was called an *Aktion*, a German word that for me defies translation. A raid, which is the most usual

English translation, doesn't begin to convey the terror I felt, and feel even now, when I hear the word *Aktion*. The Nazi vocabulary was one of euphemisms. We learned to use them ourselves. Liquidation, transport, action, selection, resettlement, relocation, labour camp, deportation – these matter-of-fact words hid the most sinister of intents, the most evil of motives. The purpose of an *Aktion* was to swoop on communities of Jews and round them up to be murdered or transported to concentration camps.

The agents of the *Aktion* were the dreaded Einsatzgruppen, special units of the Schutzstaffel (the SS, the political police and most powerful institution in the Third Reich). The four battalion-sized Einsatzgruppen, grouped A through D, one for each of the four military fronts across the Eastern European territories, fanned out in the wake of the invading Wehrmacht (the German armed services), slaughtering »undesirables« mostly Jews. In contrast to the process of rounding up Jews in ghettos – hellish holding pens where Jews were trapped in many major Polish cities and towns – before deporting them to camps, these mobile killing squads came directly to the home communities of Jews and massacred them then and there. Moving into a town, they would ask the Judenrat – the local Jewish council set up by the Nazis in each occupied town, primarily to communicate their orders to the population – for a list of all Jewish inhabitants. If the Judenrat did not or could not supply a list, the Nazis could rely on local antiSemites to direct them to Jewish homes. Local militias were recruited to help in the dirty work of hunting down, terrorising and executing Jews. In Ukraine, there was no shortage of volunteers. Einsatzgruppe C carried out the single most concentrated massacre of the war in Ukraine, with help from local militia. Over two days at the end of September 1941, about 33,000 men, women and children were taken from the Kiev ghetto out to the Babi Yar ravine on the edge of town, stripped of their clothing and gunned down. The ravine was their grave.

Two months after that massacre, at the end of November 1941, a detachment of Einsatzgruppe C descended on our town. Many years later I read that the Germans had forewarned the Judenrat in Borysław that they needed a thousand Jews for deportation. They expressly demanded that those who were unfit to work, along with rabbis, ritual slaughterers providing kosher meat and anyone else with a religious function, be handed over to them. Apparently many people refused to comply. On 28 and 29 November 1941, the Nazis, with the help of local police and collaborators, began seizing people on the streets. At that stage there was no ghetto in Borysław, and we weren't such easy prey because our homes were spread out all around the town. Those people who were caught by the police were mainly the elderly and the sick. It seems that around 1,500 people were taken. That's a number I've come across several times. In January 1942, a month after the event, I wrote in my diary that the number was 2,000. I don't know how I knew this. What isn't disputed is that Jews were driven in trucks to the forests around Borysław, to Tustanowice and Mraźnica, and shot. They fell into mass graves they had been forced to dig beforehand. I read later that only as many victims as could be executed immediately would be transported by truck to the place of execution so people would not realise what was to happen to them until the last moment.

In towns all around us there were similar stories. Martin Gilbert's *Atlas of the Holocaust*, maps the directions of the Nazi regime's murderous currents and the death tolls, region by region, month by month, year by year. In November 1941, he identifies 1,500 people massacred in Borysław, 3,000 in Lwów, 1,200 in Stryj and 2,500 in Nadwórna, all in Galicia.

The diary entry I just mentioned is dated 1 January 1942. It marks the beginning of a series of entries written episodically over the next six months. They finish abruptly on 22 June 1942. Did I stop writing, or did I lose what I wrote? I think the latter is more likely. How did I manage to hold on to these scraps of paper? Did I carry them with me, or did I leave them somewhere, with someone? I wish I could remember. I can't. But the handwriting and the language are mine. I recognise this girl, Binka.

»I haven't written for a year: What a year it has been. So much has happened. The Russians have left and now we have German occupation. I cannot adequately describe what we have been through. The day the Russians left, they demolished everything. It was terribly frightening. Everything was burning. The sky was dark and there were explosions everywhere. But that was only the beginning.

The Germans came on 1 July 1941 and 4 and 5 July are the most horrible dates. Pogrom – my God. It was so, so terrible. About 500 Jewish people are dead. How is it possible that humans can be so cruel? That they can murder, kill and maim. For a long, long time I couldn't stop thinking about it. The terrible fear. And yet life went on.

Since 15 July we are decorated and have to wear armbands with a Jewish star. We thought perhaps we would be allowed to live a little in peace. But how little did we know.

On 28 November 1941 again the same things happened. They took people from the street and also from their homes.

My God, how to survive all this? I love life. I would like to live.

A week later, we had a visit from the ›Reiterzug‹ [cavalry platoon]. They were very polite and they didn't take anything except when one of them asked me if I could do without my ring. What could I do? Naturally, I took it off my finger and gave it to him. So now, except for some small disturbances, everything is quiet.«

I wrote again on 5 January 1942:

»I wrote down briefly what's happened until now and how it has affected me very badly. I have never come across death directly until now, and I am terrified. I don't understand it. I am so afraid of death. It is terrible to think that one will never again see flowers, or forests or the people one loves. Man is nothing. If only I could really talk to someone about it, or if someone could explain it to me. I love Klara, but Klara prefers Viva I was speaking to Klara about it, but she says it is not true. So I don't know if she doesn't really realise it herself or if she is just saying that so I won't be upset. I am sad about it because now I haven't got anybody. Ilka is in Lwów and Erna is in Drohobycz, so I am alone. [Ilka's family moved to Lwów before the war, and Erna was a friend whom I'd met on holiday in Truskawiec who lived in Drohobycz.]«

I was alone, and struggling to make sense of something which 60 years after the event strains human limits of understanding. I'd never heard of genocide, a term not coined until 1944, and no-one knew the phrase ethnic cleansing. The organised murder of millions of people because their existence offended notions of racial purity was unimaginable. Yet a fortnight after I wrote in my diary about my terror of dying, the Nazis revealed their plan to exterminate all of Europe's Jews.

Planning had begun six months earlier when Hermann Göring, founder of the Gestapo (the Nazi secret police) and commander-in-chief of the Luftwaffe (the German airforce) instructed SS officer Reinhard Heydrich to begin making »all necessary organisational, functional, and material preparations for a total solution [Gesamtlösung] of the Jewish question in the German sphere of influence in Europe«. On 20 January 1942, Heydrich convened a high-level meeting at a lakeside villa in the wealthy Wannsee district of Berlin, and laid out the Final Solution [Endlösung].

In the course of The Final Solution, he explained, the Jews would be brought »under appropriate direction to the East for labour utilisation. Separated by sex, those Jews capable of work will be led into these areas in large labour columns to build roads, where doubtless large numbers of them will fall away through natural reduction. The inevitable final remainder will have to be dealt with appropriately, since they represent a natural selection which is to be regarded as the germ cell of a new Jewish development.« The word extermination wasn't mentioned. It didn't need to be. The Nazi ideologues calculated they needed to kill 11 million Jews from more than 20 European nations to eliminate a race which they believed threatened the biological purity and strength of the ›superior Aryan race‹. Their bogus race science played into centuries of religious prejudice against Jews in Christian Europe, and was supported to varying degrees by extreme nationalism, financial insecurity and fear of Communism. The Third Reich could, and did, exploit existing anti-Semitism across Europe to secure the help of thousands of individuals in murdering Europe's Jews. While not all the Nazis' victims were Jews, as Holocaust survivor Elie Wiesel has written, all Jews were victims.

I didn't understand the odds of survival at the beginning of 1942, but by the end of the year, they were abundantly clear.

IV. BELZEC

We always say, don't we, that hope is the last thing to die? The winter of 1941/42 was particularly severe. Borysław was gripped by a typhus epidemic, which lasted several months, and many people around us were dying from starvation, poverty and disease. But another pattern began to emerge over the course of that winter, and beyond. After each massacre or deportation, there would be rumours that it was the last one. That was the incredible perfidy of the Germans. In the lull between killings, we allowed ourselves to think that maybe the worst was over, that maybe they would leave us alone now. We never stopped hoping that life would get better. No, that's not quite true. We never stopped hoping that we would be allowed to live.

Of course, we were deluded. The worst was still to come: 1942 was the year of slaughter. In his book *Ordinary Men*, historian Christopher Browning writes: »In mid-March 1942, some 75–80 % of all victims of the Holocaust were still alive while 20–25 % had perished. A mere 11 months later, in mid-February 1943, the percentages were exactly reversed.« In 1942, the German focus shifted from mass shootings in fields and forests and ravines to murder much more diabolical, a more secluded and organised form of killing Europe's Jews.

In September 1941, the Nazis had begun experimenting with large-scale gassings of Soviet prisoners of war in sealed vans. By December 1941 they were van-gassing Jewish prisoners in Chełmno nad Nerem, the death camp 60 kilometres north of Lodz. During the course of 1942, they would refine the technology of mass extermination by gas and body disposal by cremation in death camps called Belzec, Sobibor and Treblinka, and at the largest of them all, Auschwitz-Birkenau. By the end of that year, four million Jews would be murdered by the Nazis, and hundreds of Jewish communities across Europe would disappear forever. But we didn't know that at the beginning of 1942.

In Borysław we had perhaps more reason to hope than elsewhere. Or at least we convinced ourselves that we did.

The German war machine was desperate for our oil, and though the Reich government forbade the employment of Jews, the German management of what became known as the Carpathian Oil Company successfully argued that Jewish professionals – chemists and engineers, administrators and mechanics, boilermakers and drillers – were indispensable for the smooth resumption of oil extraction and refinery. In other words, there was less imperative to annihilate Jews in Borysław than there was in other places. To give them some protection against random raids by the SS and Ukrainian militia, *Carpathian Oil* workers wore a badge embroidered with the letter *R* pinned to their chest. The *R* stood for Rüstungsarbeiter [armaments' worker]. That badge gave those who wore it hope of reprieve. But what the Nazis could not have factored in was the effect that Berthold Beitz – the impeccably connected young banker whom they appointed as business manager to the Carpathian Oil Company – would have on our town's fortunes.

Beitz arrived in Borysław in July 1941 as an enthusiastic patriot, backed by the Nazi top brass, among them the architect of the Holocaust, Heydrich. He was only 27, and had been employed by *Royal Dutch Shell* for just over two years. His expertise, however, was sufficiently valued for the Reich Ministry of Economy to demand deferment of his military service. He could have stayed in his office, maintaining oil production quotas and seeing to the comfort of his wife, Elsa, and their young daughter, Barbara. But the atrocities which Beitz witnessed in Borysław – and most especially the brutal evacuation by the SS of the town's long-established Jewish orphanage on 7 August 1942, when infants were thrown out of windows and children dragged from their beds and driven barefoot to the railway station in the middle of the night – apparently turned his stomach and swayed his loyalties. He was, as Rita says, a good German, though we set the bar low. A good German was someone who, if he saw you in the street, didn't shoot you.

As the director of a strategically vital oil company, Beitz was kept in the loop by Nazi functionaries in the region who notified him in advance of impending *Aktionen*. He passed on advance warnings to his Jewish confidantes who spread the alert. He also had the right to inspect Jews who had been rounded up at the Umschlagplatz [transfer point] in order to pick suitably qualified workers, and make sure that none of his R badge workers were put on the transports to the death camps. He always kept on his person a telegram from the Oberkommando des Heeres [Army Supreme Command] which expressly stated that others should make available to him »the necessary workers to maintain oil production«. No-one knows exactly how many Jews he extricated from the transports going to the gas chambers at Belzec by claiming them as »professional workers«, but it is thought to be around 250, among them Talmudic scholars, hairdressers and tailors, some in no fit condition for physical work. Beitz is also known to have hidden Jews in his office and in his home.

Over the years, his critics (a small minority) have said his primary motive was to increase the production capacity of the German armaments industry. They said he acted only to line his own pockets and that he did not put himself at any great risk in rescuing Jewish workers for the German oil industry. But those allegations were not substantiated and in October 1973, Yad Vashem, the Holocaust Martyrs' and Heroes' Remembrance Authority in Jerusalem, honoured Beitz (by then one of the leading industrialists in post-war Germany) as one of the Righteous Among the Nations, an award given to non-Jews who risked their lives to save Jews from the Nazis. On its website, Yad Vashem states that »though he never engaged in active political opposition to Nazism, Beitz's help to the Jews of Borysław directly challenged the most crucial ideological fixation of the regime«.

I didn't know Beitz personally, but Rita did. She worked in the office of *Carpathian Oil* as a book-keeper and typist. She remembers him as the most handsome man imaginable – a copy of the screen actor Robert Taylor, she says, in his brown leather coat and brown hat with its snapped brim. She still has her work papers from *Carpathian Oil*, signed by Beitz, and her *R* badge.

We had two straws to cling to in Borysław: our valuable oil and the presence of Berthold Beitz. But The Final Solution did not have any exemption clauses. Hitler had made his intentions clear. The Jews were to be annihilated. Poland, which before the war had a population of 3.5 million Jews, the largest Jewish community in Europe, was where the Nazis' moral and intellectual madness would find its fullest expression in the death camps. It was a matter of when, not if, our number came up.

The next wave of terror began building up in the early spring of 1942. We noticed different police in town, extra police. We saw them talking. Why were they here? The March *Aktion* started the way the previous

Aktion had, on the street, with the sound of running, of terrified human beings bolting from their hunters. Then came the banging on doors. I remember this dreadful uncontrollable fear when I heard that noise. I still hate loud noises; they make me want to cover my head with my arms.

I don't remember anything about where we hid. I know I was always hiding with my mother. My father and brother hid separately. It was in houses, different houses, I think. At first the Gestapo came at night. Then they started coming in the daytime, breaking into Jewish homes. How did they know which homes were Jewish? Our neighbours showed them.

When it was over, many hundreds of people had vanished from our town. This time they weren't taken away in trucks to be shot. They were taken away on trains, or transports, as they were called. The word Judentransport stripped all humanity from its cargo.

When I picked up my diary again on 4 April 1942, I wrote only fleetingly of what had happened in the preceding weeks.

»I haven't written for quite a while. Meanwhile, so much has happened. Two transports of our boys left from Borysław to go to the work camps ... We hear that horrible things have happened in Lwów. I am very worried about [my friend] Ilka. It is horrible. Life is terrible. I don't know whether we will survive this. I am normally an optimist, but even I am starting to have doubts. Perhaps, perhaps, maybe we will survive.«

We assumed that »our boys« had been taken away somewhere to work, to forced labour camps. In the harshest of conditions, we assumed. We didn't yet know about the death camps. We hadn't heard the name Belzec, and if we had, we would have associated it with a small border village about 120 kilometres north of Borysław as the crow flies.

Belzec was on the train line between Lwów and Lublin, which in pre-war Poland was an important centre of Jewish life, commerce, culture and scholarship. In other words, it was geographically well-suited for the mass extermination of Jews, placed as it was between the large Jewish populations of eastern Galicia and southeast Poland. In November 1941, the SS and police authorities began building a new ›camp‹

there. Five months later, it was ready. On the morning of 17 March 1942, a train pulling 19 sealed freight wagons, their windows grated with barbed wire, was shunted to a spur inside the camp, about 300 m from the village train station. It carried 1,400 Jews rounded up from the ghetto in Lublin. In the afternoon, another transport of Jews arrived from the Lwów ghetto. With the exception of a few men who were selected on arrival for special grisly duties, no-one who arrived at Belzec that day – or on any day of its operation – lived longer than a few hours.

Belzec was a death factory. Its only technical equipment was the train ramp, the gas chambers, deep pits for stacking the corpses and living quarters for the small staff of SS and German police officials, and guards, all of whom were either former Soviet prisoners of war or Ukrainian and Polish civilians recruited for the purpose.

It was also the prototype for two other death camps, Treblinka and Sobibor, in what was known as *Aktion Reinhardt*, the plan to kill about two million Jews in the central government area of occupied Poland. These death camps, unlike concentration camps, which were primarily centres for detention and forced labour, had no place for prisoners to sleep, no camp hierarchy, no roll call, no rations. They existed exclusively for murder. The SS and their collaborators killed about 1.6 million people in the *Aktion Reinhardt* camps between March and December 1942. More than 90 per cent of them were Polish Jews.

Belzec's primitive wooden gas chambers were the first stationary gas chambers the Nazis built. It was at Belzec that the Nazis got their industrial murder model up to speed. Experiments were carried out under its commander, Christian Wirth (called *Christian the Savage* by his SS staff), to determine the most efficient method of handling the transports of Jews, from offloading in the reception yard through to herding the victims, naked and shaved, into a ›tube‹ which led directly into gas chambers, labelled as shower rooms. Speed was of the essence. Right until the moment when the victims were enclosed in the gas chambers, they were to be under the impression that they had arrived at a transit camp from which they would be sent on to a labour camp. The few deportees whose lives were spared were ordered to remove the contorted, suffocated corpses from the gas chambers and pile them in tight layers in mass graves. The members of the Sonderkommando, as these special

Jewish detachments were called, were periodically murdered and replaced with people selected from newly arrived transports.

Transports arrived regularly at Belzec from March through to May 1942. Within a week or two of opening, the centre was killing up to 5,000 victims a day. At the end of May, the camp was closed for improvements. It reopened in the middle of June with six new concrete gas chambers capable of murdering more than 3,500 victims simultaneously. During the peak period of Belzec's operation, from July to October 1942, three to four transports per day delivered on average 10,000 people to the gas chambers.

The final transports arrived on 11 December 1942. By then body disposal had become a serious problem, and there was a more sophisticated death machine at Auschwitz to take up the slack. The Nazis wanted their killing centres to remain top secret, so when the head of the SS, Heinrich Himmler, decommissioned Belzec, he ordered that all traces of mass killing be eradicated from the site. The fences and barriers, the barracks and gas chambers were dismantled and what could be salvaged was taken to the concentration camp at Majdanek, just outside Lublin. The Sonderkommandos were forced to open the putrid, evil-smelling pits, exhume the piles of corpses and cremate them. An estimated 500,000 bodies were burned at Belzec in the spring of 1943. A young Polish historian and friend, Robert Kuwałek, who worked at the Belzec Memorial Museum, has interviewed Poles who lived in the village then, people who knew what was going on inside the camp but were too afraid to speak out. The Germans burned bodies day and night for three months, he tells me, and the stench of oily black smoke spread into the countryside for 25 kilometres around Belzec. Locals scraped fat off their windows, and covered their wells. The Germans would provoke villagers in the streets by asking, »Do you smell anything?« By June 1943, all physical evidence of the camp's existence had disappeared. The entire area was landscaped with firs and wild lupins to disguise its former use and it became the most forgotten of the Nazi death camps.

Robert told me of a conversation he overheard while he was escorting a party of Americans into Ukraine to search for traces of their Jewish heritage. One of the Americans, a man, approached a woman in Lwów. »Are you Polish, Ukrainian or Jewish?« he asked her. She replied:

»I'm a citizen of Lwów.« He asked her what had happened to the Jews in Lwów, and she told him, »They're gone.« Where? he wanted to know. »To Poland, to the United States.« The American pressed on. »Did you ever hear the name Belzec?« He started to talk about the death camp where at least 74,000 Jews from Lwów were gassed. She looked at him implacably: »I told you, they went to Poland.«

The people who died at Belzec did so in an anonymous mass. No transport lists have survived from there. For the Jews of the Crakow district, Belzec was what Treblinka was to the Jews of Warsaw. Only five people managed to escape from Belzec, and of those, only two survived the war. One was Rudolf Reder, a chemist in the Lwów soap industry before the war, whose extensive affidavit, first published in 1946 (in Polish), describes how that hellish place functioned. I can barely stand to read his unfiltered account, though it has a unique position amongst my documents. It contains all that can be told about how 500,000 people, including my mother and her family, were murdered at Belzec.

Reder was selected for the *Sonderkommando*. Here's how he described watching his Jewish brothers and sisters, acquaintances and friends being driven to their death: »Several dozen SS men used whips and sharp bayonets to drive the women to the building with the chambers and up three steps to the gangway, where the askars counted 750 people into each chamber. Women who balked at entering were bayoneted in the body by the askars, the blood flowed, and that is how they were driven in to the evil place. I heard the doors closing and the moans and screams; I heard the desperate cries in Polish and Yiddish, the bloodchilling laments of the children and the women and then one joined, terrifying cry ... That lasted fifteen minutes. The machine ran for twenty minutes, and after twenty minutes it was very quiet, the askars opened the doors from the outside, and I, together with the other workers picked out like me from previous transports, without any tattoos or insignia — we went to work. We dragged the bodies of people who had still been alive not long ago; we used leather straps to drag them to the huge waiting mass graves, and the orchestra played during this. It played from morning to evening.«

The gas chambers of Belzec were waiting for the Jews of Borysław all through 1942. Yet incredibly, there were times when we forgot that we were doomed. There would be an *Aktion*, and then things would seem to go quiet. In those deceptive, illusory lulls we would find ourselves believing that perhaps we had a chance of surviving. It's as if we thought, well, that's what happened, but now we can get on with living.

When I revisit the months from April to June 1942, I find a girl suspended in disbelief, resisting the chaos and disorientation that had supplanted the moral and physical order of her world. The news from other towns was sickening. I was lost for words to describe the misery and humiliation I saw on the streets of Borysław. And yet ... I was infatuated with my brother's friend Imek Eisenstein. In defiance of the net closing around us, I fretted about whether he found me pretty and dreamed about stroking his head. At this end of my life, I'm struck, and somewhat embarrassed, I must confess, by my simplicity. But I was a girl. I thought like a girl. I felt like a girl. I hoped against hope that my future included Imek, or if not Imek, then some other boy. I somehow managed simultaneously to hold the frisson of not knowing whether Imek liked me, and the dread of not knowing if I would live. The first, needless to say, occupied the front of my mind, while the second ate away at the lining of my stomach. Literally.

My diary entry of 4 April 1942, which opened with the first transports to Belzec, continued:

»I think that I am rather a silly little thing. Now I like Imek. He gave me his photograph and I gave him mine. I don't really know what he thinks of me. Perhaps something like ›this little girl is quite nice‹. But he has walked me home a few times. Of course, that doesn't prove anything. I am sure that in a few weeks I will laugh about it (if I am still alive), because I know that I am still very young and I am sure that I will have many crushes. But for the time being ... this is the way it is. I also know that I am not writing often enough. I shall try to write more often.«

V. IMEK

How does an older woman feel when she meets her younger self on the page, uncensored, unedited? I must confess, this young girl Binka has a lot in common with the woman I am. She's flirtatious, impulsive, opinionated and affectionate. She's aware she often comes across as frivolous, but she wants to be taken seriously. She yearns to be understood and to understand. She has an eye for style and she appreciates beauty. She exchanges berets as well as books with her friends. But she also has very definite ideas about what constitutes proper behaviour. She's self-critical, but not self-conscious. She's not one to sulk, nor feel sorry for herself, at least not for long. She knows there are others less fortunate than her. Besides, she's easily distracted from her own misery by people or situations that amuse her.

of course, in the wider context, nothing amusing happened between April and June 1942 when I was regularly filling my diary pages. Whole communities of Polish Jews were being wiped off the map. At the memorial museum in Belzec, you can stand in front of a map of Poland and watch as, month by month, beginning in March 1942, the lights (each one representing a Jewish community) are extinguished until finally, by mid 1943, there is darkness. Most Polish Jews no longer existed. We felt this darkness rolling towards us. We knew it would engulf us, and yet still there were days when I felt happy. As long as my mother was alive, I felt safe. I could still feel then. I wasn't numb with terror. And I still prayed then. I believed in God. I don't any more, at least not the God that a religious Jew would recognise. I certainly don't ask him for anything these days. I've learnt my lesson there.

I have translated these few diary entries for one reason only. I can see in them, naive as they are, the foundation blocks of the woman I have become. They don't offer many facts about what was happening in Borysław. I wish, with hindsight, I'd been a more diligent chronicler of the destruction of our town and in particular of its Jewish community by the Germans. But I had eyes mostly for what was happening in my own young life. I treasured that life. There's a bittersweet quality to these ramblings as I read them now. They record the last months of my childhood in the spring and early summer of 1942.

11 APRIL 1942

I visited [my schoolfriend] Klara and we talked ...

In Drohobycz there was a registration of women from 18 to 32 and of childless women. [The Judenrat would have been asked to register the women's details in anticipation of a new demand from the Nazis.] In Borysław all the girls are very very scared, and are looking for work. As far as I am concerned, I don't care any more. I believe in destiny and whatever God gives me. I hope it will be for the best. For the time being, I still like Imek. I saw him yesterday with Nusia but I don't think he is going out with her any more. Perhaps I am wrong. Yesterday we visited Ella – that means Josek, Imek and me. Josek accuses me of changing when there are other people around. He says I behave differently, that I start speaking very fast and so on. It isn't true. I know that I speak fast. I don't speak such a lot at home because there aren't other people there, so Josek probably hasn't noticed that I have changed and that I speak fast now. Other than this, these last few days have been quiet, but who knows what will happen tomorrow. I am worried about Ilka [in Lwów] and Erna [in Drohobycz] because I haven't heard from them.

14 APRIL 1942

Terrible weather. It snows and then straightaway changes into slush. In the morning I went to see Klara and I got very wet feet. I met Imek so we walked together. I had a small photo of myself which I gave to him and he had it enlarged. It's very nice. Still no news from Ilka. I am very worried because we hear that terrible things are happening in Lwow. My father came home and told us about the horrible things that have been taking place around us. I worry but it can't be helped. Whatever is one's destiny, it will happen. I want to live so much and I am so afraid of dying, but what can I do about it? I am trying not to think about it too much, to live every day and to think about God every day. We don't know what's going to happen, however I hope that we'll survive.

There was a letter from [my grandparents in] Hureczko. It is very difficult there. They have suffered badly. I can well imagine.

25 APRIL 1942

A few days ago I received a letter from Ilka. They are all right, but I haven't heard anything from Erna. I asked Josek if Imek is going out with anyone, and he said no. I am so happy about that because I still like him, even if I say that he isn't such a pretty boy. He is very sweet and he has a wonderful smile. I noticed his lovely smile today. I wonder whether he finds me even a little bit attractive. Quite a few girls have asked me whether I am going out with him. I think that's very indiscreet and bad-mannered because you don't ask things like that.

People still hope that perhaps it will finish soon, but I don't think so. I think that's silly. Somebody, I don't know who, said, ›Hope is the mother of stupidity.‹ A few days ago the weather was beautiful and warm. Now it's got cool again but we are already wearing ankle socks.

28 APRIL 1942

Yesterday a letter arrived from Erna [in Drohobycz]. It is okay there. The weather is terrible. It is raining hard and sometimes even snowing and it's very cold. I feel sad and blue. I don't know what to do with myself. I wish I could do something, go somewhere. God, how I wish the war would end. Aside from that, I still like Imek, more than ever. He is very polite when he sees me, but I don't think that he really cares. He is not going out with Nusia any more. He is not going out with anybody else, but perhaps they will make up again. Sometimes I really feel like I would like to stroke his hair. I would really like to see him more often. I know that I am still very young and probably, if I live, I will like some other boys as well. But just now I really like Imek. Imek was delivering summonses and he saw some Poles from the west in Derczyce in the labour camp. So they are not just taking Jews to the labour camps but also others. They say that it is only for six months, that they keep them in the camps and give them food three times a day. Hitler has made another speech and he spoke again about Jews, so there is great fear. There is nothing we can do.

30 APRIL 1942

It was snowing yesterday and to think it is already the end of April and it is as cold as it is in winter. Tomorrow is the 1st of May. I hope that nothing terrible happens. I am in a down mood again. This guy Imek. I am really preoccupied with him, and I really don't know what I see in him. He is kind, he is polite, he is nice, but actually he is just a very average boy.

I didn't see him today so I miss him. I wonder will he come tomorrow? I know that I am silly, but I can't help thinking about him all this time. There is gossip that some money came from the United States for the poor people.

[By this stage emerging information about mortality rates in the ghettos of Poland was making the pages of *The New York Times*. An article by Henry Shoskes on 1 March 1942 was titled *Extinction Feared by Jews in Poland*.]

It is frightening. There is such wretched misery in Borysław. You can see living corpses walking the street. They say that 13 people die every day and also that they are taking poor little children whom they find on the streets to the orphanage. That in addition to the pogroms and the labour camps and transports and so on. How can one survive it?

I am really not complaining. I am grateful because at our home it is still not bad. We eat three times a day while others have nothing. We have heard that something horrible happened in Stanisławów [about 5,000 Jews from the Stanisławów ghetto were taken to Belzec on 31 March, one of the biggest transports in the early phase of the camp]. I am still praying and begging God to make things better. My birthday is approaching on 8 June. Will I still be alive? I hope so.

3 MAY 1942

The day before yesterday I visited [a friend] Lusia Zuckerberg. We started to talk a bit and it developed into a nice conversation. I am so glad because I don't really have people to talk to. Ilka is so far away in Lwow. Erna is also away but she is so childish. Klara has got Viva. I am alone. I can talk with Josek of course, but naturally not about everything. He thinks that I am very silly and he says I really am not very clever, that I can't talk about serious things. Lusia . is older than me by two years, and she is clever, but she has two sides to her. She is amusing and witty and very good company but she is also serious and clever. So we talked a lot about many things, and I am jealous of her because she has got a wonderful father I don't mean it badly but I just wish that my father was like this. The other day he [my father] prepared some hot water to soak his feet and I was getting a book from a shelf and I accidentally stepped into the bowl and knocked it over. My God, you should have heard what happened. Screams and anger. I didn't do it on purpose. It was an accident and after all, it wasn't nice for me either to have wet feet. It is so sad because sometimes when I look at their life, and then I think about marriage, it's frightening. It is funny that I, being so young, should talk about love but I love my mother so much. It's so great that when I am really very scared I just cuddle up to her and feel safe. I don't have the father that I dream of but I have a mother that I totally adore. My God, how I pray she survives and that we can give her the best in life, because she deserves it.

I was walking home the other day and met Imek. We also met another Klara. She stopped us for a minute and invited Imek to come and see her, saying, 'You can come Imek. Binka will let you.' I was very embarrassed, but I didn't show it. Then Imek turned towards me and said, ›Would you let me?‹ I replied, ›Naturally.‹ How can Klara and some other girls pretend to know something that I still don't know? It is really strange but in one way I can be very serious and in another I am just a silly 15year old who only thinks about boys and so on.

Today I visited Hanka Blocka [a non-Jewish Polish friend]. We wanted to swap berets. Mine is brown and hers is navvy, but hers is too small. It was wonderful to see her home. Gosh, how elegant it is. Just to think that we used to live like that as well, that it is not as though we have always lived in a shack. Yes, those were different times, but that's in the past. Perhaps, perhaps, the good times will come again. Ah, I just remembered something. Imek has got new riding pants and he looks like something out of a fairytale. He has also got this very nice jacket and some high boots. He looks fabulous. He is very well built, broad-shouldered and very narrow in the hips and he is tall. He's fantastic. (This is Binka number two!)

5 MAY 1942

I received a letter from Ilka. I am so happy to hear from her. She also sent a photo. I love her, she is wonderful. Distance and separation haven't changed our feelings or our friendship. I wrote her a long letter and asked her to reply quickly. I wonder whether we would agree on certain things, and if we have similar tastes. I sent the letter only today but I'm already waiting for her answer.

In the afternoon I went with my mother to see Mrs Wekselberg. I wanted to go back home because I was hoping that Imek would come. We came home and Imek was waiting. I was pulling my mother to go back home as if I knew he were there. Intuition, huh? I am so surprised that I still like him so much. I never liked anyone so much before, but I don't think he cares about me. Fylypiak [our Ukrainian neighbour] is sitting at our place and talking. He is going on and on. Something's in the wind. What is happening? Why is he here?

7 MAY 1942

Yesterday a letter arrived from Etna. I love her, but I can't believe that in times like these she can still think about Janek [a non-Jewish Ukrainian boy]. I have to admit that I find him very attractive too but since I learned that he was beating up some Jews I can't look at him any more and Erna in her letter writes how much she likes him and how wonderful he is. I am going to write to her and tell her what I think about it.

The weather is wonderful. It's warm with beautiful sunshine. In the morning I went to see Viva and on the way back I bought some pierogi [dumplings]. In the afternoon I went to Imek's [with Josek] and from there to the post office and then I visited Frydka. Josek stayed there and Imek and I went over to his place. He mentioned that he met Nusia but that she looked away and that he felt awful about it. He doesn't think that she should have behaved like that and I agree with him. He mentioned that his parents were not very happy when he was going out with her and my impression is that he misses her. I would like to find out why they broke up but I don't dare ask. I still like him very much.

Josek came and we went home so it was a good day.

13 MAY 1942

Something terrible happened at home. I quarrelled with my father and he hit me in the face. I shall never forgive him for it. Doesn't he realise that he is not achieving anything by behaving like this? How can we respect him? He came home yesterday and mentioned that Dr Teicher asked if he could organise large quantities of food for [a Jewish charity]. My mother ran around, carrying quite a lot of various supplies on her back from Mra nica. Not only did she take a big risk in carrying the supplies but I don't think that he really appreciated what she did. Yesterday I cooked a little and I did quite well, and today I sold a shirt for one kilogram of wheat and two kilograms of potatoes and my mother gave me 25 zloty. Today I visited Imek ... Oh, I like him so much but I still don't know what he thinks about me. Still no news from Ilka.

30 MAY 1942

Hip hip hooray! Victory! I'm going out with Imek. He told me that he likes me very much. I am so happy. I wasn't sure until now but now it is confirmed. That's great. In eight days it will be my birthday. We were hoping that perhaps the end would be closer but it doesn't look as if it will happen very quickly. Yesterday I wanted to talk to someone but I didn't have anyone to talk to and then I wanted to write but I was too lazy, and today I don't want to write any more about what I felt yesterday and I don't want to use just empty phrases so I am not writing. I will write again soon.

15 JUNE 1942

I don't know why I am feeling the way I am feeling at the moment. I am sad actually. I am just drifting from one corner of the room to the other. I don't know what is wrong with me. When I am at home, I want to go out, and when I am out I want to get back home. I am so moody. Imek and Josek went to visit [their friend] Karol but I didn't want to go, so I went to visit Lusia. But I didn't want to stay there. Something was driving me and I had to get out again. I didn't get very far, perhaps only 20 metres and then I decided to go back home. I was missing Imek and decided I definitely had to get back. I don't know what's wrong with me really. Sometimes I think that Imek is absolutely wonderful and sometimes I just don't care about him. What do I really see in him? He isn't pretty but he is very handsome and very well mannered and terribly nice. But I still don't know how serious he is and if I will be able to talk with him about all kinds of things. I really do want someone who I can cuddle up to and talk to, someone who will really understand me.

The 8th of June was my birthday. Josek surprised me by repairing my watch. He is so good but sometimes when it comes to me, he's a bit unfair. On my birthday Lusia D. came and brought me flowers and a brooch. In the afternoon Josek and Imek took me out for cakes. They are both wonderful boys.

Lately I have been a little bit calmer but now I am starting to get a bit more fearful. Some people say that maybe it won't last very long, but others say that there is still a long way to go and it is so difficult to keep on living. We don't feel safe in the daytime or in the night-time. A few days ago [our acquaintances] the Grinszlag family was attacked. Mr Flachs [the father of a friend] has had a heart attack. He is in a very serious condition. I am praying so much to God for this horror to end, but will we survive? Ilka's father has been taken to the labour camp. It's terrible.

I am reading a very good book which I borrowed from Ducek [a friend of Josek's]. He's a clever boy but a bit naaive. I like him. Now it is getting dark, so I have to stop writing.

22 JUNE 1942

It is a year since the war started. It's hard to believe that we have been living like this for a year. You never know what is going to happen either during the day or at night. Every hour is different. We go to sleep at night and we don't know what will happen in the morning. It's horrible. I have become so pessimistic. All the ghastly news that's reaching us of pogroms in different places. Thousands of Jewish lives, innocent children, women and men. Jewish blood is flowing. And where is God? I think about that so often. Why is this happening to us? Have we sinned more than other people? Is it some kind of punishment? I am praying and praying that we should survive and enjoy life. Doesn't my darling mother deserve some happiness? She has suffered so much for most of her life, and now, when finally we have grown up and could bring her some joy, this horrible thing has happened.

I hope that God will give us a better life, but I don't really believe in it, and I am only 15 now. I think that one has to accept it, and be ready to die but I can't. I am so afraid of death. I don't understand it. How is it possible that there is nothing and that all that is left of it is just ash? When I think about it a fear grips my heart. Just to think that a week ago Mr. Flachs was joking with us and now he is dead. I am so terribly afraid.

I think that Imek doesn't like me any more. He didn't say that, but I think that's what it is. I am a bit sad about it, but I will cheer up because I know that I can be quite serious but that there is another Binka that sometimes likes one boy today and another tomorrow. I have known him now so long and still don't know what he is like. He is a very good friend, but nothing else. Ducek was here. I like him more and more each day.

VI. AUGUST-›AKTION‹

Six weeks after that last diary entry, there was a very big *Aktion*. In the build-up to the *Aktion*, we could sense something sinister in the air. The tension was palpable, and everyone was preoccupied with finding a place to hide. In the evenings, only the Gestapo were out on the street. When the round-up started on 6 August 1942, my mother and I were hiding in a storage room in a kind of warehouse, next to where we lived. We had squeezed ourselves in behind an enormous row of packages. My father and brother weren't with us. I don't know where they were. I have completely blanked out a lot of what happened on this day. I don't remember the weather, although it was summer, and probably warm. I can't recall any smells or colours, the kinds of intimate details that can rekindle a mental or emotional picture of a past event. They've gone. I've wiped them. What I can't forget though are the noises. They ring in my head. The sounds of dogs barking, boots kicking, men shouting, fists pounding, glass smashing, women screaming. The noises were overwhelming. They triggered panic and confusion, and blind unthinking fear. That was the idea.

I think we were found on the first day of the *Aktion*, which lasted three days. I remember hiding, and then this terrible noise, a hammering, smashing assault on a door. I suspect it was our neighbour Fylypiak who betrayed us, the man whom I mentioned in my diary and whose presence disturbed me. Our neighbours in this area weren't the kind we'd had before the Russians threw us out of our home. They were a different class of people, mostly Ukrainians, whom we had little to do with, and vice versa. It happened often during the war that neighbours denounced neighbours.

The Ukrainian militia broke into where we were hiding, and dragged us out into the street to join a throng of people being driven forward by SS men with their whips. Dogs lunged at those who tried to make a run for it. I clung to my mother's hand, and my mother kept a protective arm over me. Numb with terror, we walked until we reached the *Grażyna* cinema, which was used as a holding centre by the Nazis. The auditorium had been emptied of seats, and was filled to the point of bursting. There were hundreds of other people in there, seized from all over town, jammed tightly together, men and women, mothers cradling babies, school-age children like me, and elderly people who could hardly walk. The Gestapo came in the back door and started looking around. If I close my eyes now, I can see it, though there are things I don't want to remember. Children being snatched from their parents' arms and flung against the wall, thrown out through windows. I can't bear to think of it. The Gestapo started picking out girls, pointing at this one and that. I remember that my mother and I had been pushed and shoved about, and that we found ourselves at the front of the crowd. I hate crowds. You never know what's going to happen when you find yourself in a crowd. An SS man shouted at me to come forward. I shrunk back against my mother's body, and gripped her hand desperately. He hit me across the back of my head with a baton, and yanked me away from her. Did she cry out? I don't remember. I don't remember anything about that last moment I was with my mother except drowning, paralysing fear, and disbelief. It couldn't be real. It couldn't be happening.

I think there were about ten of us girls selected. I was the youngest. We were put in the back of a truck. We didn't know what they were going to do with us, whether they were going to rape us, or kill us. They took us to a cavernous warehouse in which confiscated Jewish property was stored. Jewellery, watches, spectacles, shoes, underwear, shirts, dresses, trousers, hats, coats, belts and so on. We were ordered to separate these belongings into different categories.

We stayed there working for several days. We slept on the floor and were given nothing to wash ourselves with, but we were fed. I was given the task of ladling soup into bowls. I remember having to be very careful that I didn't give anyone too much. It had to be done absolutely right. I remember one of the policemen who was supervising our work coming over to me and asking, »Are you Jewish?« I replied, »Of course. You know I am.« He said, »You don't look like one.« My eyes, he said, looked a little bit Oriental. Maybe I was supposed to take that as a compliment. I don't know. He tried to be kind to me. He told me I could have some more soup. I was terrified. I wondered what he would offer next.

On the fourth or fifth day, we were called together. We thought our time had come. To our surprise, we were told to go home. Just like that. I walked home. It was during the day, and at first I was alone, but then after a while my brother came home, and then my father. I learned that Josek had been discovered too. My brother had been rounded up by the Gestapo and taken to the railway station, and there, among the terrified mass of people on the platform, he and my mother found each other. But while she was consigned to the death wagons, he was pulled out of the crowd, selected for slave labour. He was a young man, she was a middle-aged woman. That's how it went. Just before she was loaded onto the transport that would take her and thousands of others from our town to the gas chambers of Belzec, my mother called out to Josek, »Take care of the baby.« That was it. Those were her last words to him, to us.

I stopped talking after I lost my mother. I went into a state of deep shock. I didn't know where she had gone. I didn't want to know where she had gone. The truth was too dreadful to bear, and I didn't look for it. My body and mind shut down. I felt nothing. It was as if I had turned to stone. The pain came later. My brother took care of me. He fed me and kept me clean. He washed my hair and brushed it. I could do nothing. I don't remember how long I stayed like this, but one day I got sick of being so helpless. I found a hairdresser – even though Jews were not allowed to run businesses, there were some small shops operating under the auspices of the Judenrat – and asked him to cut off my beautiful long hair.

When I came home with my hair chopped just below my ears, my brother cried. I cried. We clung to each other, crying. And then I started to speak again. My childhood was over. If I were to survive, I would have to learn to look after myself. I was no longer Mama's beloved baby. As far as she knew, my life too had been spared, and she so desperately wanted me to live.

And my father? What part did he play in my life after Mama was taken away? The strange thing is that I have very few memories of him from this time onwards. I transferred my dependence on my mother to my brother, as she had expected. With hindsight, I feel enormous compassion for my father. He was 44. He had lost his wife, Sala, an uncommonly strong, sensual, vigorous woman upon whom he had relied for nearly 20 years in one way or another. But I wasted no time on his loss and his pain. I was too needy myself and I knew he could give me no comfort. He was a weak man, with heart problems, or so I was later told. I don't know if that's true. After Mama was gone, my brother and I took certain things for granted, and one of them was that we could not rely on our father to look after us.

Our family lost its beating heart, but so did many others. Borysław's Jewish heart was literally ripped out; around 6,000 people were taken in that August Aktion from our town and nearby villages. Everyone knew someone who had been torn away from their family. My friend Róża later told me that she lost her grandmother and two aunts in that Aktion. Her husband, Marek, lost his mother and his sister. If I had no-one left to care for me except my brother who, at age 18, accepted responsibility for my survival, I was lucky. I was alive. I knew that I had been a spoilt child, and that I was much too concerned about myself. My brother was a much nicer, more thoughtful human being. I knew that too. But I missed my mother terribly. I remember feeling envious when I saw other children with their mothers. »Why my mother?« I asked myself. »Why have they got a mother, and I haven't?« I knew this wasn't a proper way to think, and that I should be happy that other children still had a mother. But I wanted to be hugged, to be kissed, to be comforted. I ached for her touch. As time went by, that ache didn't dull. I ached for anyone's touch. There's a photograph Róża has of me, taken after the war, among a group of female Russian soldiers. There's snow on the ground, and we're huddled tight together in a row, facing the camera. I have my head nestled into one of the girls' shoulders. I am a snuggler. I crave affection, and respond to affection quickly when it's offered. That's got me into trouble, of course. But my mother raised me to be loved, and who's to say that developing a healthy appetite for love in a child isn't the best protection a mother can offer?

VII. GHETTO

In the first weeks after my mother was taken, I imagined she was in a forced labour camp. That was what the Germans wanted us to think. They kept telling us that Jews who were taken for »resettlement« were going to work. I worried about my mother being cold in the camp, and not having enough to eat. Would anyone share their food with her? She used to cook enormous pots of soup for the poor. She always thought of herself as privileged, even when we were reduced to relative poverty ourselves.

We had enough food in the house because of my mother's foresight and energy in stocking up on the black market, and for a while, until it became too difficult, Josek continued going out into the countryside: we had goods to barter, which many poorer families didn't. People around us were starving, but I don't remember being hungry. Even before the war I had a small appetite and I wasn't a picky eater. (My favourite foods were, and still are, potatoes and cabbage and bread.) I took over the cooking at home because someone had to. I had no idea to start with. I was told that you could use egg to thicken soup, so I took an egg, cracked it into the soup and it floated on top. I tried to bake bread, but it was a disaster. Gradually I learned enough to feel useful to my brother and my father.

In October 1942, the Germans established a Judenviertel [Jewish quarter] in the oldest and poorest part of Borysław. The non-Jews in that area were evacuated, and rooms in their houses and apartments were allocated to Jewish families – one family per room. My brother, my father and I shared a room. In Borysław, we called the ghetto Dzielnica, the District. The town's sprawling, ad hoc growth had made it difficult to have a closed ghetto. There was no wall around the Borysław ghetto, no gates and no guards. Certain streets were nominated as boundaries, and Jews were separated from non-Jews by normal urban traffic. We knew we weren't allowed to move freely across those boundaries. Those with jobs in the oil industry left the ghetto in groups each day, and returned at night. There was a strict curfew. I don't remember anyone being shot for being out of the ghetto at night, but it was a risk that people took.

At the end of October, there was another *Aktion*, which lasted three days. Since we Jews were now living all in one place, it was easier to round us up. I don't remember where I was, but my brother, my father and I survived. There was a brief gap of a week, and then the terror started again. Continuous murderous operations, numerous small-scale *Aktionen* aimed at liquidating the Jewish population of Borysław and Drohobycz. Another 1500 people were transported to Belzec in November and December 1942, and several hundred were forced into trucks and driven to the field behind the Borysław abattoir where they were executed at point blank. Butchered like animals. My mind is empty. I can read about what happened, but I don't remember anything. I was there, but I was not there. As I mentioned, I have made myself a timeline, but these events are absent from my memory. I would have been in the ghetto. Róża remembers me there. That's where we first met each other. She shared one room with her mother, Fenka, her husband, Marek, and his father. Her cousin Imek, my boyfriend, lived next door to them with his parents, who would soon come to play such an important part in my life.

On 15 November 1942, the Germans opened a forced labour camp at Mraźnica, on the northern edge of town. Jews registered to work with the Carpathian Oil Company were required to go and live there. We called the camp »the barracks«. In comparison with concentration camps such as Majdanek, »the barracks« was a paradise. It wasn't large. At capacity it housed about 1,400 inmates in buildings set around a courtyard. Men and women slept in separate dormitories, a few people to each room, on beds they brought from the ghetto. A few prominent Jews, expert chemists and engineers and the like, lived with their families in a separate block of houses nicknamed by camp inmates as the White House. Walek Eisenstein, Imek's father, who was the head of the

Jewish police, lived in separate quarters inside the front gates. A high fence surrounded the camp but there were no surveillance towers, and workers had comparative liberty of movement. Jewish police guarded the front gate, and Ukrainian Werkschutz [armed guards] guarded the back, but in the early months, when the security was as much to keep the local population out as the Jewish workers in, workers could leave with a special pass. Later, when security was tighter, guards could be duped. But ironically, in our town it was considered safer inside the camp than outside. On the street, even those Jews who had the R badge that identified them as professionals vital to the arms industry or the refineries were at risk of being seized and deported by the fanatical SS.

My brother and my father were registered to work. I can't be certain when they went to live in the camp, because for a few months the camp and the ghetto existed simultaneously. I was never registered in either the ghetto or the labour camp, although I still have a certificate stating that Sabina Haberman is an employee of *Beskiden Erdöl-Gewinnungs G. m. b. H.* (a subsidiary of *Carpathian Oil*) and should be given free passage. It is the only document I have bearing that name, the name I was given at birth. It was a false ID to give me some protection if I was stopped. I never worked, and after my brother and father went to live in the camp, I was left alone in the ghetto. I was 15, and living one day at a time in a place from which life was being systematically extinguished. A few friends were still alive, and as far as I can remember, their situation was similar to mine, that is, our families had more to exchange for food on the black market than many of the terribly poor families in Borysław. But each day we survived was a miracle.

In January 1943 I invited a few friends to our room in the ghetto to celebrate Josek's 19th birthday. I wrote about it in my diary.

20 JANUARY 1943

Wednesday, today is Josek's birthday. I bought him a small gift and invited Lusia F., Rolek, Ducek and Imek. We were singing Russian songs. What beautiful words. We tried hard to be in a good mood, but it was very forced. I couldn't stop thinking about Mother, not even for a moment. I find it so difficult to say what my feelings are. It is a pain, incredible pain, and a longing for something good, beautiful, and light. It is a memory of the days past, it is the pain of today and the pain of this horrible life, living like animals from day to day, from Aktion to Aktion, fighting to survive, but what kind of fight is that? We are so completely helpless and they, barbarians, have everything in their might to destroy us. We have been through so many horrible things, and all the time there is blood, the blood of murdered mothers and children. And fear, paralysing fear, running, hiding, hiding in forests, bunkers, and all this in vain.

The English radio says: ›We know everything. We know about the pogroms, we know about Belzec, about all of it.‹ Mourning everywhere, prayers. Everywhere they have memorials for the murdered Jews, but what do they really know? Instead of just talk, we need some deeds. Prayer will not return my mother to me, but for the few who still have their parents, only deeds will help. We are so helpless, we do want to live, but how, and where is God?

I have a photograph which was taken on that day. It's of myself and Josek with Imek, Ducek and Rolek Harmelin. All the boys are wearing armbands. Of them, only Rolek survived the war. He married Rita, and it was from Rita that I got the photo. It was kept safe during the war by her Polish uncle, Adam Zoszak, who was married to her aunt Giza. That's another story, a great love story, but it's not mine to tell. Briefly, this uncle wasn't from our town. His wife was visiting her sister, Rita's mother, in Borysław when the Germans occupied the western part of Poland in 1939. He followed her, and they stayed in the east. He was a lawyer, but he got a job with Carpathian Oil and lived in a house next to the labour camp where he hid his Jewish wife, and her niece, and also her Jewish family's photographs. The Nazis made a clean sweep of all Jewish houses once they had murdered their inhabitants and destroyed everything, including photographs, so it's a miracle that I have an image from this period.

My father became desperately ill that winter. He contracted typhus, which swept through the ghettos in Poland and killed so many people. I've read that 2,000 people died of typhus, poverty and hunger in Borysław during the winter of 1941 and through until mid 1942. This was a year later, but the killer disease was still taking what victims it could. I remember my father lying on his bed, painfully weak, and pleading with me not to take him to hospital. Once people went to the hospital, they were as good as dead. Hospitals were the Gestapo's first stop when they were making selection for resettlement. I promised my father I wouldn't let anyone take him to hospital.

He was unconscious for a long time, and I nursed him as best I could, around the clock. I remember being in a decrepit little room and washing my father's sodden sheets daily in boiling water on top of a potbelly stove. We had nowhere to hang the washing. I don't remember how I got things dry in the depths of a Polish winter, but I knew that the bed linen had to be kept scrupulously clean, that bugs spread disease, the bed bugs that infested the ghetto. Morning and evening, I changed my own clothes and washed them and my father's. I still can't believe that neither I nor Josek got typhus.

There's a well-loved poem by Julian Tuwim about trains called *Lokomotywa* (expertly translated by Walter Whipple) which, if you recite aloud, mimics the sound of train wheels in motion. It starts slowly, very slowly, and then gains pace, faster, and then faster and faster.

> Slow – as a – turtle – with weights – on its – back,
> The train – begins creeping – along – down the – track.
> She tugs at her wagons with struggle and strain,
> The wheels begin rolling, and so does the train.
> She huffs and she puffs as she enters the race,
> And rambles and scrambles to quicken her pace.

I remember my brother and I changing the words of the poem so it was about the bed bugs. Slowly they moved, then they gained pace, faster and faster. I don't know how we found it in us to laugh about bed bugs, but we did. It gave us a break from our suffering, I suppose.

It must have been about this time that my brother was turning over in his mind whether or not to join the partisans operating under the cover of the Carpathian forest. He could have made a break from the camp. Other young men did. I didn't know much about the partisan resistance in our region, and still don't, but for a young man like Josek, the temptation to do something, anything, rather than wait to die must have been very strong. The partisans had weapons, they were fighters. He didn't talk to me in detail, but I understood there was a possibility of him leaving us. In a letter he wrote to me from the labour camp a few months later, he spoke of having decided to stay in Borysław: »... I have decided, and told Father, that I will not leave Borysław without you. When I see you I will have more definite news. So please, darling, be patient and believe that tomorrow things may change and perhaps we will survive. We have to believe in it because otherwise we won't be able to last.« What kept him from leaving Borysław was his sense of responsibility and love for me. I am sure of that.

When my father's fever broke, my brother took me to the labour camp and I slept for what seemed like 24 hours in his girlfriend Hala's room before returning to the ghetto. At this early stage in the camp's existence, it was possible to sneak in and out – the Jewish police at the front gate could be distracted. I remember my brother coming from the camp to visit me in the ghetto, and taking back cakes I had cooked to sell. I needed to earn money somehow. After my father had recovered, and was strong enough to return to the labour camp, we smuggled him back in. I don't know what month that was, but on 15 February 1943, a fortnight after Germany's 6th Army's humiliating surrender in Stalingrad after five months of heavy fighting for the Russian city, there was another big *Aktion* in Borysław. The police locked 300 people in the Colosseum, the smallest of the town's three cinemas. They were there for two days without food or water before being herded onto trucks and taken to a field behind the abattoir. Much later I read that they were forced to stand on the edge of lime pits so that when they were brutally clubbed, they toppled into the pits where they died in slow and hideous torment. Other people were deported, and others still taken to the forest to be shot, though I have no precise memories of this.

In early 1943, most probably after that February *Aktion*, the Germans closed – or liquidated, as they put it – the ghetto. By then, the only visible Jews left in Borysław were those living in the camp, Jews kept alive to work. Those of us who were not accounted for on the camp's register were either dead, or, like me, in hiding.

VIII. HIDING

There are black holes in my recollections of the next 20 months of my life. I do not apologise for that. A condition of survival was voluntary memory loss. I have retrieved as much as possible, but I was a late starter.

For many years I made no effort to piece together what had happened to me or to anyone I knew who had survived the Holocaust. I never asked questions, and nobody asked questions of me. When I left Poland in 1948 and spent nearly two years in Paris waiting for permission to emigrate to America, I met people from my part of Poland, my town even. Some became good friends. I knew they were Jewish, and they knew I was Jewish, but no-one spoke about what that meant. We were alive. Enough said. Perhaps we thought we would forget if we didn't talk. Immediately you started talking about what had happened, it became a reality again, a reality too painful to be lived more than once.

I have my diary to draw on, or rather, the bits of it which remain, but little for the remainder of 1943 until liberation in the first week of August 1944. I have some photographs, some extraordinary photographs, which I was given after the war by others who had survived. Imek is in one of those photographs, the one taken in the ghetto at my brother's birthday party. Were Imek and his family still living in the ghetto then? I know I stayed with them for a period after my mother was taken. I remember Imek lying next to me on the bed and holding me while I rocked myself to sleep. They may have stayed in the ghetto until it was closed in February, and then moved to the camp. I can't say. What I do know is that Walek Eisenstein had a particular role in this tragic period of Borysław life.

Walek Eisenstein was the head of the Jewish police. The Jewish police were, and still are, a controversial and delicate subject. They were organised by the Judenrat in each municipality across occupied Eastern Europe. Their duties included collecting ransom payments, personal possessions and taxes from other Jews, collecting people for forced labour and guarding ghetto gates and fences. The Jewish police took their orders from the Gestapo, but they made their choice to co-operate under the worst imaginable circumstances, ones few of us will ever face.

I can't speak for their motivation, but I know we all wanted to save our lives and the lives of those we loved. I didn't know the Eisenstein family before the war. I got to know Imek after the Germans banned Jewish students from attending school and Josek and I were thrown back on each other's company and the company of our friends. I can speculate that Walek was desperate to protect his wife, Pepa, and their son and only child, Imek. These are my reflections as an adult who has herself borne children. As a child, however, I didn't question why Walek Eisenstein made the choices he did. Imek loved me, and because of that, I was loved by his parents. I loved them in return.

I have mentioned that my father had a younger brother who lived in Borysław, and that our families were not close. I knew however that my cousin Benio, who was about six years my junior, had been nursed by a Ukrainian woman because his mother was unable to breastfeed him. Benio, whom I met maybe only once or twice before the war, featured more in my life during the war because of his connection with his wet nurse, Hania Proc. Hania loved Benio like her own child. In fact, she had a son whom she breastfed at the same time as she was nursing Benio. One boy she called her Jewish child, the other her non-Jewish child. From the time war broke out in 1941, Benio lived with Hania and her husband on the outskirts of Borysław.

Her husband, whose name I don't remember, was a terrible man, always threatening and shouting, and occasionally hitting her. I saw this when I went to live with them. I think my father probably paid Hania to hide me and that my uncle, Benio's father, helped to arrange it. Benio remembered towards the end of his life that Hania said I couldn't stay long because it was risky. He recalled that I stayed a month, but I'm not sure that his memory was reliable at that time.

Benio was a fixture at Hania's house, having stayed there regularly from such an early age, that the neighbours probably thought he was another child or a cousin. They were used to seeing him around. But if they'd seen me, they would have asked questions. Neighbours were always suspicious when someone unknown appeared in a house. So whereas Benio could move around freely, I was kept indoors and out of sight.

I have letters from Josek, which I think must have been brought to Hania's by my uncle. When I think how dangerous it would have been had these letters been intercepted, I am surprised at how much detail they contain. In one letter, dated 6 May 1943, Josek takes me lightly to task for being critical of his girlfriend, Hala. There's another that is undated but which I think I received in the same period because once I left Hania's I lost touch with my uncle. Josek writes on Thursday, at 8 o'clock in the evening, and starts by saying, »Darling Binuśka [which is a diminutive of my name], I received your letter. It annoys me that I can't see you but Dad says that he will go with me together, hopefully on Saturday, and I would love so much to see you and to talk to you ... Yesterday I was standing in a queue from 3 till 7 waiting for a pass« – Jews with a special pass could leave the camp premises, but they were exposed to the arbitrary whim of every German they encountered – »I thought that I would go mad, it was so terribly depressing, waiting and waiting, standing and standing. But today I am feeling better again, and I am in a good mood.«

Then he tells me that for the time being he and his friends have had to stop working on the bunker they are digging on the sly at Poldek's. Poldek Tenenbaum was a friend of ours whose house had been requisitioned by the Germans for use as the office of a scrap metal business run by a Pole called Mr. Machnicki. My brother and his friends were building a hiding place beneath a rabbit hutch in the backyard, big enough for about eight people. It was always understood that I would be among them. He continues, »... one can already hide in there. Imek will write to you about it, and I shall tell you verbally when I see you ... When Uncle comes to see you, please give him a letter. Darling, be patient. Write to me and tell me how it is there. I kiss you. Josek.«

I don't remember how long I was hidden by Hania Proc. I think her husband probably forced her to get rid of me. One Jewish child was more than enough for him. I remember their arguments. He was always threatening to denounce her to the police for keeping 'your Jewish child', meaning Benio. She told him that she would denounce him too, that he had known about the arrangement from the start, and that they would all be killed, him, her, her Jewish child and her non-Jewish child. So he was afraid to do anything about Benio. But I had to go.

I never forgot how much Hania had done for me, and particularly for my cousin. I was so grateful for the risks she took on our behalf that I sent food parcels to her after the war, from Australia, until she died. When I travelled to Borysław in 2006, my heart turned somersaults when I thought for a few delirious minutes that one of her relatives might still be alive. I was told there was a Ukrainian woman named Proc in the town, and taken to meet her. Sadly, it wasn't anyone related to my Mrs. Proc, but another sweet-natured elderly woman who invited me into her home, showed me her photographs, told me about her Polish mother, and then, with a sad shrug, let me go. All the while her husband and adult children kept their eyes firmly on the job of wiring up a satellite dish to a cramped little house so basic and impoverished it made me cringe. Borysław hasn't moved forward in 60 years. If I were generous I would say it has marked time.

Hania was probably persuaded to take me in temporarily because she knew my brother was preparing a longer-term hiding place for me. She wouldn't have known where. It was much too dangerous to reveal that kind of information. But I think I probably went straight from Hania's to the hiding place at the Tenenbaum's old house, or Machnicki's, as we called it, after the boss of the salvage business who was in on the subterfuge. When I was sent into the protection of Mr. Machnicki, I thought he was a god. I understood the huge personal risk he was taking in hiding Jews on his business premises. Everyone knew that hiding or actively helping Jews in defiance of Third Reich policy was a capital offence. But what I didn't know was that Mr. Machnicki himself had a false identity. It was only many years after the war ended that I learned his story.

I remember thinking it was odd that there was a particular German officer who came sometimes to visit the house, and that during his visits we were allowed to come up from beneath the ground to wash and stretch our legs and drink and eat in the light. As a girl, I didn't question why or how this
German knew Mr. Machnicki. I knew Mr. Machnicki as a Pole, though my friend Marek, Róża's husband, once made a strange comment to me about him, which I recalled many years later when I learned of Mr. Machnicki's true identity.

Marek ran a photographic studio in town, which the Germans, who took a lot of photographs that needed to be processed, allowed him to keep open for much of the war. Marek had taken a photograph of Mr. Machnicki, I don't know why, maybe for an identity document. I remember him saying to me one time when I met him, perhaps when I visited Róża and her mother, Fenka, who hid above the studio for a period, that »this Machnicki of yours has got Jewish eyes«. I told him not to be crazy, that he didn't know what he was talking about. Mr. Machnicki was the boss, I said. But Marek was right.

This is the story of Mr. Machnicki. I was told it first by Poldek Tenenbaum, who was hidden in the bunker with me, and who survived to emigrate to Israel, and then more recently by Henrietta Braun, my new-found friend from Brazil, whom I knew as Eva, the daughter of Mr. Machnicki's attractive young secretary, Mrs. Rysiek. Machnicki's real name was Edmund Blum, and his secretary and her daughter were his sister and his niece. Machnicki/Blum, who was in his early thirties when I knew him, was a Crakow lawyer before the war. Through his sister he knew the German officer, Herbert Szpitta, who visited us. Szpitta ran a Stanisławów-based scrap metal business, and had sent Blum to Borysław to manage its office there under the false Polish identity of Machnicki. Why? I don't know, though it seems he was protecting several members of the Blum family.

Soon after Machnicki/Blum arrived in Borysław, it was arranged that his sister, who by then had false papers identifying her as Mrs. Rysiek, would join him as his secretary. She brought her daughter, Eva, and her husband with her, though I never saw him because he spent the rest of the war hidden behind a wardrobe.

I saw Machnicki/Blum once after the war, but at that time I didn't know his true identity. I visited him when I travelled to Katowice to have my tonsils out in June 1946. He was murdered by unknown assailants about two weeks later, on 8 July 1946. Subsequent rumours suggested the involvement of an underground resistance movement. But I knew nothing of that then; to me, my Mr. Machnicki was always a hero – well-read and intelligent, tall and slim, with dark soulful eyes and a wonderful smile, a man who had invested in my future when there was no reason to think I would have a future.

IX. DISCOVERY

When I first went to Mr. Machnicki's, I was hidden in the cellar under the house. It was dark, cold, cramped and damp, as cellars are. But at least we were indoors. When the German officer came to visit, and we were allowed out, I talked with Eva, and Mr. Machnicki gave me lessons. He gave me books to read and tasks to do when I went back underground. I read a lot by candlelight. Mr. Machnicki told me I was bright, and had potential. I didn't want to disappoint him.

How long did I stay in the cellar? I don't remember. Nor do I know why I was moved from the cellar to the bunker outside, under the rabbit hutch. I didn't ask questions. I moved where I was told to move. Hiding places were hard to arrange. some people paid for places in bunkers, but I think I got a place not only because my brother was one of those who dug the bunker at Mr. Machnicki's but also because I was the girlfriend of Imek

Eisenstein, the son of the head of the Jewish police. The other people in the bunker thought of me as a talisman, a mascot. Though I probably didn't fully understand why at the time, I had some power by association – power as in one person on death row being perceived to have a better chance of reprieve than another person on death row. We were all living with a death sentence. It was just a question of when, not if, the sentence would fall.

The bunker was a reinforced hole in the earth, dark and wet, with no air to breathe, no room to move. I become very disturbed when I think about it. There was always water dripping down the dirt walls, and water on the mud floor. It was dug fairly deep, but not deep enough to give the taller adults any headroom. I was smallish, so I could stand up. There were two layers of bunks, I think, for the eight of us underground. We each had a place to lie down, and somewhere to put our food, and a hole in the ground to use for going to the toilet. The stench and the filth were terrible. Food was brought to us. We hardly ever went outside because of the risk of being seen, but when we did come up for air it was always late at night.

I don't remember much about who was in the bunker with me. There was Poldek Tenenbaum, his younger brother and Poldek's girlfriend's mother. I remember she was with us but Poldek's parents were under the house, in the cellar. That's all I remember.

What did we do down in that hellhole? I'd be lying if I said I knew. I have blocked it all out. What remains is an abiding aversion to confined spaces and low ceilings. Others may find dark houses with small rooms cosy, intimate, charming, but in me they trigger blind panic. I must have space and light and height above my head. At home in Sydney my work space is on a mezzanine floor with hard white light bouncing against white walls and a skylight above. I look out across my desk through glass that soars unobstructed from the ground floor up to the third level of our beautifully proportioned, spare modern house. I built this house when others of my age were wrapping their living spaces more tightly around them. I wanted more space, more air, more room to move. Time has erased my memories, but not my fears.

I suppose that we talked a bit and we slept and waited for our friends on the outside to bring us food. What else was there to do? Oh, I wrote. I was always writing whenever I could. But when the police discovered us, I threw the diary I'd been writing in down the toilet, into the hole in the earth, because I was afraid that what I'd written would compromise Mr. Machnicki.

Someone must have seen us coming out of the ground at night, or maybe they saw an unusual amount of food going out to the rabbit hutch. Eva/Henrietta remembers bringing us bread covered over with greenery for the rabbits. It was the Ukrainian militia who came for us, who dragged us out of our hole, terrified wretches unaccustomed to daylight, and that should have been that. I have a photograph, which is now exhibited in Berlin, of the smashed-up rabbit hutch, and another of we doomed Jews standing in front of what remains of our hiding place. In the first photograph you can see a mangled pile of clothes, bedding, some bread, and a tin bowl and cup. This is what the militia found inside our bunker and hauled up when they destroyed it. In the second photograph, Poldek, the mother of Poldek's girlfriend, and an unknown man wearing a cap are looking straight at the camera, grimly. Poldek's brother, a simple child, is grinning in the foreground of the picture. I am there too, in the background, my head turning away from the camera. My profile is somewhat blurry. I look as if I'm going somewhere. I'm not. I was trapped, but I didn't want to give the hunters the satisfaction of recording the terror in my face.

Marek gave me these photographs. The Germans took their film to his studio for processing, and he kept them. They are rare images, I'm told, though not ones I treasure for their memories, like other photographs I carried with me from the old world to the new. I keep them for the record.

We were taken to the police station, the one that was next to my first home in Borysław. We were thrown into filthy, dark cells under the station, the cells where I remembered pickpockets and drunks being held overnight when I was a little girl, when the police station next door seemed a harmless kind of place. One of the militia men on duty recognised me. He was a former schoolfriend of my brother's, a Ukrainian boy called Janek (I think he was the same Janek that I mention in my diary, the boy that my friend Erna was so keen on). He spoke to me, and apologised for not being able to help. He couldn't let me go, he told me. I said I didn't expect him to. I told him that I understood. He asked me if there was anything he could do for me. I remember this so vividly. I looked around at where I was. It was foul. I was meant to sleep there until I was executed the next morning. I asked him if he could bring me something to scrub the floor with. Janek looked uncomfortable. He said that I would probably be shot tomorrow, and that I shouldn't worry about cleaning the cell. I replied, »Tomorrow is tomorrow. Today I am alive, and I am not going to live like a pig.« I knew exactly what I meant. It was a deliberate act, a defiant act which said to my captors, »I will not buy into your assessment of me. I am a valuable human being.« It was about self-respect. Róża calls it life-oriented. She says if I had asked for a roll with butter and ham, and a chocolate, things would have turned out differently for me.

He brought me a bucket of water and a brush, and I began scrubbing the floor. Then I became aware of people looking at me through the little window in the cell, pointing to the crazy Jewish girl. When I had finished, Janek brought me something clean to lie on, some hay, I think, and I slept. I wasn't the only person in the cell. There were others from under the rabbit hutch, though I don't remember how many.

In the morning when I woke up and looked around, I was alone. My life had been spared. I am sure now, and I suspected then, that Imek's father Walek Eisenstein had intervened on my behalf. How did he know where I was? These things were known. When Jews were discovered in hiding places, the Jewish police knew. They were in charge of the labour camp to a certain degree. The Gestapo were based in Drohobycz and weren't there all the time.

I stayed in that cell for two days, maybe three. While I was kept at the police station, something very curious happened. I was told to clean up the garden. I had never worked in a garden in my life. I started working on a patch of dirt with little green things poking through. I didn't know what they were, but I had been told to clean up the garden, so I did what I was told. I am a perfectionist. I like to do things properly. I worked extremely hard. I pulled out every scrap of green that I could see, and then I got a rake, and made the soil, which is very rich and black in Poland, beautiful and smooth. I remember the sense of achievement I felt.

As I stood back admiring my work, I sensed someone standing over me. Someone very very big. It was the terrifying mammoth of a man we knew as Mittas, whom everybody said was a murderer. He was the head of the Ukrainian militia which had seized us. He looked at me, and at the bare garden bed, and then at me again. I saw this disbelief in his eyes, and then suddenly he burst out laughing. I had no idea why. It wasn't until later that someone told me I had pulled up every single one of the new plants in the police station's strawberry bed.

It was a miracle that this monster didn't shoot me on the spot. I can only think that he saw how proud I was of my work, and he was amused by the absurdity of the situation. A Jewish girl who should have been shot at dawn looking so pleased with herself for having destroyed the promised fruits of summer.

Shortly afterwards I was collected by the Jewish police and taken to the labour camp where I moved in with Imek and his family. However, I was never registered to work at the camp. Walek Eisenstein made sure my presence there went undetected.

X. THE CAMP

In the short time that I was in the camp in the late summer and autumn of 1943, I stayed close to Pepa, Imek's mother. She was the first person to offer me the affection I had craved since my mother's death. When Imek and I talked together about what we'd do in the future, if we survived, she would listen, and would say, gently, »Well, if you like each other, that would be wonderful, but first you have to study and grow up and then we'll see what happens.« Pepa was a good and decent woman, but her husband's position made her persona non grata. She was very lonely. I don't remember her ever talking to any other woman in the camp.

I could move around the camp as long as I stayed beneath the radar, so to speak, but I didn't see much of my father or my brother because they were taken to work in gangs during the day. At night, Josek and his friends, among them Lonek Hoffman, Mendzio Doerfler and Tolek Manskleid, would try to slip away into the hills where, over a period of months, they dug and constructed camouflaged bunkers beneath the forest floor. It seems incredible to think of this now. Conditions at the camp had deteriorated with the appointment of Second Lieutenant SS Friedrich Hildebrand as commandant. Each morning, after a 6 o'clock roll call, the camp inmates were marched single file under armed guard to work, and each evening they returned the same way. Rations were minimal, enough to keep them alive for as long as their labour was feeding the German military's needs. Where did my brother and his friends find the strength after a day's hard labour to walk for several kilometres, unseen, into the forest, to dig and shovel dirt, hack and haul heavy branches, and then get back down to the camp again before dawn? And why did they come back to the camp? Why didn't they flee into the woods?

The extensive forests around Borysław were inhospitable places offering minimal chances of survival. People who sought refuge there depended entirely on friends from the town, or on the collusion of peasants in the surrounding countryside, for their food supplies. There was the danger not only of being caught and shot by militia and German patrols, but of perishing from the bitter cold. Jewish members of Ukrainian or Polish partisan units could not count on the support of the local population when non-Jews were encouraged to attack Jews with impunity. And in Eastern Europe, many of the partisans themselves were deeply anti-Semitic.

The camp offered protection from the elements, and survival rations. Rita, who was in the camp for all of 1943, though we rarely saw each other because she too was marched out early each morning under guard to work, remembers the staple diet was some kind of hot water with a few frost-bitten potatoes floating in it. The bread ration was two slices of black bread a day, one to go with that soup in the evening and the other with the 'pretend coffee' in the morning. Twice a year, at Christmas and at Easter, there was meat in the soup – horse meat. Rita says that she survived on these paltry rations by going to sleep as soon as she got back from work. I don't know how Josek and his friends found the energy to do more, but they did. They were extraordinary young men.

My father had no part in these underground activities. He had recovered sufficiently from his near-death experience with typhus to be considered fit enough for slave labour, but still, the fever had knocked him about dreadfully. I remember going to see him in the room where he slept in the camp. The last memory I retain of him is of a thin, old man sitting near his bed. I realise now that he was 45 years old. I felt this awful pain in my heart to see a man who had once, in my eyes, enjoyed such strength and power, reduced to such frailty. He was as reliant on my brother as I was. All my childish anger towards him drained away. I felt only compassion for him. Even now, I find it difficult to talk about him without some shame, some guilt. I don't even remember his likes and dislikes. He died before I grew up sufficiently to see beyond his role in my life as a parent. I never knew him as a man.

I mentioned that I was vulnerable to throat infections as a child. When I was in the camp I caught diphtheria, a highly contagious disease that used to be called »the strangling angel of children«. It starts in the throat and if left untreated can end up paralysing throat and/or heart muscles. Diphtheria has virtually disappeared since the war with the widespread use of vaccines, but in the absence of immunisation it spread like wildfire through the crowded, and pitifully unsanitary ghettos in Polish cities and towns. The best available treatment was an anti-toxin and penicillin, but for most Jews even money couldn't buy medicine to save their children's lives, and hospitalisation was a death sentence. Imek's parents isolated me in an attic, and sent a doctor to visit. Walek Eisenstein bought medication for me. I don't know where he got it, but I had medication for diphtheria. I was lucky. I keep saying to myself, I was lucky. What other explanation can I find? I don't believe in God. How could I after what I experienced and saw? But at times I have such a strong feeling of being surrounded by a kind of cosmic love.

That didn't always make me grateful. Oh no. I may have been looked after by angels, but I myself was not one. I felt sorry for myself stuck up in that attic, without company. I put my frustrations into a ›letter‹, which I seem to be addressing to Josek, but I don't think I ever gave it to him.

»You say to me ›you are the good one‹. I know that is not true and I realise that I can be very mean-tempered, but I feel so sick ... I don't think that I am a hypochondriac, but because of this illness I feel terribly nervous. I was afraid that I would suffocate. It was so terrible though now it is getting better. A doctor said that there is now an epidemic and it could have been fatal. The knowledge that I can be of some help is so good for me. You can bring something to me so that I can wash it, even though I can only do it on Sunday.

It is true that I am overwrought and I cry easily but you know that I was not like that before. I think it is just because of my illness. I know that I blame a lot of things on my illness, but I don't know that you really understand how I feel. I remember that I used to suffer often from throat infections, and I also remember how Mama used to care for me. I would be lying in a beautiful clean bed with white sheets and covers, and Mama would bring me special sweets for my throat, and give me cuddles and love. Now it's cold, I have terrible pain, I can hardly breathe and the only cheerful note is that you will come, that Josek will come, and will take me in his arms and talk with me, and cheer me up. I feel so lonely. I miss you, Mama.«

There is no date on this ›letter‹, but I used the same kind of narrow ledger paper, writing across columns and in pencil, as in another diary entry dated 8 August 1943. I will come to that shortly. I also wrote poetry in my attic. I wrote to relieve my misery and to assuage my loneliness. I never expected anyone to read it, but I was sad, so sad.

I don't blame you or myself
I don't blame anyone at all
That happiness did not come to me
Just kept on rolling on
And sadness is so great
And green, green like the moss
And has no eyes
Only falling tears.

I was in the attic for three or four weeks, I think, until I was no longer infectious. There are not many other memories I have of that period. Róża, Imek's cousin, remembers that Imek and I came out of the camp to visit her and her mother, Fenka, wherever it was they went when they, as she says, »disappeared off the earth's surface in the spring of 1943«. I don't remember where I visited them, though at some stage they were hidden above Marek's photographic studio. She says that Pepa also spent several hours with them another time, and that she spoke about me as if I were her own child. It was not until after the war that Róża and Fenka became so important in my life, but even at that time Róża seems to have understood how much I mattered to Imek.

On 8 August 1943, when I wrote the diary entry which follows, I had just turned 16. The Germans had been occupying our part of Poland for more than two years. I had lost my mother. Many of my friends were already dead. My brother and my father were slave labourers. I had somehow managed to survive a pogrom, six major deportations and mass shootings, discovery in a bunker and a deadly contagious disease. And yet, I never made any particular effort to save myself. I was unbelievably placid. I didn't lift a finger to ensure my own survival during these years. I allowed myself to be taken care of.

Here is what I wrote on that day. I am not sure where I was at the time. I was still living with the Eisensteins in the camp, but I say that I am sitting outside on the grass and can hear music – there was no grass in the camp, and no music.

»Already a year has gone by [since my mother was taken away]. I've been looking through my old diaries and I can't believe how much I've changed. I think I've grown up a lot. It looks like I have started to know myself. There are so many sides to me. Sometimes I am so naive, like a small child. I get angry easily and sometimes there is a little woman growing up. But I don't really know myself very well. Goethe said, ›To know yourself is to be great.‹ I did have a very nice diary but I threw it into the toilet when we were discovered. Today there was roll call. It looks more or less like this. Approximately 1,100 people – sorry I shouldn't have said people, it is an old habit, I should have said 1100 slaves, standing, waiting. Suddenly there is movement. He is coming. Everybody stands to attention. They are coming. Two ruffians, drunk, hardly upright, horrible faces, and the slaves are standing to attention. Finally the order is given. You can go. God, how is it possible that one can treat people in such a way, to humiliate them ... Will it be ever possible to take revenge for what has happened? I don't believe that the payback will ever be enough. Perhaps some people will take individual vengeance, but I don't think we will be able to avenge the shame they have put us through.

I am sitting outside on the grass, and I can hear music coming from somewhere. I always dreamed that I would continue my piano classes. Mama and I talked of how perhaps I might study at the conservatorium. Mama, it is so painful and it gets worse and worse. It is one year and two days since you have been taken away from me, and how can I believe in God? I look at Josek and my heart is breaking.

I love him so much. He, my dearest one, is suffering so badly, I can't write any more.«

It was probably quite soon after I recovered from diphtheria that I was taken out of the camp to go into hiding once more with Aryan families. That's what we called them. The Nazis' racial ideology saturated our vocabulary. What we dreaded was it saturating our spirits too. Our last defence was our self-respect. How did we keep that when, in life and in death, we were treated as less than human? We didn't accept their evaluation of us. We refused to believe what they wanted us to believe.

We never acquiesced to our own slaughter on the grounds that we had no value as human beings. History has told a different story, about a people who put up next to no resistance to their extermination, who walked meekly into ghettos and blindly onto trains bound for the gas chambers. It wasn't like that though it suits some people to think so.

The central objective of the Third Reich's utopian vision of an Aryan ›master race‹ was to ethnically cleanse each town of Jews, to declare it *judenfrei* – literally, free of Jews. In the longer term, the Nazis wanted to rid Europe not just of Jewish inhabitants, but of Jewish blood and bloodlines, a concept they called Judenrein, which refers to purification. There would be no let-up until we were all killed, and the Jewish ›root race‹ eliminated. Did they expect us to agree to our annihilation? Did they think that the few Polish Jews who were not yet dead by the middle of 1943 would meekly succumb to the Nazi vision of a *judenfrei* Europe? On 30 June 1943, the SS and Police Leader Friedrich Katzmann filed a secret report called *The Solution to the Jewish Question in Galicia* in which he expressed surprise at the resistance of the few remaining Jews in Galicia: »There were also other immense difficulties during the Aktionen as the Jews tried to avoid evacuation by all possible means. They not only tried to escape, and concealed themselves in the most improbable places, drainage canals, chimneys, even in sewage pits, etc. They barricaded themselves in catacombs of passages, in cellars made into bunkers, in holes in the earth, in cunningly contrived hiding places, in attics and sheds, inside furniture, etc. As the number of Jews still remaining decreased, their resistance became the greater.«

If survival meant hiding down a well, or under the forest floor, or in any other number of appalling places, those of us who were offered such sanctuary were grateful for the chance to live. I know I was. I never stopped wanting to live.

And I have never stopped being grateful to those Poles and Ukrainians who resisted the Nazis' manipulation of our region's deeply ingrained anti-Semitism and risked their own lives to hide me. To my deep distress, most of their names are lost to me, if I ever knew them. Where I can, I shall remember them.

XI. THE FOREST

To begin with, I was hidden with Christian people whom my father had known through business, before the Russians destroyed his livelihood. Our family had been well regarded in Borysław and like many Jews in Galician towns, we were culturally assimilated. (The story goes that in Galicia, even the rabbis spoke Polish fluently, whereas in Lodz or Warsaw, only the intelligentsia spoke good Polish, and in Lublin, everyone spoke Yiddish.) I spoke a better Polish than many of my Polish schoolfriends, and since my looks were not distinctively Jewish, some families could be persuaded to offer sanctuary to a girl who by then was known as Sabina Kulawicz (Kulawicz was the name of my observant Jewish maternal grandparents, ironically). I learned my prayers and the Catholic catechism. Actually, I knew more about Catholicism than I'd ever been taught about Judaism. when I matriculated in 1946, I did so under the name Kulawicz and specified my religion as Catholic. It wasn't until I reached Australia in 1950 that I openly identified myself as Jewish again.

The Christian family I remember most clearly was a woman and her son. There was no husband. I remember going to church with them (when I had asked Josek for gloves, I expect I needed them for going to church). She was very kind. She fed me well. One day she took me into the countryside. We were walking towards a small village when we were stopped by police who asked where we were going. She must have talked her way out of that encounter because they let us go, and then

I remember she left me with some peasants. I was uneasy with these people. They let me sleep on a platform above a ceramic oven, which heated the room. But then the woman came back to get me. I think my father must have been worried about where I was, and who I was with. She brought me back to the town, and I was moved to another place. And then another place. And then another place. It was always a few days here, a few days there, not very long. After a time, it got harder to find places for me to stay, and I think it was my brother's contacts, his former schoolfriends, who helped find hiding places for me. I lived in constant fear of being unmasked. On 11 June 1943, Himmler had ordered the liquidation of all Jewish ghettos in occupied Poland, and the transports were rolling into the death camps from across Europe.

In Borysław, as everywhere else, the Gestapo had carte blanche to kill Jews and they had a network of collaborators willing to help them. The penalty for hiding Jews was death. I always arrived at a new place by night, but people in small towns are naturally very inquisitive, and the moment my presence in the household attracted comment and there was a chance that a neighbour might alert the militia, I left.

I remember going with the woman and her son to some kind of entertainment in a private home. There were a few other people in the room. I saw a girl, and immediately thought, ›she's Jewish‹. Nobody in that room except the woman who had brought me there knew that I was Jewish. But I remember suddenly feeling terrified. If I could tell who was Jewish, surely someone else could tell the same about me? I was also very confused. All my life up until then I'd been taught that it was wrong to lie and to pretend to be something I was not. I knew I had to do these things to stay alive, and that I would be killed if I told the truth. But I was disoriented in the extreme during that time.

About ten years after the war ended, I was in New York, and somebody put me in touch with a young woman who they knew also came from Borysław. We met, and I said to her, »I remember you. You were in that room and I thought that you were Jewish.« It was the same girl. She said that she too had recognised me as Jewish. We didn't say much to each other on that occasion. It was too strange, and too painful a coincidence for both of us, I suspect. I don't remember her name and I don't know what became of her.

If I close my eyes, I can picture myself as I was when I was moving from house to house, with my rucksack. I wore a scarf over my hair, and some kind of coat. I always wanted to blend in wherever and with whomever I was. I tried hard to do the right thing, to behave nicely so as to please these decent people who took me in. I wanted so much for them to like me. I understood that each family which gave me shelter put their lives on the line on my behalf.

My brother was my rock, my connection with the world as I was passed from one hiding place to another, always dreading the next goodbye, never allowed to know people's names because that could endanger them. I was so alone, so completely cut off. I waited in a permanent state of fear to be told what to do next, not knowing if there would be a next or if that day would be my last. I did what I was told. I, who am rebellious by nature, who always wanted to do things by myself, little Zosia, samosia, as Mama called me, became compliant, passive.

I pined terribly for Josek. He understood this, and the letter below, which I must have carried with me, though its discovery would have been fatal, reveals how painful our separation was for him too.

»Dear Binuś,

I received your wonderful letter and I am very grateful for it because you have prompted me to write. It is not that I am reluctant to write, but first of all I don't write because I really don't have time to do it and secondly while I am writing I am also trying to organise things connected with food for the forest. I am also involved in organising various things which Mendzio and Lonek have given me to do. By the time I get back [to the camp] there is of course dinner and a shower and then finally, around 9 p.m., I can visit Hala and it is then that I can relax a little.

I usually like to lie down and try not to think too much, just relax. But you know my sense of responsibility, and how I try to deal with everything that needs my attention. It weighs so heavily on me that I have to finish everything otherwise it continues to absorb me and I can't think about anything else.

Recently I have been working at Tustanowice, which was very lucky because I could get some extra milk from the peasants. I even managed to get two lunches in the canteen so I feel and look much better. I hope I will be able to visit you next week so you will see for yourself.

I think about you, my darling, all the time. I am so happy that I don't have to worry about you but then I think how selfish I am. But sometimes when I think that you could be discovered and caught, a horrible fear takes hold of me. I try not to think this way.

Don't worry, my darling. It will be all right. Recently I have become very determined, and in a way I don't even care any more. The important thing is that you survive! You don't even know yourself how much I love you. I hope that you can keep your spirits up because sometimes I notice that you are giving up. But Binuś, you must never, never give up. The most important thing is not to think too much and to have something to do. I will try to be with you as quickly as possible. I know that my presence gives you courage.

So, Binu, my dearest, hold on! I don't think you realise what you mean to me! See you, Binuś, Your Josek«

I moved such a lot in 1943. Everything is a blur in my mind. It is possible that I slipped back into the labour camp under Eisenstein's protection during the periods when my brother could not find a Christian family that would agree to hide me. I would have seen Imek then.

My brother was preparing a bunker with his friends in the forest, as I've mentioned, but I don't think I went there until the spring of 1944. I do, however, remember going into the forest another time with Pepa, Imek's mother, probably in the late summer or autumn of 1943. I remember being in the camp, and someone showing me how to wrap old flannel rags around my feet and legs. There was an art to doing it properly so that the rags wouldn't bunch up and chafe inside your boots. Pepa was a tall, slender woman, and quite delicate. I remember people were worried about whether she was up to the walk. The shelter was built into the side of a mountain. It had a roof of sorts, but no sides, and looked over a valley. I remember how free I felt up there on the mountainside with Pepa, almost as though I were on holiday. Later, when I was in the bunker my brother built, which was further into the mountains where the deciduous beech of the lower Carpathians gives way to deep, dense fir pine, I felt a much greater sense of imprisonment and isolation. But this first time I could see the sky, hear the birds. There was a little waterfall nearby that we washed in. But we stayed only a short time. Someone saw us. We couldn't tell who it was, but we could hear their voices in the valley below, shouting excitedly. We knew it was only a matter of time before word of our whereabouts reached the militia. We fled back through the forest to the comparative protection of the camp. I remember hours and hours of walking by night. I remember also that we stopped and hid inside haystacks to sleep, and being frightened as I lay burrowed in the warm dry grass, not because I feared being poisoned by the fumes that my grandmother had once warned me about, but because the Germans searching for Jews would tear into haystacks with their weapons.

The countryside around Borysław bristled with stories of betrayal, violence and murder during the war. Those of us who were hiding were never out of danger. Many people from Borysław and the surrounding villages tried to hide in dugouts and caves in the forests, and some survived, but many were betrayed or perished. We had a price on our heads. The Nazis offered strong incentives for non-Jews to capture and denounce Jews and those hiding Jews. I don't remember when exactly it became impossible to find families who were prepared to have me under their roof because it had become too dangerous for them, nor when my brother organised for me to be taken to the bunker that he and his friends had built in the forest. I estimate, from working backwards, that I must have spent about two months buried under the forest floor, and that I went there in the spring of 1944. On 13 April 1944, 600 Jews from Borysław were transported to Plaszow, a concentration camp about 10 kilometres from the centre of Crakow. Maybe my brother had heard somehow that something was about to happen, and he sent me to the forest before then. I don't remember the transport. I didn't know until much later that the Eisenstein family were on it.

For most of my life, I sealed my memories from this period as tightly as I knew how. Releasing them terrifies me, even now, and it is possible that I have confused the conditions in this forest dugout with those in the bunker under the rabbit hutch. They were both nightmarish, dark, dank tombs for the barely living.

The forest bunker was not very deep, maybe a little short of 2 m, and closed over with rough-hewn timber, on top of which were strewn branches and small trees for camouflage. I shared my confinement with about nine others, none of whose names I can remember. Again, we had bunks, with just enough room to lie down. The walls and floor were earthen, and we felt the weight of the earth above our heads. The only time we came out for air, and to go to the toilet, was at night, so while I saw the stars through the forest canopy, I never saw the light of the sun.

We were totally dependent on friends from the town to bring us food, risking their lives with each trip. We had a bit of jam and bread, I think, and some kind of tea. There was no shortage of water, and we had sugar. On good nights, someone would bring us something hot and cooked. Who were these people, these saviours of ours? I think they were mostly non-Jewish friends of my brother's. I remember only one name, Zygmunt Miskiewicz. We called him Mundek. I have his photograph. I never asked him why he helped us. I never asked anyone why. (*Conscience and Courage*, an analysis by psychoanalyst Eva Fogelman of the motivations of rescuers of Jews during the Holocaust, suggests that most people lost their bearings under the madness of the Nazi occupation when evil was rewarded and good acts punished.»Fear disoriented them, and self-protection blinded them ... A few, however, did not lose their way. A few took their direction from their own moral compass.«)

Once I was in the forest, I didn't come and go any more. Those who brought us food barely stopped to talk. We had very little communication with the outside world.

We didn't learn that the Germans were closing down the labour camp until liquidation was well underway.

The first indication we had that something was seriously amiss came in a note that Josek's friend Mendzio sent to us in the forest. I still have it. It was written in haste on a torn scrap of paper, and its contents are terrible, though Mendzio's Polish grammar is perfect, all his full stops and commas in the right places.

»Dear ones,

I will tell you everything when I see you. I am in the camp and I am not allowed to move from here. Eisenstein has guaranteed with his life that I will not run away. I hope in time, however, that I can come to see you. Do not dare leave and come into town. I will organise everything. I have money. Lonek is dead. Lonek was killed on Saturday 3rd June 1944. Be well, Mendzio.«

I was devastated by the news of Lonek Hoffman's death. Not only was he my brother's friend, but he was a hero among that group of boys because he had refused under torture to divulge the whereabouts of bunkers in the forest. Tolek Manskleid, who survived the war, described what had happened in his evidence at the 1967 war crimes trial of camp commander SS officer Friedrich Hildebrand. A bunker in which Lonek's mother was hidden was discovered by a forester, who informed the

Ukrainian militia. Lonek's mother was among those killed when the bunker was raided. Lonek was in the camp when he heard the news of his mother's murder. He found out where the forester lived and hunted him down. You could buy arms from the partisans who were in the forest. »When Lonek found out about it, he killed the forester. Hoffman always carried a weapon«, Tolek told the court. Renate Reinke reported it in her book about the Hildebrand trial, *Antworte, Mensch!* [Answer, People!]. When Lonek and Mendzio were caught by the Germans and tortured to reveal the whereabouts of other bunkers, Lonek was so badly beaten that he lost an eye. Tolek told the court, the head of the militia said that in all his life as a policeman he had never seen a man take a beating like Lonek did. He told Lonek he would save his life if he told him where people were hiding.

So now, Lonek was dead. From Mendzio's few words we understood that the situation at the camp had deteriorated sharply. The front was approaching. The Russians were getting closer. Executions would be immediate, and it would be extremely foolish for anyone to put themselves in a situation which would prompt that. Mendzio's note told us that Walek Eisenstein was in the camp. It was only much later that I pieced together what happened to Eisenstein in that spring of 1944.

He had been deported to Plaszow in April 1944, but returned to Borysław under SS guard six weeks later, at the beginning of June, with two others. The Nazis knew there were still a few remaining Jews hidden in the forests and in the town, and they wanted to spread the word that the camp at Plaszow wasn't so bad after all, and that if people went there they could work and be fed. All lies, of course.

Plaszow in June 1944 was nothing like our forced labour camp in Borysław. When it first opened in June 1942, prisoners worked for various German companies, such as the enamelware factory run by industrialist Oscar Schindler, whose famous ›list‹ saved hundreds of Jewish lives. But the SS gradually expanded the camp and its function changed. At its peak capacity, it was a concentration camp holding 20,000 prisoners. In March 1944, transports began taking Jews from Plaszow to Auschwitz and various other death camps. Thousands were also shot in the camp.

Eisenstein was brought back to Borysław to lure Jews to Plaszow with the promise of food and work. Did anyone believe him? No, I don't think so, but some people came in because they were starving to death. Why did Eisenstein co-operate with the Germans at that late stage? Why didn't he refuse? Was it because Pepa and Imek were still alive, and maybe he thought he could save them? I've asked myself these questions many times. They weigh heavily on me, but I can find no answers.

In September 2006 when I went to Crakow I took a car out to Plaszow, or rather, to the place where it used to be. Where there were once barracks, factories, warehouses, barbed wire and mass graves, there are now shrubs and open grassland where families come with their kids to fly kites and exercise the dog, where lovers stroll and the elderly soak up the sun. Plaszow has become a green lung in the midst of an expanding Eastern European metropolis. The Nazis built their concentration camp over two Jewish cemeteries. When they closed it at the end of 1944, the few hundred surviving prisoners were ordered to exhume and burn 9,000 bodies from 11 mass graves. But on a soft late summer afternoon, there was nothing more than a gentle wind to disturb those who visited the rehabilitated Nazi killing fields. I walked up to the foot of a hulking Soviet-style memorial which looms over the freeway below. I remembered those whose names were not on Schindler's list, among them Walek Eisenstein who, with Pepa and Imek, was transported from Plaszow to Auschwitz, and perished there.

I cannot be objective about Walek Eisenstein. In the few accounts that remain of this period, his name is blackened. He was a much-feared man. But I was never afraid of him. I loved him. He protected me as if I were his child and I can only conclude that he loved me, for Imek's sake. There was no connection of blood between our families, no obligation on his part to take me under his wing. But he did, not once, but several times. I am sure that I owe him my life. I cannot run away from that, and I do not.

XII. THE END OF THE WAR

In the early summer of 1944, the Red Army was drawing closer from the east. The Allied forces had landed on the beaches of Normandy on 6 June and were poised to liberate Paris. And yet the transports to Auschwitz kept rolling.

I was still in the forest, in the bunker. Mendzio had told us not to come into the town. It was my 17th birthday on 8 June, but I don't expect that anyone celebrated, nor do I know if I saw Josek that month, nor indeed who came out to see us after Mendzio's shattering note was delivered. On 22 June, 700 people were deported from Borysław to Auschwitz, though of course we heard nothing about that. It wasn't until many years later that I learned that on the same day, Josek and about 50 others from the camp were sent to Stryj, about 50 kilometres east of our town, to build an airstrip. Josek couldn't get word to me that he had left Borysław, and by the time I found out, it was too late to matter. My brother was dead.

While I was in the forest, and ignorant of his whereabouts, Josek escaped from his work unit. A man called Milek Winkler, whom I met in 1993 when I first returned to Borysław, was also sent to work on the airstrip. He saw Josek give his supervisors the slip. In the evidence he gave in the 1967 Hildebrand trial, Winkler said:»I saw him, walking away, my heart was beating when he disappeared into a cornfield.«

Where did he go? What was he thinking? I will never know. On 19 July 1944 Josek was executed by firing squad inside the camp at Borysław, on Hildebrand's order. He was 20. My father and Mendzio were shot alongside him. Hildebrand gave a speech in which he warned that anyone else who tried to escape should expect the same fate. How and where was Josek found? Did he go back to the camp to collect my father and Mendzio? Why was he caught? Why only those three? If they were caught in the forest, were they in a bunker? Were there other people there? There will never be any answers for me. I got there too late.

On the same day that my brother, my father and Mendzio were killed in the camp, Eisenstein sent for me. Someone came into the forest. I don't remember his name, though I knew him at the time. I remember that when he arrived at the bunker, there was some discussion about whether I should go with him. Some people said no. They wanted me to stay, for their own protection. But others said that if Eisenstein was asking for me, I should go. They knew he would look after me, but they didn't know why he would want me to come in. We had no news of what was happening in the town, or in the camp.

I walked out of the forest with my guide overnight. He didn't tell me that my brother and my father were dead. When I got to the camp, it was the morning of 20 July. I came into a room where Eisenstein was. He didn't say a word. He just opened his arms, wrapped me in them, and sat me on his knee. And then he started sobbing. Not crying, but sobbing. I sat for a while. He was not the same man I remembered. He was so thin. I asked him about Imek and about Pepa, and he just kept sobbing. I asked him about my brother. I said I wanted to see him and my father, because I knew they were in the camp. He didn't answer. He didn't say a word to me, not a word. Then he put me down, and said, »Stay here until I come back«, and locked the door behind him.

I was crying because he'd been crying. I didn't know why I was there. I didn't know what was happening. I was exhausted and hungry. There was some food in the room, which I ate. I probably went to sleep.

In the evening, he returned, and said to me, »You have to go back now.« No explanation, not a word about why he had sent for me, or what was happening. He handed me over again to the man who had brought me out of the forest, and we walked back.

When we got back to the bunker, it was empty. There was no-one left in the forest. Eisenstein must have known what was going to happen. The bunkers were considered relatively safe up until he sent for me, the biggest danger of discovery coming from Ukrainian partisans who also used the forest for cover. He must have known that the Germans were going to clean out the forest that day, and he wanted to save me. Why else would he have brought me down? While I was locked in that room on my own, the SS and the Ukrainian militia surrounded the forest. They brought dogs. They hunted down the Jews in their bunkers and brought them back to the camp. Or at least, that's what I heard later.

There was no alternative for me but to make the long trek back to the camp. We slept a few hours, and then set out again. My guide left me on the outskirts of town and I went on alone to the camp.

I approached it from the road, knowing there were still Jewish police there. They were usually at the front gate. I hoped that someone would recognise me and let me in. I saw a Jewish guard I knew, and told him what I wanted. He said to me, »Are you crazy? What are you doing here?«

I told him again. »I want to go in. My father and my brother are in there, and there is nobody in the forest. I want to be with them.«

He looked at me, and said, »What for? Don't you know what happened?« I said, »No.« He told me that my brother and my father had been killed two days earlier in the camp, with Mendzio. That's how I found out. He told me to get away, to save myself, but I was in complete shock. I was determined to get inside. I went around the perimeter of the camp and up the hill. I thought I could slip in the back entrance, which was less well guarded. But as I got there, two German police on horses, the Reiterzug [cavalry platoon], bore down on me, and shouted, »Raus, weg hier! [Get away, get out!] You know you're not allowed to talk to Jews.«

I'd come in from the forest with a rucksack on my back, a scarf covering my head, and boots on my feet. They saw some stupid Ukrainian peasant kid, not a desperate Jewish girl crazed with grief. I thought I'd try again at the front gate, but as I made my way down towards the road, I saw lots of German police arriving. They were surrounding the camp.

I ran. I didn't know where to go but instinctively I turned towards the town. There was nobody left in the forest. It had been cleared. I remembered those friends of ours, the Staniszewskis, with whom Josek and I had shared Christmas as children. I walked through the marketplace or what was left of it, and heard people talking about those Jews who had been shot in the camp the other day. Those Jews they were gossiping about were my father and my brother and Mendzio, but it still didn't quite reach me. My mind registered that what I'd been told was true, they were dead, but nothing about their deaths made sense. I kept walking until I reached the Staniszewskis.

I asked if they would take me in. Jurek and his mother were all right, but Mr. Staniszewski was terrified when he saw me. »One night only«, I pleaded. I would go in the morning. He agreed. I had a bath, my first bath in I don't know how many months or years. I slept in a bed, and ate with them, and in the morning I left. I remember Mrs. Staniszewski hugging me, but her husband was keen for me to be gone.

There was a park nearby, with a few trees and a little bench seat. I sat on the bench and wondered what to do. It was the morning of 22 July. High summer, though I have no memory of the weather. As I sat there, I saw about 300 Jews from the labour camp being marched to the railway station, surrounded by SS men, Ukrainian militia and dogs. I was sure someone would recognise me and ask me to join them. I hoped they would, because then I would not be so alone. I would belong somewhere, with the Jews, going to wherever they were going. I had nothing to live for, no prospect of a future. Everyone that I loved was dead – my parents, my brother, and Imek, as far as I knew. But I didn't have the strength or the will to pick myself up and join them, and nobody in that tragic remnant of Jewish life saw me. Or if they did, no-one called out. No-one seemed to know me. There were many people from surrounding areas, including Drohobycz, in the camp at that time, people who had been driven in from the forest by hunger and people who had been flushed out by terror. I sat there watching the whole transport pass by, and I didn't care what happened to me. Later, I found out that this was the last transport of Jews from our town, that the Nazis had liquidated the camp and sent everyone left there to Auschwitz.

I stayed on that bench, trying to think. I suppose I hoped to save myself, though what I remember most clearly is how utterly helpless and abandoned I felt. Then I thought of Mr. Machnicki. He was the only person I knew who might help me. When our bunker under the rabbit hutch was discovered, the Germans didn't look any further. They never found the Jews who were hiding in his cellar. As far as I knew, they were still there. I went to Mr. Machnicki's, and he took me in. I hid in the cellar for the next 17 days. I remember nothing at all about that time. I don't remember who else was hiding with me apart from a girl called Mala, about two or three years older than me, and an older woman called Anda Katz. I must have asked Mr. Machnicki to let me in, but maybe I stopped talking after that, as I'd done after my mother was deported to Belzec. I am sure I went into shock. This was the only time during the war that I was conscious of being hungry. We survived in the cellar on a lump of sugar each day.

We knew the Russians were approaching. In those final weeks we could hear the armies shelling each other, the booms of the artillery. Those who could see the sky say it became redder. When my brother escaped from his work gang at Stryj, I can only imagine that he wanted to be with me when the war ended. That's what I like to tell myself. But I will never know.

XIII. LIBERATION

On 6 August 1944 – two years to the day since my mother and I were seized – Mr. Machnicki came down into the cellar to tell us he'd seen German police and soldiers, many of them injured, packing up and fleeing. He'd also seen quite a few Ukrainians running away too. The next morning the Soviet troops rolled into Borysław as liberators. There was no dancing in the streets, or kissing on street corners. We were utterly spent of energy, both physical and emotional. The Jewish survivors who started to emerge once it was clear that the Germans had gone had ghastly pale faces, emaciated torsos, swollen limbs. Some were unable to walk because they'd been confined for so long. They came out from under bedroom floors and in between walls, from down wells and up chimneys, from under the ground and up in attics, from every cramped, lightless, inaccessible space a human body could fit itself into. In comparison with others, I was in relatively good health. I could walk upright. I was starving, but everyone was starving by then, Jews and non-Jews.

Compared to the Germans, the Russians were a shabby lot. Their long grey coats smelled. But oh God, how glad we were that they had finally arrived. We wanted to touch them, and they wanted to touch us. I remember being surprised to see so many young girls among them, exotic beauties from the further reaches of the Soviet empire, from Georgia, Kazakhstan and Uzbekistan.

There were degrees of ambiguity about where allegiances stood after liberation. We Jewish survivors kept our heads down, and said very little. We had grave doubts about whether anyone would believe us. Anti-Semitism didn't leave town with the Nazis. Ukrainians and Poles who had hidden Jews didn't want their neighbours to know. They asked the people in their cellars to wait until dark before they left. As for the Russians, well, they were the same lot who, not so very long ago, we had called oppressors.

I will say here that the number of Jews who survived from Borysław's pre-war Jewish population of about 15,000 is variously estimated at between 250 and 800. I myself have more often heard the lower figure though I'm told by historian Robert Kuwałek that 800 survivors from our town gave testimonies shortly after the war. I am not a historian. I am a survivor, and at the time I wasn't counting. I was looking.

Everybody was looking for someone. I knew there was no-one left for me but all the same I went out into the street to see who I could find. While I was out walking I met Marek, Róża's husband. »Have you got anybody?« he asked. When I told him I was alone, he said, »Come, you'll be with us.« He took me by the hand and led me home to Róża and her mother, Fenka, like a lost puppy. I'd first met Róża, Marek and Fenka in the ghetto when they were living next door to Imek. Although I did not know Róża and her family very well, there was never any question of whether or not I would stay with them. Marek presented me as a fait accompli.

Marek had reopened his photographic studio and the business was quickly up and running. All soldiers like to be photographed, and the Russians were no exception. He, Róża and Fenka had moved into an empty flat nearby. The flat had one bedroom, a kitchen with a sink and running water, and an outhouse. Marek retrieved some furniture and personal belongings he had left with a Polish friend while he was in hiding. They had a table, several chairs, some pots and pans, and a white kitchen cupboard in which to put their clothes – not that they had much to wear. Fenka had only one dress. Marek had trousers made of sackcloth, dyed navy blue by Fenka. Róża had a dress made from her school uniform, a good coat (likewise her former school coat) and two slips. She shared her clothes with me. We took turns wearing her dress and the coat, and she gave me one of her slips. Washed in the evening, and ironed in the morning, our slips soon grew threadbare. Fenka patched holes in them, and soon it was hard to tell the fabric from the patch. I still have mine. I shared Fenka's bed in the kitchen. She slept with her feet near my head, and I slept with my feet near her head. Róża and Marek were in the other room.

I adored Róża, who was seven years older than me. I didn't know much about her background but there was always an air of mystery about her. Her father had disappeared in the Soviet Union many years earlier, and she and Fenka had had a hard life because of that, even before the war. Róża was very beautiful; tall and slim with high cheekbones, finely arched eyebrows, lovely green eyes, a wide sensuous mouth and thick blonde hair. She was also an intellectual and her intelligence and erudition impressed me even more than her haughty elegance. She gave me books to read – Proust, Goethe, Dostoevsky, Balzac –

and I read them in the hope that whatever she had absorbed from them would transmit itself to me. I wanted so much to be just like her. But Róża and I have opposing natures, and however hard I tried, I could never impress her. Nor could I charm her with my joie de vivre.

My schoolfriends, the Fleischer twins, Nina and Luka, used to tell me that I was the only one who could cheer them up, but my ready smile and laughing eyes seemed to irritate Róża. I found it difficult to understand myself sometimes. How was it that everyone was dead, and yet I wanted to go dancing? I felt guilty for being alive. I was engulfed by the enormity of my losses, just as Róża was. But I was so hungry to live, and my sunny nature just seemed to bubble up around the sides of my despair. Róża didn't understand that my light-heartedness was only a veneer, and because she didn't seem to see or acknowledge my suffering I thought she didn't care about me. She was a young married woman wanting to make up for lost time, and her husband had brought into their home a troublesome teenage girl. I was an orphan who desperately needed someone to love, and to love me. We got caught up in a spiral of her resentment of me and my envy of her. She had her mother, she had Marek. I had no-one, and Róża kept me at arm's length.

When I read back over the diary I kept while I lived with Róża and Marek, I am reminded of how complicated our relationship was. She did her best with me, but there was always something about me which got on her nerves, right from the beginning. Perhaps it hurt her that Imek was so fond of me. I don't know. We've never spoken of it. In any case, it was through Imek that I became so inextricably bound to Róża. She loved her cousin Imek deeply. They were both the only children of their mothers, the Samuely sisters, Fenka and Pepa. Róża struggled with me long after Imek was gone, for his sake.

My heart bleeds for all of us, Róża and Marek and me, as I pour over the cheap school exercise books I used as diaries. The sentences are crammed so tightly on the page and my pencil script so faded that I strain to make out the words even under strong lights and using a magnifying glass. We were all crippled by the burden of our grief, yet to speak of that grief was impossible. We wanted so much to pick up the threads of normal life – to work, to study, to build a home, start a family – and yet the problem was, why? And how? We all wanted to believe that the moral universe as we knew it before the war had been restored. Yet even I, young and immature as I considered myself, and as Róża considered me, recognised that all preconceptions about what it meant to be human had been shaken to the core during Hitler's war. Still, we didn't speak about good and evil. We spoke about whether I should be allowed to go out dancing, and at what time I should be home.

My diary began again in January 1945. I was 17, and in common with many young diarists, much more preoccupied with the state of my heart and mind than with the state of the world around me. I failed to mention, for example, that the Germans surrendered to the Allies on 8 May 1945, although I am certain that there were big celebrations in our town. I began that year in very bleak mood.

5 JANUARY 1945

›One has to forget. Enough of mourning.‹ I read this sentence in a book called Byron that I am currently reading. I tried. I went to celebrate the New Year. I don't agree. I can't forget.

I continued at greater length the next day.

6 JANUARY 1945

So yes. The year is 1945, and already it is five months since we were liberated. I can hardly believe it. I can hear the voices, I talk, I touch. I know that the Russians are here. I cannot describe the state I am in. At any moment I think I will wake up from sleep, and that the illusion will break. It's some kind of very painful apathy. I sit, but I don't have the strength to get up, and my thoughts go round and round in circles. Josek is dead. Dead? What does it mean? I can't accept death. I don't understand it. Is it only me who finds it so difficult to understand? The first time I came close to death was when Lonek was killed. I fought his dying, I wanted to take away its power; but I lost. So I kept asking questions. What does it mean to die? He is not alive any more? I talked to older people. I asked them, ›You, my elders, the clever ones, the wise ones, what does it mean that he is not alive any more?‹ Never. I am so afraid of this word, of its howling emptiness. Such a cold horrible word. The older people, who normally would say to me, ›you are so young, you don't understand‹, stood there looking at me, silently, and walked away, because they too did not have an answer. And then came despair, terrible despair. I cried, silently at first, and afterwards there were no more tears. Now I can even laugh occasionally, but the pain is so dreadful, so I sit and write, but I don't really know what I want. To live? Just to survive? To live without having any desire or any aim? It doesn't make sense.

It didn't make any more sense the next day.

7 JANUARY 1945

Out there, in the camp, there is freshly turned earth and a pit. My brother is lying there but the pit is too short, so my brother's legs are bent. Sorry, it isn't my brother, it's my corpse. Once he was alive, he was so strong, and so beautiful, so strong he got the first bullet, and he wanted to run, he wanted to live. He waved his hand, he was saying goodbye to life. The second bullet killed him, and then just the cold corpse. Green grass, goats graze on it and in the pit is my brother. Dear God, I think I am going crazy. I want to scream out loud, 'People, do you know that out there is my brother?' But the people are silent, they don't hear me. They have enough of their own problems. I am eating a tasty piece of bread and my brother is dead. I am holding his photograph. His beautiful smile. I remember ›Dear Binuś, you don't know how much you mean to me.‹ I can't bear it. Not true. I know I am crying now, but soon I will be able to laugh again ... It is two years without my mother. I remember how I cried, ›Mama, where are you?‹ And now, Josenku, corpses are silent. God! Do I still believe? The other day I asked a soldier, ›Do you believe in God?‹ ›Absolutely‹, he replied with conviction. Then, with such surprise, he asked, ›And why not?‹ Can one still believe? Where is God? And my brother is dead?

In February, it rained. I wrote: »There is a lot of mud, black, ugly, clinging to you. It is hard to get out of the deep mud. It is grey and it is sad. It agrees with my mood, with my thoughts and my feelings.«

And in March, I was desperately seeking solace in the smiles of orphans. By then I was working as a teacher's aide at the Catholic orphanage we called St Barbara but which the Russians renamed Children's Home.

13 MARCH 1945

I should find some satisfaction in working with the children, and in trying to teach them how to grow up to be a good human being (but I myself don't really know how to do this). And there is some happiness in every lovely smile that I get from them, and every good word that I exchange with them, and when I can see their smiles and a bit of happiness in their eyes. I try but there is not too much happiness. There is a lot of pain and there are so many orphans there and I too am an orphan. I shouldn't feel sorry for myself, but I am longing so much to hear a few kind words. I am so sad today.

Recently, as a result of a labyrinthine series of connections, I received a copy of a diary page, dated 22 April 1945, at the bottom of which my name, Binka Kulawicz, was signed. Nearly eight months after Borysław was liberated, I was still hiding behind the Polish-sounding name I had adopted during the war, probably in the spring of 1943 when I began living with Christian families. Above my name was a short poem by Adam Asnyk, which I had written out from memory for the girl who kept the diary and who, like me, was Jewish, though I didn't know it at the time.

For noble hearts is
The pleasure most blessed
When they bring joy to
Those sad and distressed.

The woman who faxed me the page of her old diary lives in Brazil. She was that girl, a Holocaust survivor like me. Her name had long ago slipped from my memory, but her image had stayed fixed. I could place her in the Tenenbaum house in 1943, with her mother, and the man I now know to be her uncle but who, at the time, I knew as Mr. Machnicki, her mother's employer and my protector. Occasionally we were allowed to come out for air, and it was then that I must have played with the girl called Eva, but whose real name I now know is Henrietta. When our hiding place under the rabbit hutch was denounced to the Germans, I never expected to see Eva, or anyone else, again. I expected to die. But here I am, more than 60 years later, integrating into my timeline a document so precious that I am still absorbing its meaning and the meaning of Eva/Henrietta's reappearance in my life.

I need to retrace my steps. Shortly after the Russians arrived, I went to the military headquarters to try to join the army. I wanted revenge. I wanted to kill Germans. I was interviewed by an officer. I told him that I wanted to fight the Germans. He asked why. I told him that I had lost everybody, and he looked at me, and said, in Russian (it sounds so nice in Russian), Duroczka, ty maja [silly little girl]. I'd be dead ten times over before I ever saw a German, he said. He told me to finish school and grow up to become a decent human being. I remember thinking that he was a good man, because if my mother were still alive, she would say the same thing.

So I went back to high school. That was hard. I resented any kind of authority, and after my experiences, I found it difficult to concentrate. On top of everything, I was expected to sit alongside and be friendly with other students who only a month ago might have killed me, or denounced me.

I worked during the day and went to school in the evening. I walked the 3 kilometres to school after finishing work at the orphanage, and was back home by about 9 pm. On Saturdays I helped Marek at the studio, developing film. Because the job at the orphanage was a government job, and paid so little, I knitted for extra money. It was difficult to buy wool after the war. I used a thick carpet yarn salvaged from old rugs that had been picked apart. It was coarse, and made my fingers bleed. I knitted at night, and kept a ledger of what I was paid: 80 roubles for gloves, 350 roubles for a sweater and so on. I also recorded what I spent. Looking back at my accounts, I see I went to the cinema in Drohobycz, I bought some clogs and a blouse, I went to the doctor to have my knee x-rayed, I had my shoes repaired. Marek and Róża were generous to me, but I felt I had to pay my way. It's not the hardest thing in life to earn a living. What I found much more difficult was earning Róża's respect.

There were soldiers in town, and I was an attractive young girl. My body had recovered quickly after the war. I wanted to go out and have fun. Yes, I was grieving, and my pain was deep and acute, but my instinctive response, as it has been at other times in my life when I have felt the earth subside beneath my feet, was to keep moving. I am an extrovert. I like to be among people. Good company distracts me and warms me. In March 1945, I met a young Russian officer called Pasha and he took me dancing. Two months later, when our romance foundered on Róża's disapproval of my behaviour, I covered page after page, trying to understand what it was that I wanted from my life.

13 MAY 1945

Pasha. He came into my life unexpectedly. We went dancing, and he brought me home, and as usual to say goodbye I held out my hand for him to shake. and then I don't know how it happened, but he kissed me. At first I wanted to run away, but then he kissed me again. It was my first kiss, and it gave me pleasure though I don't understand why

Two months have passed and I have been going out with him. Pasha is not a young boy. He is 27 and I know that he is a grown up man and he desires me. But I know that I will not become his lover. So now, I question myself, do I love Pasha? I don't know. I do know that I like him very much. I went to meet him at the barracks and it was a cold day, so he asked me in. I have never cared about what other people say, however to go into the lodgings of an officer isn't the done thing. He asked me why I was making things so difficult. He says he loves me. How can I explain to him that he is a Russian and that he doesn't understand how I feel and that I can't marry him?

I am very young and I still don't know what I really want to do with my life. I've been thinking of my mother and of how she always wanted us to have the things which she didn't have. I loved her so much. She was my mother, she was my friend, and she hoped that we would have a happy life and a career. She believed in me and she trusted me.

Imek's relatives have given me shelter. They feed me, they clothe me, they try to give me the crumbs from their hearts. Do they understand me? I don't think they think about it, they have enough of their own problems. I have become a person incapable of enjoying life. What will become of me? I am uneducated, not particularly intelligent (though I don't like to admit it to myself), I don't know why I should go on living. I am afraid to express my opinion because I might say something stupid. What can I do to build up some belief in myself? I always wanted to study journalism and to write, but I don't think I have either the talent or the intelligence for it ... Marry Pasha? I couldn't. I am so grateful to them [the Russians] for liberating us but they are so different. I am by nature extremely impulsive and I am guided by my emotions and not my brain. I don't know how to put the brakes on. I miss my mother's guidance so much. I don't think I have met anyone else who is as undisciplined or as confused as I am. But there is one good thing about me, which is that I can accept the situation I am in. And also, I don't judge people because I know that you never know what people are really like. Even after all the horrible things I went through, I still trust people. Something is happening in my life now. I think it's some sort of crisis. It frightens me .

A couple of weeks later, I failed to come home one night and the low-level tension always present between Róża and me erupted into the open.

26 MAY 1945

I went over to Pasha's place and we lay down on his bed and I put my head on his chest and I fell asleep. I couldn't believe that I was actually there, sleeping, in an officer's room, on his bed, all dressed and with my virtue intact. I got home at about five in the morning, and then it started. ›Where were you? What were you thinking? What were you doing?‹

I knew very little about the ways of men for a girl my age. I hadn't had much of a chance to learn the game of love. I had lived through a war in which the basic rules of civilised society were turned on their heads. My priority in those years was not wondering whether a young man's eyes and hands might wander too far, but figuring out who I could trust with my life. Would this person shoot me, or would he spare me? My relationship with Imek was nurtured in the most abnormal conditions and was always very protected. I thought I was mature, but really I was still very childish in some respects. But how was I to learn about love? And from whom?

Sometime before this meltdown over Pasha, Róża had quarrelled badly with Marek and she walked out on him. When I came home, Marek was there with a man who sometimes worked in the photo lab, an awful man who made advances towards me. I asked where Róża and Mama (as I called Fenka) were. Marek said they had gone and were not coming back. The other man, Mr. L., said something along the lines of, ›Well, you know women. They're all talk. They'll be back.‹

I went searching for Róża and Fenka and eventually found them at a friend's place. When I went in, I was probably smiling because I was so pleased to see them. Róża turned to me and said,»What are you looking so happy about? Go home, go back to Marek. You can take my place there, in everything.« I started to cry. I said to her,»How can you say something like that?«

I went home, still crying, and Marek asked me what Róża had said. I told him that she wasn't coming back. Mr L. kept saying,»Oh yes, they'll be back, don't worry.«

He was right. Róża came home the next day, and in my diary I wrote about hearing her and Marek laughing and making jokes behind their closed door. There was no apology to me. When Róża came out, I said to her,»I'm not going to stay here. I hate you, Róża.« I said I would look for another place to live. Then Marek came over to me, and said that Róża had told him what she'd said to me the day before.»That was horrible«, he said.»She hasn't got the grace to apologise to you, but I'm not going to let you go. You're like family.«

I was so confused and hurt by this incident. How did love work? How could Róża say that I could take her place in everything? Didn't she think of me as a child? She certainly treated me like one. Why else did I expect the worst when I got home so late after going out with Pasha? I remember being too scared to knock on the door, and sitting outside, crying, until Fenka found me. That's when Róża made her terrible scene. When she was done with interrogating me, she asked me if I was planning to go out dancing that night. When I said I was, she told me I wasn't going anywhere, and that I had to study. If I left the house, she said, I needn't come back, and that she didn't have anything further to say to me.

27 MAY 1945

Always the same. So it is not just a question of not letting me go dancing, it is just that she is absolutely not interested in how I feel or what I think and all that I am going through. It is just a certain kind of upbringing that matters. But this kind of upbringing is all wrong, particularly for me. Even if my mother were to treat me this way I would rebel because I am stubborn and rebellious by nature.

8th June is my birthday. It looks like it's going to be a great one. In a few days I shall move out of here. After the words that have been said, life at home is impossible. It is a great shame that it should end like this. I wanted to remain friends. It would be better for me perhaps to live separately. Perhaps I could rebuild faith in myself. Here, I feel so small, so worthless, Róża is everything, the cleverest one, the best one, the nicest one. I am crushed by her superiority. She is so perfect. Mama, please help me. Save me. I have no-one.

Four days later, I finished writing about what had happened that night when Pasha called to collect me to go dancing.

1 JUNE 1945

Pasha came in and he started a conversation with Marek. He said that if Marek didn't want me to go out with him, then he would not come over any more. But [first] he wanted to explain that he was very serious about me, that he was an officer and that he was trusted with other people, and that Marek should trust him too, that he was serious and respectable, and that he was a Communist. I can just imagine how much that conversation amused Marek. Finally I was allowed to step outside with Pasha and he told me that I had to make a choice. Either it was books and studying or it was Pasha and marriage.

In the morning I asked Róża, ›Is there anything that you would like to say to me?‹

›No‹, she said. I replied, ›All right, in that case, I will go, but I think it will take two days for me to find somewhere to live.‹ I put on my coat and went towards the door and then she stopped me. ›Binka, wait, sit down.‹ And then she started talking, saying that I was still so young, so immature, and worst of all, stubborn, arrogant, willful, conceited and very difficult to manage (that's enough to start with). I agree that I am young and immature, and that I make mistakes, but isn't that normal at my age? All I really need is some praise. What she calls stubbornness I would call a strong will. She says I am conceited when I really don't believe in myself. I am really not conceited at all, just the opposite. And to cover up for having so many doubts about myself, I pretend, I act, and she calls that arrogance. So I wanted to tell her all that, but I was afraid, and didn't know how to say it. Róża said, ›Just talk straight, without elaborating.‹ But I kept saying that I found it so difficult and I didn't know, but obviously she finally understood me. Then she said that maybe she had made a mistake in saying all those things, and she asked if I wanted to make peace. I said, ›What a question.‹ Of course I wanted everything to be all right again. So my attempt at independence fizzled out and now of course I question myself again and I really don't want to leave because I don't want to be totally alone. Pasha? I do miss him. Maybe I will see him when I go to the movies, but now my priority has to be exams. Probably I won't pass them. Very sad. I don't have a clue in algebra, geometry and physics, and Ukrainian. I don't need them anyway. We'll see.

That was it with Pasha. Róża made my choice for me, but it was the choice I would have made if I'd been as honest with Pasha as he was with me. The truth was that I didn't want to be the wife of a Russian soldier, moving from town to town, organising our life in terms of five-year plans, taking whatever the Communists dished out. I still had my dreams. I went back to my books, and when I sat my exams in mid June, I passed.

With school over, I took a job in a delicatessen in nearby Drohobycz. I was happy to get the job. I didn't have any skills to speak of, and I was paid better than at the orphanage. The deli owner, Mrs Spiegel, gave me board during the week, and on the weekends I hitched a lift back home to Borysław. I did everything at the deli — I opened the shop, prepared food, served behind the counter, cleaned, and so on. The Russians were moving back east, having taken Berlin, and we sold them vodka and tasty snacks. I worked long hours but I earned what I considered a fortune, about 100 roubles a day. Even so, I was tempted to steal. I remember it well. The shop took a few thousand roubles a day and there was no cash register. I wore an apron, and put the money in a big front pocket with a zip. I thought if I just took 100 roubles more, I could buy myself things I wanted, like real shoes (the ones I wore had wooden soles) and a warm coat. I was so ashamed of myself for even thinking like this. What would my mother say? Mrs. Spiegel trusted me. My shame was enough to control the urge to steal, though it didn't stop my wanting the shoes and coat.

It was around the time I got the job in Drohobycz that the remains of my brother and my father and Mendzio were exhumed by whatever Russian enterprise had taken over the former camp. The next and final entry in this diary was dated 3 July 1945:

»By mistake they dug out the graves of my father and Mendzio and Josek and they have moved them to the cemetery. There was no-one to dig the graves there so I approached some Jewish people and I begged them to come and they buried them. I wanted to look, but I was afraid. I stood there. I appeared so calm, but I was completely paralysed. The moment the coffin hit the ground I broke down. I felt like screaming, screaming, ›Be careful, be careful, that's my brother, my brother.‹«

I couldn't talk about my grief. I couldn't even write about it. I needed others to speak for me. I remembered the first verse of a poem I had once read. I wrote it into my diary. Then slowly, line by line, the whole poem came back to me. It expressed exactly how I felt. It's called, simply, *Pain*. The poet is unknown.

> By night through silent woods
> Through empty field and plain
> In clouds of silent mist
> A hermit walks, the Pain.
> Through field and valley he treads
> From far arrives he now
> Bearing a blue and silver plough.
> A child sleeps in the valley
> Wrapped in nightly mist so deep
> Tormented and grieving,
> The weary heart sleeps.
> The Pain comes clad in mist
> And tears the sleep apart.

He grasps the plough in both hands
And drags it through the heart.

XIV. DESPERATE TIMES

By the summer of 1945, the boundaries of central Europe were once again shifting. Our part of Poland was pushed behind Ukraine's redrawn western frontier, thus becoming part of the Soviet Union, and Poland was compensated for its losses in the east by gaining former German territories in the west. Borysław's Polish citizens were given the choice of staying and becoming citizens of the Soviet Union or registering for repatriation to Poland. Róża and Marek registered for *repatriation*, and included Fenka and myself on their papers. We were all on stand-by to go to Poland. There was hardly any warning given of when the transports to the west were leaving. You had to be ready to pack up and go when your number came up.

I was still working at the deli in Drohobycz and normally coming home at weekends. At the end of September 1945, Mrs. Spiegel asked me if I would travel to Kiev to buy extra supplies for the shop. She knew someone who would take me. His daughter had died during the war, but he still had her identity papers. I could use her documents to travel and to buy goods that were hard to get outside the big cities. It was an offer too good to refuse. Kiev had been badly damaged during the war, but it was the metropolis, historically the most important city in Ukraine. The furthest I'd ever been from Borysław was Lwów. »I haven't seen anything yet and I am already 18 years old«, I wrote in my diary on 29 September 1945. »I'm starting to believe that perhaps I do have a little bit of luck.«

We left the next day. I didn't have a chance to let Róża and Marek know I was going. We weren't in telephone contact in those days. I didn't know how long I'd be away, but I was sure I'd see them in a few days' time.

As we sat on our suitcases at the Drohobycz station, waiting for the train to arrive, I scribbled in my diary:

»Russian soldiers are lying all around us, sleeping, their dirty high boots sticking out, their guns lying all around, their backpacks tossed everywhere. The simple soldier's life. Somebody is playing a harmonica and they want me to dance. Everything is so new and so exciting.«

On 4 october, I was in Kiev, which Eastern Europeans think of as the birthplace of Russian Orthodox Christianity. I wandered, as a tourist, into one of its famous churches, and sat on a pew, soaking up its mystery and its beauty. I feel as though I have gone back a thousand years. It is very quiet in here. Occasionally a priest walks through, with his long beard and high hat. It looks like a movie, so unrealistic to me, I made notes about the religious paintings I saw, their period and the names of the French, Italian, German and Dutch painters, and included a potted history of the church, far older than any I had ever been into. Kiev gave me my first taste of what lay beyond provincial life, but I didn't have long to savour it.

By 12 October we were back in Drohobycz delivering the supplies to Mrs. Spiegel, and then I returned to Borysław. I knocked on our door. Someone I didn't know answered. »Where is the H. family?« I asked. They weren't there any more, I was told. They had gone to Poland. While I was in Kiev, Róża and Marek were notified that they had to leave for Poland on the next train. They explained to the authorities that they couldn't go then because I was away for work, and that they expected me back any day soon. But no-one wanted to know. »You go now, or you don't go«, came the reply. They had no choice but to leave without me. I don't blame them. I never have. That was what happened in those times. You did what you had to do.

So, there I was in Borysław, by myself again, homeless, with no family, and no identity papers. Technically, at 18, I was still a minor. When Róża and Marek and Fenka arrived at the border, I later learned, they had a lot of trouble because my name was on their papers and I wasn't with them. Finally, my name was crossed off their papers. Officially, I didn't exist any more.

To this day, I have a dread of goodbyes. So often things change between when you say goodbye and the next time you see a person. I didn't see Róża and Marek again for about six months. That's how long it took me to find the means to leave Borysław. And when I did finally leave, I paid a price that even now makes me squirm.

I returned to Drohobycz and Mrs. Spiegel took me in. I could stay with her as long as the shop was open, she told me. But she too was waiting to leave for Poland. My life went on. I worked long hours, and when I had the energy, I went to the movies or out dancing with Russian soldiers. I lived in two zones. On the outside I was keeping myself busy, on the inside I was leaden, weighed down by my losses and abandonment. I wrote in my diary on 23 October:

»Another day, another evening. My life is so grey. The whole day in the shop, listening to the sick compliments and the lies, and pretending to smile but feeling such terrible pain in my heart. It's already three years since my mother died, and a year since the death of my brother and my father and Lonek, but I still can't accept it. I can't understand the concept of death. Sometimes I see a mother hugging her child, and I am envious. I want so badly to feel your arms around me, but it wasn't meant to be. I have to learn to accept it. I know that life is going to be difficult. The winter is coming. I have to try to get some clothes to keep warm. I want to study. I would love so much to have my own room, nice and clean, and a place for my books. But how? And then I start to feel guilty. Am I too concerned about myself?

But I am only 18, and my brother was only 20 when they killed him, and he wanted so much to live. He too had the right to live. Is there any punishment?«

Mrs. Spiegel closed her shop on 22 November 1945 when her *repatriation* notification came through, which left me without a job. I wrote:

»I feel so sad. I don't know what to do about this. I found some sense in working. It gave me pleasure earning my living. I do need some money. I will sell the things which I don't need and hopefully I will be able to leave [for Poland]. I don't know where I will go ... Will I go to Róża and Marek or to Zygmunt [Zygmunt Miskiewicz was the friend of Josek's who had brought food to the bunker in the forest]. I am afraid to commit myself to anything but I would like to see Warsaw. Something will turn up, as they say.«

I went back to Borysław, although I knew virtually nobody there any more. Most people had either left, or were preparing to leave for Poland. Without papers, I couldn't get a job, or leave the country, and I could be arrested at any time. I had nowhere to live.

On the street, I met Mala, the girl who had been in the cellar with me at Mr. Machnicki's when the war ended. She said to me, »As long as I am here, you can stay with me.« She had a room very close to the bridge which was the central meeting place in Borysław. The room had two single beds, a potbelly stove, a table and a basin, and a place to hang clothes.

Mala was working in a canteen where, if you paid for soup, you got free bread. She used to steal the bread and bring it home. I had a little bit of money saved from working in Drohobycz, so in the morning we would buy some milk and eat the bread. I didn't eat at lunch or at night. Mala could eat at the canteen.

I should have known better, but after a few weeks, in my desperation, I decided to go to the police and tell them what had happened. I hoped they would give me some papers if I explained my situation. The Russians were different from the Germans, I thought. They treated Jews as human beings. I went to the police station (the same police station where I had been thrown into the dirty cell two years before and which was next to our old family home). I was shown into a large room, and interrogated under glaring lights by a police officer who sat behind a desk. What is your name? Do you have any papers to prove it? Why not? Around and around, exactly the same questions to which I gave exactly the same answers. I began to panic. What would they do with me? Suddenly the lights were turned off, and another officer walked into the room and asked my interrogator to leave. He beckoned me to pull my chair over to the desk. He was older than the other man, and looked kinder. He could see I was frightened, and tried to calm me down. He asked me to tell him once more what had happened, and what I wanted.

I told him that I was Jewish, that all my family had been killed and that the family I had been living with had left for Poland while I had been in Kiev. I told him I needed papers, and that I thought the police would help.

He looked at me in much the same way as the officer at the army headquarters had done. »Silly child«, I remember him saying. »Haven't you learned anything yet? Why would you trust the police to help you?« He was Jewish. He had lost some of his family in Russia. He told me that children like me, children who had lost their parents and had no-one to care for them, were regarded as a nuisance by the state. Feral children, we were called. I could be arrested and exiled, and nobody would be any the wiser. He couldn't give me papers, he said. What he could do was let me go, and strongly advise me never to come anywhere near the police station again. So I left.

I was back where I started. People told me that the only way to get papers was to buy them, but I didn't have enough money and I couldn't get a job without papers. A man I knew offered to cut me in on his black market cigarette run. His name was Dunio. He was going to Lwów, he said, and I could go with him and buy cigarettes to sell in Borysław and Drohobycz. He asked me how much money I had. I told him, and he agreed that we would go to Lwów together.

It was December, and already cold. Lwów is about 100 kilometres from Borysław. We went by truck; Dunio sat in the cabin while I sat in the open tray at the back. I froze. By the time we arrived, it was dark and we needed to stay overnight. That's where, in my innocence, I came undone. He must have assumed I would sleep with him, but I locked my door. I heard him banging, trying to get in, but I shouted at him to go away.

In the morning, he went out and bought cigarettes, which he divided between our two rucksacks. Then he told me that we should return to Drohobycz and Borysław separately. He would go first. I didn't understand why at the time. It never occurred to me that someone who had survived what we had survived would want to hurt me. When I arrived in Drohobycz, I went to the shops he had told me to go to. They said they didn't need cigarettes, that they'd already bought them from Dunio. Everywhere I went it was the same. There I was, with a rucksack of black market cigarettes which, if I were caught, would have been enough to have me sent immediately to Siberia. I had no money. I'd given it all to Dunio.

On the road which led out of Drohobycz towards Borysław, there was a corner where people congregated to hitch a free ride. I waited there with the crowd until an army truck pulled over. I went to climb onto the back of the truck with the rest of the people, but the soldiers in the cab invited me to sit inside with them. Me and my rucksack.

They weren't ordinary soldiers. They were NKVD, the secret police. They thought I was a lovely girl, or so they said. They asked me my name and then they asked me what I had in my rucksack. I was terrified. But what could I do? All they needed to do was open the rucksack to see if I was lying. So I told them the truth. I said, »Cigarettes«. They roared with laughter. »Cigarettes?« »Yes«, I repeated, »Cigarettes.« They thought I had a great sense of humour. What a good joke. They didn't ask me to open my rucksack. I got out of the truck in Borysław with my heart pounding and waved them goodbye.

Dunio had done the dirty on me in Borysław, too. Nobody wanted to buy my cigarettes. In the end, I sold them for half what I paid for them. At least I got some money back. I was desolate. I had no idea of what was going to happen to me now.

When the war ended, some of the Jews who had fled to Russia in 1941 with the retreating Soviet army, and had survived the war in Russia, returned to Borysław. I did not know any of them, but at the end of 1945, when there were so few Jews alive in the town, we got to know each other. They took me on as a problem to be solved – a young Jewish girl, without papers and alone, without male protection, in a town full of Russian soldiers. There was an obvious solution to my dilemma – at 18 I was old enough to be married. It wasn't what I wanted particularly, but since well-meaning people who were older than me thought it was what I should do, after a while I began to think along those lines too. I wrote in my diary on 26 January 1946:

»Up until a few months ago I couldn't imagine getting married and accepting that loathsome ordinary life. But now I am thinking about it. People around me are saying it is time to get married. Perhaps if there hadn't been a war and there were different conditions I would not have made this decision but I have no mother and I am alone, so the time has come.«

I don't remember how I was introduced to Heniek. He was one of those Jews who had spent the war in Russia. He was about ten years older than me, pleasant looking, and with a kind heart. People thought we would make a good match. I was open to thinking so too. Heniek is ideal husband material, I wrote in my diary. He is honest, unspoiled and he loves me. He worships me. But I could see there might be problems in our relationship. Heniek was a very simple guy, I wrote, not like the boys I'd known until then. I described him as uneducated and uncouth. His first language was Yiddish, and his Polish was awful. I turned myself inside out trying to justify why I should be interested in marrying him. I decided that I had matured. I wrote:

»... until now I would not have even looked at someone like this. But I realise that the important thing is to create a home and eventually a family. I don't try to convince myself and I've told him that I don't love him, but I hope that in time love will grow. I am finding an excuse for everything; for instance, education is very important, but it is not everything and this is something which can be acquired. Manners can be learned and when he starts speaking Polish with me and reading in Polish he will learn the language too. Besides, the ideal doesn't exist and people who have only good qualities and no faults don't exist.«

For the next month, I swung between being optimistic that things would turn out all right with Heniek and being assailed by terrible doubts about whether we would have anything to talk about. I wrote about a dream in which my mother warned me, Think hard, my child, about what you are about to do. I was stung by the knowledge that people were gossiping about how Mala and I lived, two girls on their own who went out dancing with Russian soldiers. They don't know the truth about me really, but they are very critical, I wrote.

 The clincher was this: I had always wanted to have a pair of real shoes, not wooden ones, but shoes made of leather, with leather soles. Heniek bought me a pair of leather boots, and I accepted them. In my moral universe, a girl didn't accept an expensive gift from a man without reciprocating. I felt guilty about the boots, but I wanted them. I agreed to marry him.

 For many decades I found this episode in my life embarrassing, and deeply shameful. I never spoke about it. I judged myself harshly for what in today's language you might call a survival strategy. But that's not how I thought of it at the time. I was far too much of a romantic to admit even to myself that I was taking a husband because he could provide me with papers. That would have seemed calculating. So I talked myself into thinking I was marrying because it was the right thing to do. However, I must have known that Róża would see right through my arguments, and find them wanting.

A few years ago, Róża returned to me a letter that I wrote to her and Marek on 17 February 1946 in which my news about my looming marriage is disingenuously buried.

»I am sending this with somebody who is leaving on a transport from Borysław. I apologise for the problems which you had on my account. I am sorry again but when the chance to go to Kiev presented itself I didn't think that there would be a transport while I was away. You can't imagine how stupid I felt when I walked into the house and there were strangers there. I can't obtain any documents, neither a passport nor an evacuation card, not only because of my age, but also because I am registered as already having left for Poland. If it hadn't been for the problems it caused, I would have enjoyed what I saw in Kiev. It was really interesting. I saw so many old churches and beautiful buildings. So once more, please please forgive me.

Róża! I really don't know why I love you so much. I am worried about your health [Róża was pregnant when she left Borysław and gave birth to twin daughters in November 1945] and I hope that you are all right. I have so many questions. I want to know how you are. Has Marek opened his business? Does he have a lot of work? How is your apartment? There's been quite a change in my life. It is possible that I will get married soon. I would like to think and to believe that fate caused my delay in leaving Poland. My future husband will be absolutely wonderful. He is so good and so nice but there is one difficulty. He is uneducated. He arrived here from Russia and you don't know him. Róża, I like all your relatives, Beki and Hetty and Poldek, but you are the only one I love the way I do, and it is your opinion that matters to me. In whatever I do I immediately think, ›What would Róża think about it?‹ I don't want to remember all the angry words which passed between us and the doubts which you have had about me. All I want to think about is how much I miss you and how much I love you.«

Why did it matter to me so much what Róża thought? I worried about Heniek being uneducated, but I felt my own lack of education keenly too. I'd missed three critical years of high school because of the war. I loved learning, but I had a lot of catching up to do. In my eyes, Róża was so much more cultured and knowledgeable than me. I admired her. I took it as read that her opinion was better informed than mine, and I was plagued with doubt about my own judgment, and about my future prospects.

I was married on 3 March 1946. I borrowed a dress for the wedding, which was held in a private home. I lost the address and took a while to find the place. I don't remember anything about the ceremony, other than that someone with the right to marry us conducted it (it was a Jewish wedding, not a civil marriage) and that there were witnesses. All I wrote in my diary that day was: I got married. I feel very strange about it. I can't believe it. I tried to make him happy and to please him.

After the wedding, I went back to the room I shared with Mala. I know it sounds odd, but I never knew where Heniek lived in Borysław because I didn't go there. It's hard to understand today, even for me. But these were not normal times. People had been through horrendous trauma. They were lonely. They grabbed onto whoever was close and willing. Often they married within a few days of meeting each other. Heniek was never my boyfriend, in the normal sense of the word. I knew nothing about him. I never met his family. All I knew was that he was kind to me, and that seemed enough to begin a marriage with. I'd seen little enough kindness during the war. Two weeks after I was married I wrote, Generally speaking, I could say that I think I am happy. The concept of happiness is questionable, because how many really happy people are there?

We left for Poland soon after the wedding, bound for Wałbrzych, the Silesian town where Róża and Marek and others from Borysław had been resettled. Heniek added me to his papers as his wife. He also added my 12-year-old cousin Benio, at my insistence. I don't remember when I found out that Benio had survived the war with Hania Proc, and that he, like me, was an orphan marooned on the wrong side of the Polish border. I don't understand why, when I was expecting to leave for Poland with Róża and Marek, I didn't ask them to take Benio with them. Maybe I hadn't yet discovered that he had survived. Maybe. In any case, at some stage I ran across Hania, and when she learned that I was leaving for Poland, she asked me, »What are you going to do with Benio? You can't leave him with me. He can't grow up here. He has to be with Jewish people.«

Benio didn't want to leave, the poor child. He barely knew me, and Hania was the only person who loved him, and whom he loved. Hania brought him to the station and forced him onto the train, screaming and sobbing. I felt terrible taking him away, not knowing myself what our future was. But Hania had made it quite clear to me that any future would be better for her Jewish child than being left behind in Ukraine.

XV. MARRIAGE

When we arrived in Wałbrzych in the spring of 1946, the town was midway through an identity change. Many people still called it by its German name Waldenburg but there was no doubt about who owned it now. The newcomers, mostly Poles from the east, were snapping up the goods and chattels of departing Germans at bargain prices. People couldn't travel with many possessions, so they were happy to get whatever they could for their furniture and silver and so on. They walked out of their apartments and their businesses. That was the way it was after the war. You took what you could, where you could.

Wałbrzych largely escaped damage during the war. It's a pretty enough little town, which in recent times has shucked off its coal-mining past, and now markets itself to the world as a dreamland for mountain-bike riding and a source of affordable educated labour. Goethe reputedly drank in a wine bar in the market square during a visit in 1790, but the town's main attraction is Książ castle, which was built as a fortress by Polish princes in the 13th century and converted in the 17th century to a luxury palace by one of Prussia's richest families, the Hochbergs, then known as Fürstenstein. Three centuries later, the Soviet army destroyed it and then a cash-strapped Polish government restored its rich interiors. Such are the turns of history which we who were born in this part of the world read as normal.

Heniek found us a place to live, and got on with business. I had no interest in what he did. Some kind of dealing, I supposed. He gave me plenty of money, and we ate well. We even had a woman who cooked and kept house. What more did I need? Ah, that was the problem. What was it that I needed? So much, but most of all, I needed to undo what I'd done. What had I been thinking? Heniek and I came from two different worlds. We had nothing to say to each other. Róża and Marek didn't want anything to do with us as a couple. Their thinly disguised disdain for my marriage cut me to the bone.

In May 1946 I wrote in my diary:

»My God, what did I do? I have ruined two lives, my own and that of this good, decent man with a golden heart. I blame myself for it ... People are all saying now that they knew it wouldn't last and that I will leave him in no time. But before, when I talked to them, and asked them for advice, they told me that this was the right thing to do. My dear God, Mama, what shall I do? I am not yet 19, how am I going to live and how can I cause so much pain to someone who is so kind to me? He can't understand what is wrong. Is it so important to have all these conversations that I am missing? And what is all this talk about not having anything in common? ... He can't understand. I have everything I need, a good standard of living, so what am I dreaming of? I don't know how I am going to get out of this. Mama, what am I going to do?«

Heniek thought I was the best thing that had ever happened to him. He would have showered me with gifts if I had asked for them. But I didn't want anything, and least of all sex. He wasn't unattractive, but desire was suffocated in my tangle of self-recrimination. I have blocked all memory of our physical relationship from my mind.

Nina and Luka Fleischer, my schoolfriends from Borysław, were living with their parents in a little town called Kłodzko, formerly known as Glatz, about 50 kilometres south of Wałbrzych. We corresponded. It must have been obvious from my letters how unhappy I was.

In a letter dated 11 May 1946, Nina wrote:

»My dearest crazy old girl ... Binuś, I don't want to upset you or have you be angry with me, but I can see that you already have enormous doubts. I've been thinking so much about it and I have to say it's not possible for you to be and to live with a man who is so inferior to you intellectually. I know that he is good to you and I know how important this is for you, especially you, who is always lacking love, but I don't think that you can continue to stay with him. Once again, forgive me for saying this, but I think that the truth even when it's painful is more important than untruth.«

She wasn't telling me anything I didn't know myself. On 19 May, Nina wrote again, in reply to a letter from me: »I was so afraid that you would take me the wrong way ... but I can see that you understand exactly what I was thinking.«

At this point in her letter, Nina broke off to make brief mention of her plans to convert to Catholicism. I must have told her that I didn't think it was a good idea. Don't condemn me for that. Perhaps you are right but I have gone too far, she wrote.

I myself wasn't admitting to being Jewish – it didn't feel safe to do so – but I couldn't see why anyone would want to convert. What for? To live the rest of your life under a false identity? I couldn't do that. It was always important to me to be truthful, and very painful for me to hide the truth away. That said, I didn't underestimate the fear which I believed was driving Nina into the arms of the Catholic church. The roots of Polish anti-Semitism go very deep, and immediately after the war, Jews continued to be vilified and terrorised in Polish villages, towns and cities. I've read that over the course of 1946 and 1947, as many as 1,500 Jews who returned from the death camps or from hiding were murdered in Poland. The most notorious killing spree took place about six weeks after this letter of Nina's, in the city of Kielce in central Poland (about 300 kilometres east of where I was living). Kielce had been gutted of Jews during the war, but by the summer of 1946 about 200 Jews had made their way back to the town, where most of them were housed together in one building. On 4 July, a mob of local residents brutally attacked these survivors with iron pipes, stones and clubs, killing 42 and wounding about 80 others. The Kielce pogrom triggered a huge wave of panic among Polish Jews, dashing remaining hopes for a Jewish revival in Europe's graveyard. Jews began pouring out of the country. Over 60,000 Jews left Poland between July and September 1946 with the implicit encouragement of the Polish government, which was granting passports valid only for exit purposes.

So, as I say, I knew why Nina didn't want to be Jewish, but I was uncomfortable about denying who and what I was. I'd survived by passing as a Christian, and to some extent, I was still doing so. But I didn't want my future to be based on a lie. Nina went ahead with her conversion and we never talked further about it.

In her letter, she returned to the subject of my marriage.

»You are writing to me about feeling guilty for marrying. Dearest one, there is no guilt there. You were alone. You didn't have anyone to advise you. What else could you have done? Personally I would have to marry someone who was intellectually superior to me. He wouldn't even need to be good. We have been through so much, but now I don't have time for being high-minded because it won't get me anywhere. One of my friends told me that if she doesn't matriculate she will kill herself. But then I remember our life for three years during the occupation. After this ›life school‹, and after we saved ourselves from the hands of the Gestapo, what can happen to us now?«

As well as my problems with Heniek, I had to consider what to do with my adolescent cousin, Benio, who blamed me for taking him away from Hania. I couldn't keep him. He spoke Ukrainian, and his Polish was bad, too bad for him to go to school. There was an orphanage not far from Wałbrzych that had connections to the underground, which was helping Jewish children emigrate to British-controlled Palestine. Benio eventually resigned himself to going to Palestine, and went to stay in the orphanage while he waited for a place on a ship. He arrived in Palestine sometime in 1947. It must have been before the huge furore over the *Exodus* because after that, the orphanage stopped sending children to Palestine. (The *Exodus* sailed from France on 11 July 1947 with over 4,500 Jewish men, women and children on board. Before it reached Palestine's territorial waters, the ship was intercepted by the British navy, which was clamping down on illegal immigration. There was a violent struggle, in which some people died, and the passengers were transferred to navy transports which returned them to displaced persons (DP) camps in Europe. The incident escalated, causing the British significant embarrassment, and played an important part in the eventual recognition of a Jewish state in 1948.)

In the middle of 1946 I found out, through the Red Cross, that my American uncles were looking for me. The Red Cross magazine carried advertisements placed by people searching for lost relatives. I bought one, and at the top of the list was an appeal for survivors of the Kulawicz family. I was so excited that I remember running back to where we lived, and falling over and hurting my knees. My mother had four brothers in America: Sam, the eldest brother who had left Poland after the First World War, lived in San Francisco; Adolf, her favourite, who had come to say goodbye to us in Borysław in 1936, lived near Sam; Harry was in New York; and Jacob in Argentina. By 7 July 1946 I had received a letter from my uncles in which they said they would do everything possible to arrange for me to come to the United States. They also gave me permission to organise the sale of my grandparents' house and small landholding at Hureczko, and to keep the money from the sale. Since I was hoping to leave Poland for the United States as soon as possible, I travelled to Przemyśl and did the deal as quickly as I could through a lawyer there without even visiting Hureczko. I thought there was nothing left for me in that place. Nothing I could bear to face, that is.

Sixty years later, I found the courage to return to Hureczko. I went not just to chase the shadows of the dead. I went to remind myself that my grandparents and their large family had once lived there. As it turned out, the dead were absent even from the civic death register. In the municipal office in the centre of Przemyśl, two obliging young women gently broke this news to me one morning after they'd spent the best part of an hour climbing up and down ladders on my behalf, hauling down narrow bound ledger books from high storage cupboards and scanning their beautiful handwritten script for the nuggets of official information I sought. I gained something from their effort, the date of my parents' marriage in Hureczko – 30 January 1923. But then the trail went cold. There were no death records kept in 1942, they apologised. That's when the liquidation of the ghetto began.

All Jews living in villages surrounding Przemyśl were forced to move into the city's Jewish district by the summer of 1942. The ghetto was sealed on 15 July, trapping between 22,000 and 24,000 people inside. The Nazis began their systematic extermination of the captive Jewish population of that place on 27 July 1942. I have to assume that my grandparents, Chana and Joel Kulawicz, my Aunt Nesia and her husband and daughter, Sala, and my Uncle Bernard and his wife and two children died at Belzec, with the majority of Jews from the Przemyśl ghetto. I've read that only 250 Jews came out from hiding to meet Przemyśl's liberators on 27 July 1944.

I used a tourist brochure I picked up at the hotel reception in Przemyśl to locate the village where my grandparents had worked the soil, husbanded their animals and raised their seven children. The Polish countryside was a pretty soft green, layered with cultivated fields, water courses and trees still holding their leaves. At the turn-off signposted Hureczko, my driver, Adam, stopped to ask a group of teenage boys lounging around on their bicycles to direct us to the centre of the village. They fell about laughing, and pointed down the road, under the railway bridge. We spent the rest of the afternoon and well into the evening following a cascade of equally obtuse directions.

At the first house we came to, a woman was working in a suburban replica of Monet's lily garden, complete with a Japanese-style pagoda and miniature arched bridge. I asked if she had heard of any Jews who had lived there before. She leaned over a rough-sawn Mexican-style fence, and calmly considered my question. »Yes«, she told me, »there used to be Jews here, but they were all killed. All murdered.« Her voice and her face gave away nothing of her feelings about this crass truth. She sent her husband to help us. He took us on a wild goose chase and then he left us with barely a goodbye. After that, we bounced from house to house, criss-crossing the terrain backwards and forwards, with me being pulled along by an intense longing to find something, anything, which would confirm for me what I knew: that my grandparents had lived in this place. We felt ourselves being watched by people behind gates, behind lace curtains. Finally my instincts led me to a piece of land I thought I recognised. The modern two-storey farmhouse meant nothing to me, but I felt a strong tug towards a particular line of trees, and the way the field rose to meet them. The people in the house hadn't heard of the Kulawicz family, but they knew the name of the family who had owned the place since the war ended. Later that evening, a meeting on a windswept backstreet in Przemyśl with a beaten-down man with small eyes in a block of a head confirmed my hunch. He was the son of the people to whom I had sold my grandparents' property. I still had the documentation from the sale. He'd never lived there, he said, his arms folded defensively across his chest. He didn't know if the house was still standing. He thought not. He'd sold half the property to his tenants, the people I'd met.

So this was the place. As we drove out of Hureczko, the sky, which had been strewn all afternoon with high wind-blown clouds like the underbelly of a sheep, turned a triumphant gold. It was such an incongruously beautiful sight as I took in the complete obliteration of my family's life from that bucolic landscape. The pain and despair which I felt each time I asked yet another implacable peasant if they remembered my family, and my question was answered with a shrug, or a vague wave of the hand in the direction from which we had just driven, sat over me like a pall as we headed out from Przemyśl the next day towards Ukraine, towards Borysław.

XVI. RÓŻA

I was still married to Heniek when I went to Przemyśl in September 1946 to negotiate the sale of my grandparents' property, and obviously quite depressed. I wrote in my diary on 18 September:

»The worst for me is the loneliness. I can't deal with it. I drown in it … There is no-one I can confide in and I keep trying to understand myself. I've realised that I will have to learn how to overcome my tendency to resignation … [that] basically I don't really believe in myself and I don't believe that I am strong enough. I haven't seen Heniek for a few days and I don't miss him. There is no possibility of continuing our life together.«

Soon after I returned to Wałbrzych from Przemyśl, Heniek gave me an excuse to leave him. I jumped on it, feigning distress but feeling huge relief. I had suspected there was something going on between him and our housekeeper, which didn't bother me at all. As long as he left me alone, he could do what he liked. But one day I came home and found them together, and I had the justification I needed to walk out the door. I said to him, »Look, you just get on with your life, and I'll get on with mine.« I had my own identity papers by that time. I took only what belonged to me – my clothes, a lovely jug, which I used as a vase, an embroidered tablecloth and a warm blanket. I'd bought those last three things with my own money when I was working in Drohobycz. I didn't want to go back and live with Róża and Marek, and I had nowhere else to go, so I went to the orphanage where Benio was staying. I suppose I thought I could go to Palestine too if all else failed.

As it was, I didn't stay long at the orphanage. My friends Nina and Luka tracked me down, and brought their mother with them. Mrs. Fleischer didn't waste her words. I was to get my things, and come home with her and the girls. So once again, I was saved.

Nina and Luka were at high school in Kłodzko, studying for their matriculation. I wanted to matriculate too, but I also had to earn some money. I applied for a job as secretary to the director of a timber mill. I remember the interview well. I came into the office of an elderly (in my eyes) man who, after he'd asked my name, proceeded to quiz me on my secretarial experience. I told him I had none. He persevered. »Can you take shorthand?« he asked. »No«, I told him, »but I could write very fast.« »Can you type?« he asked. »No«, I said, »but I could learn.« I was a very quick learner, I assured him. »Do you know what's involved in secretarial work?« he asked. »No«, I said, »but if you told me what to do, I could do it. I could do anything.«

I told him that I had to have a job. I had lost all my family in the war. He said he couldn't employ me as a secretary, but he sent me out into the field for six weeks to learn about the business, every little detail of it from the forest to the timber yard. I was so eager to learn. I wanted to show him that he could trust me, that I wouldn't let him down. After those six weeks, he made me his assistant. I wasn't paid particularly well. Poland was now a Communist country and this was a government business, and I was the most junior of employees. But I was well treated. I went to school in the evening. My days were long. I studied hard – I remember sitting with my feet in cold water and a cold compress on my head, trying to stay awake by drinking black coffee, and still falling asleep with my books. Still, Nina and Luka and I went out dancing when we could. I was a hopeless saver. Whenever I had a bit of money, I'd spend it. For example, I bought myself a beautiful coat when the money from the sale of the house at Hureczko came through. I thought of it as caring for myself. I remember Mrs. Fleischer once saying that the difference between Nina and Binka was that if I had saved 900 złoty, then in no time at all I would have 10 złoty. By contrast, if Nina had saved 10 złoty, in no time at all she would have 900 złoty.

I wrote to Róża and told her I was living with the Fleischers. Whatever I was doing, I always let Róża know. I considered her and Marek to be my family. I think I received Róża's reply at the end of 1946 or the beginning of 1947. The letter I have isn't dated. I have re-read it many times.

»Listen to me, my little one. I am not feeling very well and I am in bed so it's very difficult for me to write so I'll be very brief. I'm not surprised that you have landed at Fleischers. In a way I expected it because you always choose the easiest way, but for me that is not a solution. You can't stay there longer than if you were a guest, and you cannot be a permanent guest. Even if you pay for your keep, as far as I'm concerned it is not the end of the problem. Sure, you will try to read and you will knit to earn some money, but those things will take only a few hours of your day. What will you do with the rest of your time? You will paint your face, you will fix your eyebrows, you will look in the mirror and decide that you are pretty, and then you will start to take away Nina's friends. You don't understand the difference between living life and having a good time. You will commit another stupidity, so be careful. It will be at least a year or more before your papers arrive and you can leave [for America] but you can't sit back and wait for that. When the Fleischer family leaves [the Fleischers were talking about moving somewhere else] you will be on your own again. You have to learn to look further than to the next dance. Even though you are with your friends, you are responsible for your own actions. Show me finally that my feeling for you is based on something other than knowing that a man who loved you [Imek] was dearest to me in the world. I don't expect the impossible from you. From the first moment of our relationship you have continuously done things that I condemn. If I didn't walk away from that relationship, it was obviously because I thought that you were capable of and had potential for other things. I haven't forgiven you yet for your marriage and now you have done something else that I don't approve of [leaving Heniek]. But if you have already done this, then behave as agrown-up. You are only 19 years old, and you have already managed to cause pain to at least two men. [Which two men? Did she think I had hurt Imek?] Do you think that you won't be punished for that? I don't want to frighten you, but your irresponsible behaviour makes me angry. You sit there at Nina's place, and do you think that is the epilogue to your marriage? You have to stand on your own two feet. You have to study, but during your free time from work, not from play. The details I leave to you, but I expect you to tell me those details very soon. I know I've caused you pain, but our relationship is mainly based on that.«

That letter shredded me. I was ready to kill myself. I thought she was probably right. I did often look for the easy way out. I had made a mistake with my marriage, and I didn't have the guts to live with that mistake. But she was wrong about Imek. What did she know? She wasn't even there. She was in hiding for most of the time when we were boyfriend and girlfriend. I loved Imek. We had hoped to have a future together. Why did she say these things to me? I still don't understand it. I must have written back to her and told her how hurt I was by her insinuations. When she replied, she was as remorseful as she had been critical in her previous letter.

»Little one, with whom I have more problems than joy. I received your last letter, a bit of a flick on the nose. You are right. I am right. And Heniek is also right. Everybody is right. Everyone who is interested in this matter has their way of looking at it. Do you remember the story of the Egyptian and the crocodile? In case you can't remember, I'll tell it to you again. An Egyptian woman was doing her washing in the Nile with her baby very close by. A crocodile snatched the baby away. She cried and begged him to give her baby back, and he said to her, ›I will give your child back if you can guess what I intend to do with it.‹ ›Well, you will eat it‹, said the mother, and when the crocodile smiled, she asked, ›Did I guess?‹ The crocodile said, ›Yes, you guessed.‹ And she said, ›Well, you have to give my child back to me.‹ ›No‹, he said, ›I can't do that. If I give the child back to you, that would mean you didn't guess because I didn't eat it. And so I have to eat it, to confirm what we agreed on.‹ ›No‹, said the mother, guided by her love. ›You will give my child back to me because if I didn't guess it, then you have to give my child back, and if I did guess it, you still give it back to me, because this is what we have agreed on.‹

It's a complicated story, but neither in life, nor on the stage, should one come out of the parts that we play. Because I did that I deserved to be taught a lesson by you. And now that's over, I will go back to my part as an observer. There's an old saying that one person can help another to love together, but to cry together is very difficult. That's all we can do, even for the ones we care about. Each of us has to carry his own burden. Obviously I should not give advice. I myself don't take it from anybody. In any case, it wouldn't have changed anything in my life. I'm suffering from a bad case of self-hatred. Your letter was a salve to my wounds. Be well, you foolish little thing. Try not to do things which might provoke me again. Give me your little cheek and I'll kiss it.«

My friends, like Nina, could never really understand why I allowed Róża to be such a strong influence in my life. All I can say is that I had no mother. Even though Róża was more the age of an older sister, turning to her became a habit, like a daughter turning to her mother for approval. I brought my third and fourth husbands halfway across the world to be inspected by Róża (only the fourth, a man many years my junior with whom I've stayed these past 30 years, passed muster).

Róża and Marek took me in when I had no-one else, a 17-year-old orphan with an insatiable appetite for love. I clung to them as to life itself, and I put Róża on a pedestal. I needed a woman to look up to, and she was everything I hoped to become. For her part, she saw me for who I was, right from the outset. She knew that wherever, and whenever, I found myself out of my depth, I would learn to swim. I wasn't afraid of the fast current. I would use it to take me where I wanted to go, and if it proved too strong for me, I would go with it and wait for the water to bring me back to shore. She knew I wouldn't drown.

I've been back to Poland several times since I emigrated to Australia in 1950. Each time I have visited Róża and, while he was still alive, her husband Marek. There is no-one who matters more to me in my mother country, the country of absences. But even now, I don't know what Róża thinks of our relationship. I confuse her, I think.

I think my openness to men, and to the life of the senses, frightens Róża. Lots of things frighten Róża and she puts them in a cupboard, and shuts the cupboard door tight. She's as frightened now of what will happen if the cupboard flies open as she is of what's in the cupboard. I'm different. I tend to bring the things that frighten me out in the light and examine them. That way they don't have so much power over me. But I can't convince Róża to see the world the way I do. I never could.

I remember in the '70s, when I was between husbands, and I went to stay with Róża in Warsaw. I was travelling with a friend from Sydney, a German-born artist called Jutta Feddersen, who wanted to meet my friend, the great Polish sculptor Magdalena Abakanowicz. We flew from Germany, and on the way our plane was diverted to Prague because of bad weather. During those dull hours in the airport lounge in Prague, waiting to take off again for Warsaw, we two women struck up a conversation with a couple of Polish journalists. We all enjoyed ourselves, and I gave them the phone number at Róża and Marek's where Jutta and I were staying. Shortly after we walked in the door, there was a call for me and an irritated Róża demanded of me, »Who is calling you in Warsaw? You have only just arrived, and you already have a phone call?« I told her that we had met these interesting men on the plane, and they wanted to take us out. Róża couldn't understand that. It wasn't the way she did things.

Life hasn't been kind to Róża. Her relationship with Marek was fiery and intense, driven by ideas and an ideology of which I could never be a part. I wasn't made like them. I went in the opposite direction, in every sense, though I kept coming back to them like a homing pigeon. Róża didn't expect me to do that. What she has never understood is that I loved her for her sake. She thought that after I left Poland I would want to forget them because they reminded me of the saddest period of my life. She's told me that. She has told me several times how lucky I was to escape from their household. I didn't see it that way at the time. I do now. Theirs was a sad household, tragic even.

I wanted Róża and Marek to emigrate to Australia. I begged them to come, but they were intellectuals who valued the currency of the Polish language, and didn't want to exchange it for another. They wanted to make their contribution. There were other terrible times after the war, more waves of government-inspired anti-Semitism in 1946/47, and 1968/69, which drove out most of those Polish Jews who had hung on. But Róża and Marek wouldn't leave Warsaw.

I wanted so much to be part of their family. After I left Poland, and life became easier for me, in a material sense, I made many offers to help. But Róża didn't want my help. She still doesn't. In rejecting my help, she rejects me. She is saying, »You are not one of us.« Not part of the family.

XVII. JANEK

I didn't steal Nina's friends, as Róża had predicted I would. I didn't have to. There were plenty of nice boys in Kłodzko because there was an army base nearby. We girls would go out dancing together, and sometime towards the end of 1946 I met a Polish officer called Janek who was my first serious boyfriend. Yes, I had loved Imek, and I had thought of marrying Pasha, and I had married Heniek, but Janek was different. I could imagine a future with him.

Janek wasn't a professional soldier, but had interrupted his law studies to do his military service. He had an intellectual intensity that I admired. Physically, he was tall and slightly built, fair with handsome, lean features. By the end of March 1947, he had finished with the army and returned home to Pabianice, just outside of Lodz, and was writing regularly to me. In one letter he said he thought that I should join the Polish Socialist Party (PPS). I told him I didn't want to (he became involved in the party machine). I visited his family at the end of April, and he told me his parents liked me. I liked them too. Their home was such a beautiful cultured environment. His father was a prominent socialist and had friends at the highest level of Poland's post-war government. After Janek's departure, I was meeting other boys in Kłodzko, but I promised Janek that I would be faithful to him. Though we were not formally engaged, he and I had slept together. It was implied by his parents that they would be very happy if we were to become engaged.

I started to think about what it would mean to marry a Pole. I hadn't told Janek that I was Jewish. Janek and I spoke about every subject under the sun, but we never spoke about my past. He and his parents knew that my family had been killed in the war, but many Poles lost their families too. They knew I was from the east, and that I had relatives in the United States who were trying to get me papers. But again, many Polish families had relatives in America. They never asked me directly about my experiences in the war, though I remember we spoke about Auschwitz where his father had been held as a political prisoner.

Around this time, I discovered (I can't remember how) that I had an uncle of sorts living by the Baltic Sea in a small village called Skarbinowo, not far from the port of Gdańsk. He said he was related to my mother. I didn't really know how, but I was happy to have any relative, and I went to visit him a few times, once with Nina and Luka. At the beginning of July 1947, while I was in Skarbinowo, I wrote Janek a letter in which I tried to express what our relationship meant to me.

»Before we were together I thought that silence could express only loneliness and the pain of loneliness. When I was hurt, I didn't want to talk, I was silent. Silence could also mean resignation. But since staying at your home with you and your parents I know that silence can also express the feeling of completeness. When you were so close to me, words failed me. I couldn't really talk, all I could do was just nod my head. This kind of silence is more expressive than thousands of words. One can be silent when one is in despair, or agony or unhappy. But then there is the most wonderful fine delicate shade of silence when one is so happy that one doesn't need to talk and when for the most unbelievable brief moment one can hear two hearts beating in the same rhythm. I hope you won't laugh at me. I don't know whether it is the sea or the sky or you, but you gave me your permission to write about everything, whatever

I felt or wanted to say. I don't know how long it will last and how long we will be together, but I know that I want to tell you this.«

My happiness seemed perfect. But within less than a month, something had happened which shook me so deeply that things were never the same between us. It's hard to make strict sense of my comings and goings after all these years. I can't remember exactly when I visited Janek and his parents in Pabianice. Was it on the way north to Skarbinowo, or was it on the return trip? Or both? In any case, while I was in Pabianice, visiting Janek, he and I went out to a restaurant with a couple of his friends. As we were walking home, we crossed a small street and a strong smell of garlic and onion wafted out from one of the houses. Onion and garlic is nowadays more often associated with French and Italian cooking, but in Poland, Jews ate onion and garlic. One of the boys said, »The Jews smell.« I froze. I thought Janek didn't know I was Jewish. I remember his reaction. He turned on his friend sharply, and said, »How could you! Aren't you ashamed of yourself? Haven't you learned anything yet?« The other boy mumbled that he didn't mean it, that it was a joke. But the damage was done. Janek's friends came from the same social circle as he did, the Polish intelligentsia. If we were going to have a future together, these were the sort of people we would be mixing with and who would influence our life together. I couldn't escape the sadness that grew inside me. I wanted to forget about the past, I wanted to live, but I couldn't continue to live a lie.

In a letter to me dated 31 July 1947, Janek wrote that we needed to talk. He couldn't believe I was planning to leave Poland. He knew that I had been corresponding with my American uncles about getting a visa. So it wasn't just my vague departure plans that were bothering him. Something in our relationship had shifted, and he felt it. I knew what was disturbing me, but couldn't bring myself to speak about it for fear of what it meant for us.

I don't know how long I agonised before I wrote, breaking off my unofficial engagement to Janek and at the same time telling him that I was Jewish. I'm guessing it was several months because the letter I received in response to mine is dated 15 November 1947. It is one of my most treasured possessions. Janek wrote:

»My little darling!

This is a very difficult letter for me to write and I don't know where to start. I want to talk about matters which you mentioned in your last letter and I want to tell you that I was aware of that from the very beginning of our relationship. It is such a complicated thing and I couldn't understand why you didn't talk about it . I remember our wonderful holidays, brief as they were, and I remember when I asked you, ›What is the matter with you, darling?‹ You seemed to be somehow distant, and you replied very briefly, ›I've thought about our relationship and I think it will be better this way.‹ I didn't want to insist, but it was so difficult for me to understand, and particularly when we said goodbye to each other and you didn't even want to turn your head to look and to wave to me. We are grown-up and we have to be honest with each other. You expressed certain opinions about me in your last letter so allow me to express my observations about you. I know that you probably have had a difficult past and you don't want to think about what has happened, but you have to if you want to build and think about the future. I think that you need a life without special worries. You spoke so often about your need for stability and a home, but those opportunities were offered to you, as well as the chance to study. I was happy to hear about your uncles in America but I would have been much happier if you had stayed in Warsaw and studied.

Binuś, I just want to add a few sentences which will have particular meaning since your last letter. I want to tell you that not only did I know that you were Jewish, but that my mother and my father knew as well. And if you consider the warm and unassuming welcome you had into our home, consider that it was offered in full knowledge of the fact that you were Jewish. Once more, it is so difficult for me to believe that you could have even for a moment thought that we would behave differently towards you. I understand it was hard for you to write but we just want to tell you once more that you have always been for us the same Binka that we loved so much and that we knew who you were.«

Janek berated me for not trusting him. It is difficult for me to even forgive you for thinking that I would have behaved differently had I known that you were Jewish, he wrote. That proves how little you knew me, and perhaps you don't really want to know me better. Perhaps he was right. Perhaps it wasn't the courage to tell him I was Jewish that I lacked, but the courage to know him better. Perhaps I was scared of what I might find. Anti-Semitism was so pervasive in Poland then. People openly spoke of what a pity it was that Hitler hadn't finished off the job he had started, and of how all the Jews should be killed, or at the very least expelled from Poland. But not all Poles are anti-Semitic. I was a victim of my own prejudice. I was afraid that Janek would stop loving me because I was Jewish. I didn't trust him, so I cut him off before he could cut me off. Possibly what I was thinking was, ›We are free now. I don't have to wear an armband. Why do I have to talk about it?‹ I didn't want to talk about what it meant to be Jewish. Not at that time. It was too painful. We promised each other that no matter what happened, we would write to each other for five years. The last letter I sent to him was from Paris, where I was in transit, waiting for permission from the American authorities to immigrate. He replied, and begged me to write back. »I have already forgiven you«, he wrote. But I was already committed to another man. A man who knew there was no need to say anything, who knew enough not to ask. A man who had worn an armband, too.

XVIII. ZDENEK

Róża's birthday falls on 7 June, the day before mine. In 1947 I went to Wałbrzych for a few days for a joint celebration. She had decided she wanted sausages for our birthday dinner, so we went shopping together. While she was inside the delicatessen making her choice, I waited near the door. I noticed a man behind the counter looking at me, an older, good-looking man with a small moustache and penetrating eyes. He unnerved me a bit.

I was in Wałbrzych again two months later, and some friends of Róża and Marek from Borysław, the Heiligs, invited me for coffee and cakes. I went, and that man from the shop was there. He was clever. He'd worked it out. He knew that Róża was from Borysław, and that the Heiligs were too, and he'd asked them who the girl who visited Róża was, and if they could introduce us. That's how I met my future husband, Zdenek Wolanski.

Initially I wasn't interested in him. I was still going out with Janek, and besides, I had my sights set on getting to the United States to study. I had already organised my passport. I didn't think anything serious would develop with this man. But it did.

After I broke off with Janek, I wanted to feel someone's arms around me, to have someone care about me, and someone I could care about. I was so frightened of being left alone. If I suffered from many terrors during the war, the terror that endured was the fear of being abandoned. I craved human touch, human warmth. Zdenek made it clear that he liked me – and I fell in love, almost as an expression of gratitude. I fall in love easily. Maybe not now, but in those years, yes. As soon as I thought that someone was showing an interest in me, I very quickly attached myself to them. I felt safe with Zdenek, who was 10 years older than me. He had a confident, sophisticated man-about-town manner, which was not only very attractive, but also reassuring.

He had grown up in Poland's second largest city, Lodz, a major industrial and textile centre, and was 22 when war broke out. I never knew what he did before the war. It obviously didn't seem important to me. During the war, he had been in the Warsaw ghetto and fought in the 1944 uprising. He belonged to one of the smaller resistance organisations, the Polish People's Army (PAL). He never spoke to me much about what happened to him, but I know he lost his parents, an older brother and his girlfriend during the war. After Warszawa was liberated, he and his younger brother, Henio, went to Czechoslovakia to join their sister, Hela, who had gone to Prague to study medicine. Many young Jews emigrated to study between the wars, when Polish universities limited the number of Jews they would enrol, and thereby saved their lives. When Zdenek and Henio returned to Poland, they came to Wałbrzych because of the opportunities offered in the new territories.

By the time I met him, Zdenek was financially quite well-off. He and his brother Henio owned the butcher's shop, which was also a delicatessen. He lived in a comfortable first-floor apartment in the middle of Walbrzych, and Henio, who later married a girl I knew from Borysław called Lusia, lived on the floor below. Zdenek drove a big Mercedes, and knew a lot of people. But it wasn't his money or his influence which persuaded me to marry him. I loved him, and I expected to spend the rest of my life with him.

He knew about my Jewish marriage from the outset, and that I needed to get a divorce. He said he would fix it. Heniek agreed to the divorce, but told Zdenek he would have to pay for it. I don't know how much. I asked Zdenek to leave me out of it. Many years later, when we quarrelled, he would say, »I paid for you. I own you.«

There were no more Jewish weddings for me. We got married at the Wałbrzych Town Hall on 4 February 1948. It was a small affair with only a few people invited. I kept a note, written on a tiny piece of card, which Zdenek gave me on our wedding day: »My dearest wife, Binuś, I wish to always see you as happy and smiling as you are today. Your loving husband, Zdenek.«

Róża was more approving of this marriage than the first, but not completely so. She still thought I should be studying. Because I was so desperate to live up to her expectations, I always tried to keep learning, and I'm grateful to her for that.

I couldn't have been happier in those early days of our marriage. I didn't need to work any more. Zdenek would get up early to buy meat at the markets, and as soon as he'd gone, my German shepherd dog, Dolma, would come into my bed. It was perfect bliss lying in bed with Dolma, and my books and maybe a box of chocolates. We had a German housekeeper, Frau Rauschke, who cooked for us and for Zdenek's many men friends who dropped by for food and company at all hours of the day and night. He had kept an open house before we married, but to regain some order I wrote out on a big piece of paper that breakfast was from 9 to 11, lunch from 1 to 3, and dinner from 7 to 9, and that anyone who came late wouldn't be served.

Róża and Marek lived nearby. I passed much of my time with Róża and Fenka and playing with the babies, Kaja (Karolina) and Jasia (Joanna), whom I adored. I had money, though I had to ask for it, and I could spoil them. I still have a letter from Fenka, dated 1948, in which she thanks me for a dress I had bought her, even though her birthday, she wrote, was still a long way off. I knew that I was going to get it because I liked it and you wanted me to have it. I loved Fenka, and she loved me. I wish you to meet in life only those who can see you the way

I know and see you, she wrote in that same letter. I would always be for her the little girl who had shared her bed in those first months after liberation. I understood what you were going through even though you didn't talk about it. I know who you are, and this is the girl that I know and I respect. And then she wrote something that I remember her saying many times, and which I too have taken as a kind of mantra. I belong to people who, in love and in friendship, do not look at either age, or colour of the skin, or nationality.

On 14 June 1948, the French consulate in Warsaw advised that it would look favourably on my request for a transit visa for France, on the condition that I had a valid passport. I did, but its expiry date was rapidly approaching. I didn't want to lose my passport, so in October 1948, I left for Paris, alone. Zdenek had applied for a passport after we met but it was only once I got to Paris that I was able to organise a visa for him. I didn't have to persuade him to leave with me. Vast numbers of Jews were leaving Europe in those years, fleeing continued anti-Jewish violence, the intransigence of Communist governments which refused to restore pre-war property and the ruins of Jewish communities destroyed by the Holocaust. For Zdenek, the question was not if, but only when and how he would leave Poland.

Paris. Finally. It was the West, it was life, it was culture, it was Enlightenment. But first, it was a brothel. I was met at the station by a friend of Hela, Zdenek's sister, and because there was a transport strike on, we left my luggage and began walking, looking for a hotel. I had bought a few American dollars on the black market before I left, but my zloty were worth nothing in France. On my limited budget, the hotels were all of a certain sort, with rooms rented by the hour not the night. Finally I found a room, with a mirror on the ceiling. I'd never seen anything like it. That night, I got very sick, and as my fever took hold and I drifted in and out of consciousness, I was aware of beautiful girls, and handsome black men coming into the room, bringing me food. I had never seen black men before. They called a doctor for me. When I was well again, and had moved to a nearby hotel, the girls would greet me in the street. *Sabine, ça va? Tres bien, Sabine?* they would call out. (Later, when Zdenek arrived, he asked me,

»How do you know these girls?« I told him, but I don't think he believed me.)

Friends in Poland had given me the name of a couple, Niuta and Max, who might help me find somewhere to live. I tracked down their room in another small cheap hotel, the sort you used to find all over France, very basic, with a squat toilet in the corridor and nowhere to shower or bath. No-one answered my knock on their door, so I walked in uninvited. A woman emerged from under the bed. I was as startled as she was. »What are you doing there?« I asked. She stood up, brushed herself down and replied brusquely, »I live here, but what are you doing here?« (It transpired that because the room was so tiny, she stored her belongings under the bed in a suitcase.) Niuta and I eventually became close friends, and we both ended up living in Sydney. But on that day, she took me to see the concierge who found me a room.

Before Zdenek arrived, I had the run of the town. I was in seventh heaven. Everyone who was anyone was in post-war Paris – the philosophers and poets, the Communists and the painters, the spies and the singers. I can't say I rubbed shoulders with Jean-Paul Sartre and Simone de Beauvoir, but I breathed in the same air. I did meet Juliette Greco, who was singing in a Left Bank café then, and Jean Louis Barrault, whose work with avantgarde and classic theatre helped revive French theatre after the war, sometimes dropped by our university theatre group. I enrolled at *Alliance Française,* and hung around the student canteens where I could eat cheaply and meet other people my age. I hovered, shall we say, at the edge of Parisian intellectual life. That was exhilarating enough for a wide-eyed girl from the Polish provinces. Of course, I met other émigrés, including young people who came from my part of the world, but we never talked about our past. I still had questions, the ones I've carried around with me right up until now, but mine was a very intuitive search in those days. I thought I could find the answers not necessarily by asking directly, but by mixing with people.

Once Zdenek arrived in Paris, my student life stopped, except for French language classes at the *Alliance,* which he considered useful. He expected me, as his wife, to help him with what he was doing, and to knuckle down. The *American Jewish Joint Distribution Committee,* known as *JOINT*, looked after Jewish migrants passing through Paris, and offered skills training courses. Zdenek learned to be a cutter of men's shirts, and because he was so clever, and good with his hands, he was soon teaching others. He got a job with a shirt manufacturer and after a while, when my French was good enough, we started making men's shirts ourselves, on the side. I didn't sew, but I was the go-between, scurrying by Métro between Zdenek and the two or three outworkers who sewed for us. And I ironed the shirts. I was good at ironing.

We stayed in Paris for almost two years. With the help of a contact of his sister's, Zdenek was able to bring a few of our things out of Poland – Persian carpets, a few nice pieces of furniture, a lot of my books, and a beautiful silver cutlery set, which we sold to raise cash. Eventually we rented a flat, but while we were still at the hotel, I had a shocking accident. We weren't meant to cook in our room, but because we couldn't afford to eat out, we improvised with a Primus stove. One night when I was trying to cook some meat, I got impatient with how long it was taking and added more fuel to the Primus. It exploded in my face. I was badly burned, and hospitalised. When my skin began to heal, the itching was unbearable. The doctor had warned that my face would scar wherever I touched it, so when I came home Zdenek used to tie my hands next to me at night so I wouldn't scratch. Even when the skin was healed, it would turn purple when I was cold, and red when I was hot. The doctor recommended exposing my face to the sun. We had an acquaintance with family in Nice, in the south of France, so I went there for a while. Zdenek came to Nice briefly towards the end of my stay, and I have a photo of us there, so young, with me wearing an off-the-shoulder white broderie anglaise blouse he made me to go with two skirts, one white with blue polka dots, and the other blue with white dots.

Zdenek was a possessive man. I didn't recognise his jealousy as such at first. I just thought he must love me very much to want me to himself. In Nice, I remember, I had made friends before he arrived, and he was upset. I could sit somewhere, in a bar or at a café, and someone would smile at me, and I would smile back. I didn't see anything wrong with that, but it was enough to start an argument with Zdenek. He wanted me to concentrate on him, while I was eager to embrace the world. From the beginning, we had problems with this. »Why don't you grow up?« he would demand, though it was my sunny, childish nature which had attracted him in the first instance. I was growing up. I was learning, but when I had grown up, he didn't like it.

But I am running ahead of myself again. In Paris, we met a friend of Hela's whom I admired very much. Edita M. was a striking-looking Czech woman, considerably older than me, who lived in an elegant apartment. She was a woman of independent means, with a married lover in London and a son who was a pilot in Israel. She liked to spoil me with little gifts, perfume and the like. She also taught me something about money which I've never forgotten. Soon after we met, she lent Zdenek some money, quite a lot of money. When he asked why, she said, »You'll give it back to me when you have established yourself. But when you have money in your pocket, you talk differently to people. You feel much more secure. I don't want you to feel that you are penniless.«

There was a very long queue of Poles waiting to emigrate to the United States, and we had no idea of when we would be able to leave. There was no question of being able to stay permanently in Paris, and the French authorities didn't want us getting too comfortable. We had to regularly renew our transit visas (which allowed us to stay temporarily in France), proving each time that we were still waiting for immigration papers to the United States, which had tight quotas for Poles. Meanwhile, tensions between the two new superpowers, the Soviet Union and the United States, were rising. The Soviet Union had triggered the first crisis of the Cold War on 24 June 1948 by cutting off all road and rail routes going through Soviet-controlled territory in Germany and blocking access to the three Western-held sectors of Berlin.

For over a year the Allies flew supplies, including food, coal and machinery, into Berlin. At the height of the Berlin airlift, one Allied plane landed every minute in Berlin. On 4 April 1949, the Western powers signed the North Atlantic Treaty, the beginning of NATO, which stated that an attack on any one of them would be an attack on them all. The USSR lifted the blockade on Berlin on 11 May 1949, but threat of war seemed constant. I knew I couldn't go through another war. Importantly, for my state of mind, I was pregnant, and the allure of being in limbo, even in Paris, was wearing thin. I would never belong in France, I knew that by now. I needed a home, a place where Zdenek and I could build a future for our family, and not be reminded of the past.

In the early spring of 1950, I was on the Métro when I saw an enormous colour-drenched poster of Bondi Beach. *Come to sunny Australia!*, it said, or something like that. I went home and said to Zdenek, »I know where we're going. We are going to sunny Australia.« We knew someone who had already emigrated to Australia, so we wrote and asked him to sponsor us. It was easy to get a visa. The Australian government's slogan at the time was populate or perish. The perception after the war was that Australia's small population was inadequate to defend such a vast land, and from February 1948 it opened its doors to people wishing to leave war-torn Europe. It all happened so quickly for us. By June 1950 we were sailing towards Australia as assisted migrants on the Italian ship *Surriento*, catching one of the early waves of Australia's massive post-war immigration programme.

While we were in the throes of organising our departure from Paris, *Gone with the Wind*, starring Vivien Leigh and Clark Gable, had its French release. I'd read the book and I didn't want to miss the movie, the biggest romantic blockbuster of the past decade (it had played in London continuously for four years from 1940). Who knew where Australia was, and if they showed movies like that down there? *Gone with the Wind* is a very long movie, and Zdenek was already home by the time I got back from the cinema. He was furious. How could I go to a film at a time like this? We didn't even know where we were going, and so on and so on. I told him that we were going regardless, and I couldn't see what was so wrong with going to the movies. Years later, he'd say to me, »But you went to see *Gone with the Wind*«, as if to demonstrate definitively my lack of seriousness.

Zdenek and I were a combustible pairing, but I had high expectations of our life together. When those expectations fell short, I usually blamed myself. On the ship to Australia, I wrote about my uneasiness with our marriage in a diary that I didn't read again until many years later. When I did, I was devastated to find in my early forebodings so much of what was to cause us grief later on.

»We've been underway for a week. I don't know what's wrong with me. I'm so unsettled and I cry a lot. I don't know why. Is it because I am pregnant? Any little thing sets me crying. Zdenek tells me I don't think enough about the important questions of life, and usually corrects me. Does he ever dream? Is he always so matter of fact? Actually I can't find fault with him. He is a good husband, very energetic, thinking about business all the time, but somehow we don't understand each other. There are so many things I would like to talk about but to him they are not important. Am I to blame? We don't talk to each other. Our conversations turn into quarrels which end up with me crying. I don't recognise myself when I become hysterical and angry, which I regret afterwards and am ashamed of. I hope and pray that everything will work out between us, but so many little things upset him. Zdenek takes offence easily. He doesn't like me to make any comments. He is always convinced that he knows more than I do, and that he is right and he says that I am so willful and obstinate. But I can't stand the anger and the loud voice and I react badly. It would be so much better if Zdenek could praise me a little and if he could make me laugh, and then I would react differently. I have such an enormous need for tenderness and for kindness, and he doesn't understand that. He thinks that he can make it all up in bed but it doesn't work like that for me. It upsets me that after the daily quarrels he expects that everything is all right again, and that we can slide from anger to caresses. I know that I'm over-sensitive, but I can't change it. I don't know if it's only Zdenek who is like that or if this is typical of all men. Is everything based on physical desire for them? If I am not emotionally ready for sex, I can't feel anything. I still don't know how to behave with Zdenek … I feel so lonely. There's no-one to talk with about it. Fenka is so far away, and I can't write about it in any case, and my mother is not here. I'm expecting a child. I think I felt the first movement yesterday. I can't believe it. Perhaps I will not be so lonely any more. I am afraid of the future and there is so much that's waiting for me. Oh God, how I hope that everything will be all right with Zdenek. I'm so unhappy after every quarrel. I don't want to live, nothing makes sense. What will happen to me?«

I was probably feeling particularly sorry for myself when I wrote this. The pregnancy was making me feel sick. I wasn't eating because every time I sat up I would vomit. Eventually, the ship's doctor recommended to the captain that he find us a better cabin, and we travelled the rest of the way to Australia in first class. I remember that Zdenek was cross with me because he suspected, rightly, that I had charmed the doctor. But we both enjoyed first class a lot more than the cabin in the bowels of the ship, which we had been assigned as assisted migrants. We shared a common taste for comfort.

XIX. BONDI

We sailed into Sydney Harbour on 23 July 1950. I put my anxieties about my marriage where they belonged, out of sight, and greeted the New World with my brightest smile. Sydney was shrouded in thick rain. Sunny Australia indeed. The rain continued for weeks, but we headed for Bondi anyway. In those days, its cheap boarding houses were a magnet for European migrants.

Zdenek found a job quickly in a big shirt factory in the city, leaving me to fend with a landlady who, every time she saw me, thundered, »You can't have the baby in our boarding house.« I told her in my mangled English that I'd rather have my baby on the street. I hated being so vulnerable. Australians for the most part responded to the confusion of new migrants with gentle forbearance but some dished out their instruction as if we were errant schoolchildren. One morning, after I'd kissed Zdenek goodbye at his tram stop, as I usually did, a woman came over and told me sternly, »You don't do that here.« I could barely understand her, but I knew I'd done something very wrong from the way she wagged her finger in my face as she spoke. Someone told me afterwards that in Sydney you didn't kiss men in the street. This wasn't Paris.

On the walk home from the tram stop, I often stopped to watch the progress on a block of flats that was nearing completion. One morning, a man asked me why I kept staring at the building. I told him I didn't speak English. »Yiddish?« he asked. I shook my head. We communicated in broken Polish-Russian, and I understood that he was the owner of the building. Zdenek spoke Yiddish, so I brought him to see the man. I wished that we could live there but he told us that all the flats were taken. At the last minute, however, one prospective tenant backed out. So, eight months after I'd announced to Zdenek in Paris that we were moving to Australia, we had the keys to a new two-bedroom flat in Bondi.

Around this time, Zdenek and I were walking up William Street towards Kings Cross when a tram stopped, and out tumbled two people who were as shocked to see me in Sydney as I was to see them. My brother's friend Rolek Harmelin and his wife, Rita, were on their way back home to Kings Cross after delivering some film (they ran a 24-hour processing service in those days) when Rolek looked out the tram window and saw me. Rita still remembers what I was wearing – a red jacket with plaid lining, completely reversible, with a little scarf. I loved that jacket. I'd bought it in Paris, and it always made an impression. That day, it caught Rolek's eye, and brought about an extraordinary reunion. It transpired that Rita and her father, who had survived Auschwitz, had only recently arrived in Sydney to join Rolek and his parents who had immigrated a couple of years earlier. I had just been speaking to Zdenek about Rolek's father, Dr Harmelin (he had been our family doctor in Borysław), and saying how I wished he were able to deliver my baby. And here he was, in Sydney. As it turned out, he was still studying for his Australian medical qualification and wasn't yet practising, but even talking to him made me feel closer to my mother.

I wanted very much to be a mother. Josephine was born in November 1950 after a long and difficult childbirth. When I opened my eyes to learn I had a daughter, I said to the doctor, »I know.« Zdenek was working long hours, but I was too busy to miss him when I got home from the hospital. We had taken in a boarder, and as well as caring for the baby, I provided him with breakfast and dinner. His board covered our rent. I was pleased with myself. I thought I was helping. But there were moments when I definitely wasn't much help, like the day I lost a lot of money.

My uncles had been reimbursed for my unused plane ticket to America, which they'd paid for, and had forwarded the money to me. I cashed their cheque, and put the money in my bag to give to Zdenek. On my way home, I called by the Karitane family care centre with Josie. I was very nervous about handling her, and gratefully accepted the nurses' help. While I was waiting in line to be seen, Josie started crying. I went outside to where I'd left her pram and put down my bag while I rummaged around for a dry nappy, still holding onto my screaming baby. Then I went back inside to change her. By the time I realised my bag was still outside by the pram, it and the money had gone. I was hysterical. The nurses tried to calm me, telling me I'd lose my milk if I kept up my sobbing. I was such a crybaby. When Zdenek came home from work, he was so good about it. »It's only money«, he said. »Don't worry.« But I did. We had been counting on that money and we went without what we'd planned to buy with it.

We didn't go without for long, however. Zdenek worked a lot of overtime, and often brought home double his normal wage. But he really wanted to work for himself. The question was, doing what? I had a suggestion which I had carried with me, literally, from Paris. One day I'd stopped to watch a man doing a pavement demonstration. I was intrigued. I bought one of his products and took it home to show Zdenek. 'Who on earth is going to wear one of these?' he said scornfully. It was a clip-on tie, still a novelty back then. I packed the tie when we came to Australia, thinking that some day he might want to start his own business, and that he might find the idea useful.

Zdenek took another look at the tie, and decided it had potential. He was good with his hands, as I've mentioned, and creative. Later, much later, he used those abilities to make sculptures, but the challenge of the clip-on tie was purely a technical one. He completely changed the way it worked. The Lido clip-on tie was our great invention, and we patented it, and defended the patent.

Zdenek stayed at his job at the shirt factory to start with, and we made the ties at home, me with Josie on my knee. Finding the materials for the ties was my job, as was selling them. The department store menswear buyers didn't know what to do with a woman selling men's ties. I remember how politely they rebuffed my pitch. »It's very interesting, madam, but not really our cup of tea.« I would look at them blankly, and say, »Tea? No tea. Tie!« My English was still coming along.

We got our big break from Neil Glasser, who at that time was running Scottish Tailoring in the city. He became well known as the driving force behind the revitalisation of one of Sydney's grandest colonial landmarks, the Queen Victoria Building. He's a gadget man. Even now, when he is no longer young, Neil's eyes light up when he talks about the incredible technological progress flooding out of China. He loved our tie, and offered to distribute it nationally.

I found a wonderful satiny-looking material in a range of deep colours dotted with tiny points, and we made our first small fortune with the Stardust tie. We leased factory premises in East Sydney. We were a tiny team at first – Zdenek was the cutter, we employed two machinists on site, and on top of that we had a small stable of immigrant outworkers. Neil Glasser lent us some money for our first Holden car, which I drove for deliveries, and picking up finished ties. I started going into the office. Actually, I was the office to begin with. I wrote the jingle for radio advertisements, *Catch her eye with a clip-on tie*, and did demonstrations. I talked to journalists. »Waiting to use the mirror while her husband tied his tie gave Polish-born housewife Mrs. Z. Wolanski her bestseller idea for ties which clip on«, they wrote. It was a better story than the original. Zdenek kept improving the technology of the clip-on tie, and by 1956 we were travelling to the major textile centres in Italy and importing custom-designed, handwoven fabrics for our ties. Zdenek left the design side of things to me.

I may have coloured my hair red and played with bold colours in my own wardrobe, but I pitched my choice of fabrics for our market. This was the Menzies era. Australian politics were conservative, and Australian men dressed safely. Only occasionally did I misfire. I remember once putting together a beautiful collection of green ties. I've always loved green. It's bright, it gives me hope. Nobody would buy my green ties, which had a bit of blue in them. I was disappointed, and puzzled, until someone asked if I knew the old proverb *blue and green should never be seen*. I didn't, and it didn't make sense to me. I kept the samples in my range anyway. All of a sudden, everybody started picking up my green ties. It was St Patrick's Day. Saved by the Irish. But from then on I was careful with my green selections.

The business grew strongly and quickly. By the time our son Phillip was born in December 1954 we owned a house in Dover Heights in the eastern suburbs, we were leasing a large warehouse and a showroom at Circular Quay, the hub of Sydney Harbour, and had employed an office manager, the formidable Miss Molly Carter, who was always impeccably groomed in a white blouse, tweed skirt and sensible flat shoes of the best quality. Everything I know today about office administration I learned from her.

Zdenek insisted that I continue to work with him. There was no question of staying home with the children, or studying art and languages (as I wanted to). For my part, I insisted that the children always had somebody to come home to. We employed a live-in housekeeper and a cleaner, and when Phillip was born I hired a nurse.

I enjoyed working. I thought I could be more useful in the business than doing menial chores around the home. But I wasn't paid. Not directly. I always had to ask Zdenek for money, and gradually that became a source of deep resentment for me. It wasn't that I lacked for anything. Zdenek liked me to dress well, and I bought imported European fashion in Double Bay. I had my own car, and accounts at the major department stores. As a family, we water-skied and snow skied. We kept a motor boat for outings on the harbour. We took holidays in Surfers Paradise in Queensland, then still relatively unspoiled by mass tourism, and in the Blue Mountains, west of Sydney. We entertained a lot, and had a beautiful built-in cocktail cabinet and music cabinet made for us by Paul Kafka, a noted furniture maker. Kafka had studied design at the Academy of Arts in Vienna before the war. His pieces, now collectors' items, were made from expensive Continental wood and decorated with fine inlay work. A stave and a sprinkle of notes ran across our music cabinet. Martini glasses, bottles and glass tumblers danced over the polished veneer of the cocktail cabinet. For the bedroom, Zdenek commissioned a set of extremely shallow drawers, and in each drawer he put only two folded shirts. He was vain, and fussy about his clothes.

We both doted on our children, though I had more responsibility for them day to day. When I came home from work, usually about five, but perhaps later, I would ask them to give me half an hour to myself. I would go to my room, change, shower, shift mental and emotional gears, and then it was their time until they went to bed. I tried to bring them up as my mother had brought up me and Josek. I loved seeing them growing up, learning, developing. They were very affectionate, and we talked a lot together. They spoke English as their first language. I didn't even try to teach them Polish. We had a succession of housekeepers of different nationalities and it was more practical for them to speak English at home. They went to local public schools. I never considered sending them to Jewish schools, nor did I talk to them in those early years about their Jewish heritage. It didn't seem important at the time. Zdenek was more connected to the Jewish community, and more observant than I was. I made sure they were exposed to good music. Josie learned piano, but Phillip only ever wanted to play soccer. Zdenek was a sportsman and took Phillip to watch soccer from when he was a little boy. That's how he met his closest friend, David Lowy, whose father Frank Lowy founded the property giant *Westfield*. Phillip and the Lowys have stayed involved together in football, albeit at a much higher level these days.

Today the accent is on women having careers. I worked, as my mother had worked, because I wanted to help my husband, and because we were migrants. I was driven by the need for financial security rather than self-fulfillment. We had nobody to fall back on except ourselves. That said, I always enjoyed and learned a lot from the people I worked with. We employed a nice mixture of people, mostly other migrants. The only thing I didn't like about working was having no time for myself. The weekends were family time, and they were lovely, but Zdenek was careful about who I mixed with. I didn't have many Australian girlfriends. He was afraid they might influence me.

I was open to influence, as Zdenek feared. Germaine Greer was still a schoolgirl in Melbourne as the decade flicked over, and Betty Friedan's bombshell *The Feminine Mystique* was not published until 1963, but anyone with their ears and eyes open would have picked up the early rumblings of the women's liberation movement which was about to erupt in all Western societies. I myself never joined the bra-burners; I wasn't interested in that, but I had started to think about what I wanted for myself.

Zdenek didn't suspect how important Teresa Schrotter was for me at that time. His sister, Hela, and her friend Edita in Paris, had put us in contact with the Schrotters, Robert and Teresa, or Terci as we called her. They were a Czech couple considerably older than us and well established, having left Europe before the war. Robert became our accountant and Terci became my friend. They lived in Bellevue Hill, one of Sydney's most sought-after eastern suburbs, in a tastefully furnished home, so very different from most homes I was visiting at the time. Terci loved art, and the theatre, and knew a lot about both. She was kind and loving, and adored my children. But she also had a mind of her own, an independent outlook, and she encouraged me to think about what I wanted to do with my life. If I wanted to study, she said, then I must find a way to do it.

When Zdenek began buying commercial properties, it started with our needing bigger premises for the business. We bought a building in Kent Street, in Sydney's CBD, and put in a beautiful new showroom. *Lido House* was a big development, and a successful one. We then bought more property near Chinatown. Yet as we became more financially secure, I wanted to pull back from the business. My interests were changing. I questioned how much money we needed, how much money anyone needed. He couldn't understand what I was talking about. He would ask me why I couldn't worry about the business as much as I worried about my books. I was worrying about the end of the world. Nevil Shute's *On the Beach* and Mordecai Roshwald's *Level 7*, both apocalyptic science fiction novels, had detonated in my psyche and set off profound tremors.

I didn't write as regularly any more to Róża and Marek in Communist Poland, though I never forgot to telephone Róża on her birthday. They were working hard and bringing up teenage daughters, but neither of those reasons fully explain why we didn't have so much to say to each other. Róża wrote in one letter that I had become a stranger to her, referring, I think, to my immersion in the capitalist West more than my physical absence from her life. I think she thought I was superficial, and my life in Australia extremely shallow.

It's true that in those years we were absorbed in commerce, in building a decent standard of living for our children and in having fun. No-one said it, but fun was something we felt we deserved after what we'd survived. And like all New Australians, we were busy trying to fit in. Australia's growing comfort and prosperity in the 1950s and '60s gave people like us no cause for complaint. Eventually, all our friends from those years achieved reasonable levels of affluence, but Zdenek and I were more successful, and sooner, than most. We were the golden couple in our circle. I can say that without too much embarrassment. He was the successful businessman, and I was his glamorous wife. We had everything to look forward to, and no reason to look back.

I remember checking in to a very good hotel in Honolulu on our first trip away in 1956. We had taken out citizenship as soon as we could, and were travelling on Australian passports. The girl at reception looked at my passport, and then at me, and asked, »Are you Australian?« I said I was. »You don't look like one«, she said. By then I was fluent in English, and I said to her, »What do Australians look like?« She answered, «I don't know, but you don't look like one.«

My Australian citizenship was one of the few things that stayed intact when my marriage started to unravel. That, and being a mother. They were my anchors in the new life I had staked a claim to on the opposite side of the world.

XX. DIVORCE

I had put my anxieties about our marriage on the backburner when we arrived in Australia in 1950, but they hadn't died a natural death while we were establishing a foothold in this new country. There's a Jewish custom that if you're having problems within the home, you should either talk to a rabbi or to very close friends about it. We didn't have a rabbi, so towards the end of 1963, when our marriage difficulties could no longer be ignored, Zdenek decided we should talk to Rita. He complained of how I made life so difficult for him. I didn't behave or dress as a wife should (there was a particular pair of high pink boots ...). I was over the top. I was provocative. I suggested that since he didn't approve of my behaviour in company we needn't go out. For my part, I was happy to sit at home in the evenings after work and read books, and to see less of my friends. But the quarrels continued. I remember saying to him, »Look, we don't go out any more. I'm with you all the time. What is it now?« He replied, »I don't know what you are thinking.« That nearly killed me. Did he want to control my mind, too?

Every marriage breakdown has its own heart-breaking history, and very few make for pretty reading. Ours followed an excruciatingly tortured and painful course over the next two years. By 1965 there was nothing left in the marriage for me. We didn't talk any more, and Zdenek made it quite clear through his actions that he didn't trust me. He could see that we were growing apart and he thought that by making me totally dependent on him, I would be afraid to leave. I wasn't allowed to develop as an individual. He didn't want me to study, or do anything independently of him or the family. I understood he was afraid of losing me, and that his controlling behaviour reflected his own insecurity. But he didn't understand who I was. I needed to learn, to explore, to take risks, to connect with the world. Róża had understood that about me. It infuriated her, but she understood who I was. Zdenek had an image of what he wanted in his wife, and as long as I conformed, there were no problems. But the moment I stepped out of line, I had to be punished in some way.

Women with children did not leave their husbands in the mid 1960s, or least, no-one I knew of. I was unhappy, but back then who had heard of women thinking they had a right to happiness? People who had survived what I had survived did not court disaster by letting go of every bit of emotional and material security they had amassed. But I looked at it differently. I had survived the Holocaust. Didn't that give me an even greater responsibility to sort out what was important in life, not for my sake, but for my children's sake?

I continued going to work, but there was no relief from misery there. I had no-one to talk to. I was afraid of going crazy. I scribbled notes to myself on pieces of paper, as I'd always done.

»How does it feel to be really loved? Just the way you are, for what you are. Perhaps full of faults, and stubborn, and sometimes childish, maybe, and yet loved, in spite of it, and maybe for it. Not for your virtues, but for your faults. Not for your maturity, and calmness and clear-thinking, but for all your emotions, even quick anger. I don't really know but I do so terribly want to be loved for myself. I am lonely. It's quiet now. Everyone is asleep. I can't sleep. Tears are falling and I wish I had someone to talk to without reservation. Why are things the way they are now? Why don't we understand each other? Why these ugly quarrels and angry words, and continually hurting each other? I cannot go on like this. I can't stand it. I can't live without love, without kindness. Why is so much expected of me all the time? I know that I have my faults, but I'm really not bad. There is so much love in my heart. I don't want to get bitter. I can't, for the sake of my children if nothing else.«

I went into freefall when my marriage collapsed. I had no safety net. Weight fell off me to the point where people thought I was dying of something (it turned out that I had a stomach ulcer). I was depressed, and prescribed anti-depressants, which I continued taking for several years. In May 1965, by which time things between us had become ugly, I went away for three months. My friend Niuta, whom I'd first met in Paris, wanted to visit her father in Poland and asked me to go with her. Zdenek agreed. I hadn't been back to Poland since I left in October 1948.

I know I must have gone to see Róża and Marek, because there was no-one else there for me, but I don't remember anything of that visit. I was so beaten down when I left Sydney, and what I most remember is the relief of not being with Zdenek, of escaping his bombardment. I do however clearly recall going to Crakow to visit Niuta's father, a retired lawyer and a serious art collector who introduced me to early Italian painting. But most of that trip is a blank for me. It was respite, not resuscitation.

When I came home, everything was the same, and then it got worse. Zdenek barred me from going into the office. He said he didn't trust me any more. That hurt me more than anything that had gone before. We had always trusted each other. It was around this time that I thought, for the first and only time, of killing myself. I was driving to see the doctor, and I was so miserable, in such agony, that I thought if I just did a certain thing, I'd be dead. I pulled over, terrified of what I was thinking. I just wanted to disappear, to not have to deal with anything any more. I felt a complete failure as a wife. I blamed myself for our tragedy. All that kept me alive was wanting to be a good mother to my children.

By the end of 1965, we had parted. Divorce was unthinkable, but living with Zdenek would kill me so I took the penalty I knew I could bear. It wasn't light in those days; this was before the 1974 Family Law Act asserted that men and women should bear equal responsibility for a marriage breakdown. If the financial penalty was harsh, I feared it much less than the social penalty that I knew would be extracted. I knew I could earn a living, somehow. But I was terrified of being alone. Once Zdenek moved out, our large circle of friends and acquaintances withdrew from me. The phone rarely rang. The few calls I got were from husbands, and they were of no interest to me.

I stayed in the house at Dover Heights with the children. I wasn't cut off without a penny, but I had to figure out how to make money. I didn't have a profession. Zdenek had always run the business side of things for us, but I had absorbed a lot from working alongside him. By 1966, I had set up my own import company. I got on a plane and went to Italy, where I had made contacts through the tie business, and found some expensive women's lingerie I thought I could sell in Australia. There was nothing like it in the stores at the time. Doing business came easily to me. I like people, and business, in the end, is about working with people. Sometime later, when I was in Hong Kong, I saw some pretty rubber gloves, with flowers on them, and I brought those back to sell. I worked from home, but I was still in touch with Miss Carter, and she helped me with typing and invoices and so on. I didn't make a lot of money, but I got by until our divorce was settled.

We were divorced by mutual consent, which was extremely unusual in those days, but that's what we asked for, because there was no-one else involved. The court accepted our application. I didn't ask for maintenance. I didn't want to be a kept woman. But I did want what belonged to me. In my opinion, during all the years I'd worked with Zdenek, I hadn't been paid. So I got a settlement, not maintenance.

After the initial distress and shock had subsided, I started enjoying my freedom. I had lost all my old friends, with the exception of Zdenek's brother, Henio, and my sister-in-law, Lusia, whose support I will never forget. But I wasn't alone for long. I find it easy to make friends. I've always liked men, but what I wanted then was companionship rather than another husband. In the spring of 1966, I met Henry who was a perfect companion.

Henry was several years younger than me. He came from a long line of antiquarian booksellers, and worked in the family business. After all the hectoring I'd had over the years from Zdenek about my preference for books, I was in my element with a bookish man. It was a healing relationship for me, on all sorts of levels. Henry was my equal, my friend. He encouraged me to do whatever I wanted to do, and he had a great sense of humour. Whenever I was down, my kids would say, »Let's ring Henry, we need Henry here.« They loved Henry because he could bring back the mother they remembered. I began to laugh again with Henry.

As the calendar year flipped over to 1967, and I was beginning to feel brighter about my future, the darkest part of my past came back to claim me. I received a summons from the Bremen County Court dated 2 January 1967, which asked that I come to Germany the following month to give evidence against the former SS officer Friedrich Hildebrand, camp commandant in Borysław during the war, who was accused of ordering the execution of my brother and my father and Mendzio Doerfler in 1944. I had learned about Hildebrand's impending trial some months earlier. I think it was Klara Dauerman, a concentration camp survivor whom I knew through my sister-in-law, Lusia, who brought the case to my attention. She was onto all these things. I wasn't.

I had already submitted a written declaration to the court, probably with Klara's help. But the summons explained that the court could take into account in its verdict only evidence given in person at the trial and that my appearance in Bremen was absolutely essential in view of the importance of the case.

The tone and import of the summons shocked me. I was frightened both of the court case itself and of going to Germany. I had been there with Zdenek to buy material for the ties in the textile city of Krefeld, but whenever I saw someone my age, or older, I would wonder what he or she had been doing during the war. The thought of facing Hildebrand in the dock terrified me. But I knew I had to go to Bremen, and that I would have to tell my children before I left why I was going. Until then they knew almost nothing about my past.

By the late 1960s, tens of thousands of former Nazis and collaborators had been tried for crimes against humanity. The highest profile war crimes trials had taken place immediately after the war at Nuremberg where, in 1945 and 1946, the International Military Tribunal had tried 22 Nazi leaders, and sentenced 12 to death, including Number Two, Hermann Göring, and the Nazi governor general of occupied Poland, Hans Frank. Others got life or lengthy prison terms and three were acquitted. The Allied occupying authorities continued to try Nazis, and by 1949, had convicted over 5,000 war criminals. In subsequent years, the Nazi hunter Simon Wiesenthal tracked down over 1,000 Nazi war criminals, the most famous of whom was Adolf Eichmann, the head of the Gestapo's section on Jewish affairs, who had supervised the extermination of Jews. He was put on trial in Jerusalem in 1961 and executed in 1962. But still many Nazi criminals had not been brought to trial or punished. They had returned to normal lives in German society. Among them was Friedrich Hildebrand. I wanted him to be punished.

I'd thought a lot about the question of revenge for many years. I didn't want all Germans punished, but I wanted the guilty to be punished. My brother and my father had been dead for more than two decades, and their murderer had not only survived, but had been allowed to rebuild his life. I owed it to them to go to Bremen.

XXI. HILDEBRANDS TRIAL

Bremen is a prosperous port city 60 kilometres inland from the North Sea, in the northwest of Germany. It's packed with galleries and museums, opera houses and concert halls. Beethoven's first symphony had its premiere in Bremen in 1802. At another time I might have lingered in the historic market square, considered to be one of the most beautiful in Europe with its opulent Renaissance and baroque facades. But I was in Bremen for one purpose only, and I was oblivious to my surroundings. I had no interest in what the Germans had to show me of their Hanseatic heritage. I was put up in a modest hotel on the Weser River (the court paid for the cost of my return journey to Bremen, and all associated expenses, including the possible loss of earnings). At breakfast I started a conversation with a young Polish-speaking woman who said she was a witness in the Hildebrand case. »Did you know the Habermans?« I asked her. She said, »Yes, I knew them. I also knew Binka very well.« I didn't remember her at all. »Really?« I said. »Yes«, she replied. I asked her what her name was. I don't remember it now, and I didn't recognise it then. She asked, »Who are you?« I told her, »I am Binka.«

I don't remember her reaction, but I was upset. This young woman said she knew me, and she didn't. I wondered how many other people were coming to Bremen at the Germans' expense to give evidence about the past, and how reliable their evidence would be (more than 200 witnesses were brought from North and South America, Israel, New Zealand and Australia, Poland and France to give evidence in this trial). In my mind, it was essential that their evidence was truthful to ensure that the case against Hildebrand did not fail.

The Bremen courthouse, or Gerichtshaus, is a grimy 19th century brick and stone building in the Gothic style, its ornamented facade rich with allusions to Christian allegory and the symbols of justice. I know this from my subsequent visits to Bremen to see my dear friend Renate Reinke, whom I met during the trial. If I had never returned, I couldn't have described the courthouse, except to say that someone took me there. The whole ordeal returned me to a state where my senses were paralysed.

In my memory, I was on the witness stand for half a day, but Renate assures me it was only 30 minutes. Maybe I was in the court for half a day, waiting. Her recollection is certainly better than mine. She sat in the courtroom for the entire duration of the 11-month trial, trying to piece together the truth of what had happened in our obscure little corner of Europe. In the book she subsequently wrote, called *Antworte, Mensch!* [Answer, People!], she describes my appearance as follows:

»Again a new day of hearings started. Of the six witnesses, only one appeared: the daughter and sister of the two murdered Habermans, father and son. While the court was waiting for the interpreter, the court dealt with the files of the witnesses who had not appeared and during this period, the only witness was sitting at an angle in front of me. Behind me, the gallery was filled with students from three classes, who still filled the room with restlessness.

Very sure of herself and self-confident, very tastefully dressed, that was my first impression of the witness. But as I saw her close up, and as I observed her, her inner tension transmitted itself to me. I noticed how she clenched her small hands in her lap, her knuckles showing white and sharp. But the face stayed composed and motionless. What must she have felt as she heard the names out of the files, names of fellow sufferers from the hardest time of her life? ›Not attending because of illness‹, that was the most common reason. What a difference between the students who were waiting restlessly for the first of the witnesses to take the stand, and who were not aware of the presence of the daughter and sister of the murdered Habermans, and this witness. She was fully concentrated, and the focus of her big dark eyes was either on the judge or on her hands. Nothing else seemed to exist for her.

Finally she was called into the witness stand. She was the youngest witness in this trial, only 36 years old, the manager of an import and export company for women's garments in Sydney.

Calm, relevant and clear, her statement [began]: I will try to testify as much as I can remember. Yet I wanted to forget.«

The 65-year-old man sitting before me in the dock looked so ordinary, so reduced in his civilian clothes. I remember the gut-wrenching fear which used to grip me in the camp whenever Obersturmführer der Allgemeinen SS Friedrich Hildebrand appeared in his immaculately pressed uniform, and his high shiny boots, brandishing a riding whip in one hand and a pistol in the other. On his orders Jewish girls had been torn away from their mothers and Jewish boys executed at point blank. Here, in the courtroom, the former Gestapo officer was stripped of his terrifying authority. But I recognised him. I never doubted who he was.

Hildebrand kept his eyes cast downwards all the time I was giving my evidence and during my cross-examination – except on one occasion. His defence lawyer had a copy of the photograph I have mentioned, the one taken of myself, Josek, Imek, Ducek and Rolek in the room in the ghetto on Josek's birthday in January 1943. The lawyer said to me, »Well, you all look very nice here, very clean.« I knew what he was getting at. Here was a group of fresh-faced, well-groomed youngsters. Life in the ghetto couldn't have been that bad. I answered him bluntly: »Not all Jews are dirty, you know.« The typical German saying filthy Jew rang in my head. Hildebrand raised his eyes, and looked straight at me. I looked at him. I couldn't even hate him. I felt nothing for him. But most of the time I tried not to think that he was there, in front of me.

I think I was a good witness, a truthful witness. I told them I wasn't there when the shooting happened. I found out about it only when I tried to enter the camp. Other people told me my father and brother had been shot. I didn't see the bodies. I saw whatever remained of them when I moved them from the camp to the Jewish cemetery in August 1945.

I appeared to be self-contained, self-assured, but actually I was feeling dreadful. Before I came to Germany I threw out all my Valium, which I had been using for several years, since my problems with Zdenek had escalated. I decided I had to have a very clear mind, so I got rid of all my pills. But my stomach is my weakness. I thought my ulcer was better, but in Bremen my stomach was in agony. After I had given evidence, a woman approached me. She looked as provincial German women did in those days, conservative, unremarkable. I wasn't paying much attention to her. I was deep in my pain. I thought she was probably a journalist, and I told her I wouldn't talk to journalists. She said that she wanted to help me, that she'd been in the courtroom and she thought from watching me that I seemed to be in pain. She offered to take me to a pharmacy. That was how I met the radical and remarkable Renate Reinke.

I went with her to a pharmacy, and afterwards she asked me what I was going to do now. I said I would go back to the hotel, and she asked me if I wanted to come back to her house. She said, »I don't want to ask questions. You don't need to talk. Just sit down and have a cup of tea and relax. You don't have to stay for dinner.« That was the beginning of my healing, the first step I took towards crossing the bridge. Before that, I was immobilised by fear and by distrust of all Germans. Renate, the daughter of an SS man, was responsible for helping to open my mind.

Renate was present every single day of Hildebrand's trial, listening to 'reports of agony and suffering, misery and hatred, 11 months of shameful, oppressive resurrection of the past', as she wrote of her project. She was almost crushed by the experience, but like me, she felt she had to be there. She had unfinished business with her father which drew her to delve into the history of the part of the world I had grown up in. Her father, Werner Hilliges was an SS commander of a concentration camp in Innsbruck, Austria, during the war. In 1948 he was sentenced to life imprisonment for war crimes, but was released in 1955 under a prisoner exchange agreement. Six months later, he committed suicide. He never acknowledged the wrongdoings of the Nazi regime he had served. Quite the reverse. Until his death, he maintained a stance of profound martyrdom and fidelity to Nazi ideology. Renate had loved her father, and even until his death thought of herself as being close to him. But as the years rolled by, and she and the rest of the world learned more about the extent of the Nazis' crimes, her dead father became stranger to her by the day. Of particular interest to her was a gap in his war record for seven months during 1943. She remembered, very faintly, that he had been in Ukraine from May to November that year, and that when he had returned to Innsbruck he had fallen ill, and behaved extremely oddly. During this time, she learned later, he had written a letter requesting a release from the Gestapo. But his wife, Renate's mother, had intercepted the letter at the postbox. She believed that once her husband's fever had broken he would regret sending it. He stayed with the Gestapo until the war ended, and in his war record, there was no mention of his being in Ukraine in 1943. During those seven months, he was said to have been on sick leave.

Long after his death, Renate wondered what her father had seen, or taken part in, in Ukraine which had triggered his (temporary) breach of faith in the Nazi cause. Her every day was infused with a deep sadness, which she found difficult to hide, even at work. When she heard that an SS officer was to be tried in Bremen, her home town, for war crimes committed in Ukraine, she resigned from her secretarial job, and joined a German-Jewish society that was charged with taking care of the witnesses in the Hildebrand case. She took her responsibility very seriously. With great courage, she approached Jewish witnesses at the trial, including me, and gently offered her friendship. Why? She saw our pain, understood it. She too had pain.

I went back to her house and had tea. I was grateful for the security she offered, for the peace and quiet. I met her husband, Rudi, whom I liked very much. That of itself was important. He was German, and a man, but somehow I felt at ease with him. I didn't question him that day about what he had done in the war, nor ever did. Even now, I don't know what Rudi, or his parents did in the war. There was something in his bearing and behaviour which inspired my confidence, and those questions never came up.

I think Renate and I met once more, the next day, before I left. I was in Bremen only three days. I remember walking with her, in the rain, beside the river. Even as a child, I loved the rain. I always had an urge to get out when it was raining. I remember my mother bringing me gumboots and a raincoat and a hat, and saying to the maid, »Let her go«, and I would go out, maybe for half an hour. Then I would come home, and the maid would dry me off, and I was very happy. As I grew older, I recognised that I could think better in the rain. I get some kind of emotional relief. I love the water.

I think it was in that second conversation that we spoke about my children. Renate remembers that I told her that my children were my whole world. She says she felt my connection to the children very strongly, that they were my ropes through life. They were. But Renate who was born in the same year as me but into such different circumstances also became a rope for me, a rope that led me towards the belief I have today, that we are each individually responsible for how we deal with evil in our world.

Renate has tried very hard to atone for her father's guilt. Some others perhaps did not. But I continually asked myself, how can she be responsible for what her father did? She tells me she still feels guilty for having been blind and deaf as a girl. She winces at the memory of how, after watching a Hitler Youth propaganda film her father brought home for her, she swore never to speak another word to Jews. She had a schoolfriend in Berlin, a Jewish girl she used to play with in the street, and from one day to the next she stopped talking to her. »I don't remember exactly what the film was about, but I remember how I reacted«, she told me, »and for this I feel guilty.« But Renate wasn't responsible for what others did. She wasn't responsible for the deaths of my parents, and my brother.

When the trial was over, Renate kept in touch with every witness who was willing to accept her friendship. She wrote her book, and paid for 1,000 copies to be printed. The German-Jewish society she was involved with bought 200 copies and sent them to every witness. I tried to have the book translated into English, but couldn't get the project off the ground. Maybe it was ahead of its time.

We have corresponded for nearly four decades, and continued to do so until her death in 2009. She was always glad to see me. She kept photographs of my children and my grandchildren in her albums. I was as close a friend as any she has, especially since her beloved Rudi's death. She sayd we're made from the same wood. Her smile was still quick and warm, and though the long fingers of her beautiful hands, which Rudi loved to adorn with rings, were gnarled with arthritis, and her body, once athletic enough to reach alpine summits, was painfully hunched, making the most ordinary of physical tasks complex, she never complained. At 80, Renate remained an extraordinarily compassionate and passionate woman.

Hildebrand was convicted of murder. 16 eyewitnesses confirmed that he was the one who gave the order to shoot and kill my brother, my father and Mendzio, who were executed by three guards in front of the inmates during roll call. He was sentenced to life imprisonment, though I didn't know where he served his sentence until I asked Renate recently. She said he went to a high security prison in Hamburg. One more Nazi killer put away, but so many millions died. The thought keeps nagging at me. We can't blame a whole nation but it's important to keep chasing down war criminals, even now when they are old. They committed those crimes. They should be punished.

I needed to see Hildebrand called to account for his crimes. But then, when I had given my evidence, I returned to Australia and tried to put him out of my mind. I needed to do that too. I had to keep on living. I wanted to keep on living.

XXII. ADRIAN

I wear the star sign of the twins on a gold chain around my neck. I'm a typical Gemini character, if you want to believe in these things. I have to be doing more than one thing at a time, and what I'm doing has to challenge me. I'm confident I can learn, and I work hard. Why shouldn't I succeed?

In the years after Zdenek and I parted, I had to remake myself. I'd spent 17 years deferring to his greater commercial experience. I had to learn to trust my own judgment if I were not only to survive, but to prosper. I began investing in property when I got my settlement from the divorce. I bought a block of flats in the western suburbs of Sydney to give me an income. Around the same time, I did a short course in interior decorating. I liked design, and thought I could do it well. I didn't get a formal qualification like my friend, interior designer Babette Hayes, but this field is not regulated in Australia. You can get ahead without the bit of paper.

Sometime after I bought the flats, the agent whom I'd used suggested that we buy something together. Paul was a Russian, quite a bit older than me, and married with children. I decided I could trust him. Great idea, I said. I thought we could buy something old and renovate it. The problem was, I didn't have any more money to spend. I told him I could get a bank loan.

The lawyer who had seen me through my divorce, Sidney, helped me with the loan application. Then I made an appointment with the bank manager. Our conversation began with him asking me for my husband's name. »I haven't got a husband«, I replied. »Why do you need my husband's name? This loan is for me.« He looked at me strangely, and said, »This bank isn't in the habit of giving loans to single women.« To which I replied, »What's a single woman? I'm in the process of divorcing. I would have thought it was high time you changed your policy.« In Australia in the 1960s, women were routinely asked to have their husbands or a male guarantor sign for a loan, even when they were the sole earner. I'm not sure that I realised this. I did things the way I thought made sense, and took others along with me.

The bank manager and I continued talking. He asked me, »So, do you have any children?« I said, »Yes, I have two children.« He wanted to know who was looking after them, and I told him that I was. Then I said to him, »What about you? Do you have any children?« He told me he had seven. I was amused, and said, »What's the matter with you? Are you a Catholic, or don't you believe in contraception?« He seemed taken aback, and asked, »Do you always talk like this?« »Like what?« I replied. I didn't think there was anything special about our conversation.

I got the loan, in my own name. Paul and I set up a fifty-fifty partnership. The only rule was that every purchase required two signatures on the cheque.

Our business grew. We bought properties and renovated them to sell, and sometimes we did a building from scratch ourselves. We weren't very big, but we were profitable. I liked that. I liked my independence. And I liked the way we were operating. I was design conscious at a time when many developers were builders who didn't recognise the importance of design. We didn't employ architects, but we consulted them. What we built were better than average, and they came in at a good price.

At the beginning of 1968, I did what I'd dreamed of doing for so long. I enrolled at Sydney university to study fine arts. I had the property business going with Paul, and I was also doing some decorating. (Sidney had introduced me to some of his Greek clients who, after initial scepticism, accepted my proposal for a different colour scheme for some flats they were building. To their surprise the flats sold very well, so I got more decorating jobs from other Greek builders.) I was going out with Henry who poured balm on my heart and restored my spirit. Henry didn't stay overnight. He had a flat near the bookstore in King Street, in the city, and I sometimes stayed there, although I made a point of always being at home in the morning for the children. I was quite prim and proper like that. But it was 1968, a year of pivotal social change, if ever there was one. So, maybe it was inevitable that I was going to meet Adrian Van Der Linden, or someone like him, although at the time I thought there had never been anyone else like Adrian.

We met at a party. I was there by myself and a very handsome man approached me. I'm no good at small talk but I was engrossed by this man's conversation, so much so that at a certain point I realised we had been talking too long, and that I should move on. Afterwards, when I asked around, I found out that he was married, and there was a lot of gossip about the marriage being stormy.

We met next at a dinner given by a painter after the opening of his show. Adrian knew a lot of artists and writers. He manoeuvered to sit next to me in the restaurant, and again we talked non-stop. When he rang me a few days later to ask me out, I told him that I didn't go out with married men.

Adrian pursued me. I held firm, until the time he told me he had separated from his wife. Then I let him into my house, and informed him that I had a boyfriend. He said, »You never told me.« I said, »Why should I have? It's no concern of yours.« But I was very attracted to him. I told Henry I had met someone I liked, and Henry said, »Well, people come and go.« Adrian kept ringing. He said he and his wife had applied for a divorce, so we went out, and I fell in love. Again.

Adrian was like a hurricane. His incredible sexual energy knocked me off my feet. For me, who had paid such a high price for my independence, meeting somebody like Adrian was dangerous. I didn't know how to deal with this turbulence. Our love felt unsafe, right from the beginning. I didn't expect it to last long.

When I told Henry that I'd fallen in love with Adrian, he said he would make it easy for me. He would wait for me. He too didn't think it would last. So that's how it started.

Adrian was nine years younger than me. Actually, after Zdenek, all my boyfriends were younger than me. He'd arrived in Australia from Rotterdam in 1958 as a casual reporter for the *Rotterdams Nieuwsblad* to report weekly on the experiences of migrants. In his words, the contract was terminated owing to insufficient newsworthiness of reports. From 1959 to 1966 he lived and worked in Brisbane where he met the portrait artist Andrew Sibley, who remains a friend. Adrian was a painter too at that time. He could have been a good painter, if he'd stuck with it. He had a lot of talent, but he was an impatient man, and he wanted success quickly. He was great at starting things, but not at finishing them. Everything had to be done fast. Adrian lived fast. He was a playboy. Life in Adrian's orbit was intensely exhilarating. It was a rush. He needed the rush, and I, who likes to be in control of myself and my circumstances, allowed myself to be swept up by the force of his appetite for life. Anything was possible with Adrian, and I was seduced by his belief in himself and in his ability to re-imagine the world as he wanted it to be.

Adrian was also the first person who wanted to know everything about me, about the war, about my survival, about my parents. We lay in bed in his house in Paddington and talked for hours. It was like a cleansing of the horrors. I, in common with many survivors, had recurring nightmares. Occasionally when I slept at his house, I would scream out in my dreams, and he would wake me and say,»Now, tell me now, immediately. What is it?« As I opened up to him, my dreams began to disappear. For a while, he was having nightmares instead. I have a letter he wrote me from those early years.

»Dear Sabina, I shall make up to you for all the hurts and pains that mankind and humanity and life has given you. I shall give you nothing but pleasure in return for all the pain you have received. You are safe now, my darling. Never shall you fear again. Darkness is over: You are now in the light.«

I was 41 when I met Adrian, and just beginning to live in my own skin. Through him, I discovered that I liked sex, a lot. And I developed a strong social conscience. The late 1960s were the years of anti-war protests, of thalidomide, of animal liberation and women's liberation, of civil rights and human rights. Adrian had opinions on everything. I suppose he was an anarchist. I wasn't politically active. I have always been averse to joining organisations of any kind. However this is when I began contributing, particularly to causes supporting children.

Both of our divorces came through more or less at the same time, towards the end of 1968. Adrian began saying that this was more than a love affair, that he wanted to marry me. I didn't want to marry, full stop. It was becoming more commonplace by then for unmarried couples to live together. I couldn't see why we needed to marry. I didn't want any more children. I still felt enormous guilt about how my children had suffered during my marriage breakdown. Moreover, I already knew that Adrian wasn't ideal husband material, as I had so naively judged my first husband, Heniek, to be. He had no respect for the traditional male breadwinner role. He wanted money; he loved the luxurious things that money could buy, but he had no idea how to earn it himself.

The problems with money began when Adrian and I decided to go to Europe to live, indefinitely. How were we going to live? Who was going to pay? Adrian was an artist without a steady income. I earned a lot more than he did, and I didn't feel bad about supporting him. I felt he was writing well – stories, a novel, a play – but writing well and being published are two different things, particularly the way he wrote, without taking much advice. So we talked about it, and I said, »Look, I'll make you a loan, and when things improve, you will pay me back.« It was a substantial loan. We kept our accounts separate.

I sold the house in Dover Heights, with everything in it. I was in such a whirl, caught up in my feverish love for Adrian. Josie was doing her Higher School Certificate, and she remembers that her bed went under the hammer, complete with her HSC notes, which were in the drawers underneath. We had to chase those down. I wound up my involvement with Paul. I told him, »I've fallen in love, and I'm going overseas.« Both he and Sidney tried to persuade me not to cash up, but I was determined. I wanted my new life with Adrian so much. In the end, I sold my share of the business to Zdenek. Before we left for Europe, as a gesture of goodwill, and a compromise of sorts, I changed my name by deed poll to his name, van der Linden. And, of course, I dropped out of university. I had to. There was a choice to be made.

We had all these dreams of what we were going to do together. We would spend our days writing, sitting opposite each other at either end of a long table. We would live in a chateau. Josie, who was 18, would study in Paris, and Phillip, who was only 14, would finish school in Australia and spend his holidays in Europe with us. We sailed from Sydney on 2 December 1968 and disembarked in Holland where I met Adrian's family. He decided he couldn't live in Holland. We went to Belgium, looking for an affordable chateau, but I said I couldn't live in Belgium, I wanted to live in France, where I could speak the language, but not necessarily Paris, so we went south, to the landscape of the Impressionists. We rented a gatekeeper's house, which looked like a little chateau, at Tourrettes sur Loup, one of those impossibly pretty villages in Provence, between Cannes and Vence. We didn't get very far into our year in Provence however when Josie, who had enrolled in the Sorbonne, decided she missed her boyfriend and her friends, and said she was going home. Phillip had by then returned to school in Sydney. I reminded Adrian of the first of the two conditions of our relationship, that he should never put me in the position where I had to make a choice between him and my children. My children, I had told him from the outset, would always come first. It wasn't a difficult decision for Adrian to follow me back to Sydney. He didn't speak French, and he resented being incommunicado, even in a painter's paradise. Adrian always needed an audience. Our relationship was still new, and we were very much in love. So we came back to Australia at the beginning of July 1969.

XXIII. QUEEN STREET

This second arrival in Australia felt, to my surprise, like a homecoming. I had needed to go back to Europe with the intention of staying in order to discover that it was not where I belonged. Australia was no longer my place of refuge. It was my country.

Australians were now far less isolated from the events which shaped the world than they had been in the immediate post-war period. Nineteen sixty-nine was a big year. It was when the first American astronauts walked on the moon and the Woodstock festival was held, when the *Boeing 747* jumbo jet made its debut flight and the Stonewall riots launched the gay rights movement, when Yasser Arafat became leader of the Palestinian Liberation Organization and Australian media baron Rupert Murdoch bought the British tabloid News of the World. My friends in Australia were hungry for change. The social turbulence of the decade that was about to close had destabilised the political establishment and though the conservatives would hang onto government in Canberra until 1972, a new era of radical social policy was on the horizon. In 1967, Australians had voted in a referendum which finally saw Aboriginal Australians given citizenship, a long overdue correction to the colonial perception of Aborigines as a primitive race doomed to extinction. The two million migrants who had poured into Australia since the end of war, many of them from Eastern European and Mediterranean countries, had already begun to change the core composition of Australian identity from solid British to something much harder to put your finger on. I was part of that change, and I liked it.

Adrian and I started afresh in a rented house in Double Bay. Adrian, I already knew, was not the providing sort, so I went back to the bank and started investing in the property market again. A year after our return, I bought a stunning penthouse in Double Bay, with 360 degree views, and its own direct lift. Josie had moved into a flat with a friend by then, so Adrian and I lived there with Phillip and a pair of Siamese cats called Romeo and Juliet. The other occupants of this building told me I couldn't have my cats, so I told them, »Well, you take them and kill them.« I kept the cats.

Interesting things happened at that penthouse. Adrian, who, like Phillip, was a soccer nut, designed a game of table soccer, which became the focus of their relationship. There were marathon games in which Phillip and his friends played Adrian and his friends in 72-hour stretches. Adrian did everything to excess, including smoking a lot of pot, which disturbed me, not only because it was illegal but also because I didn't want.

Phillip following his example. I asked him not to smoke at home. Yet at the same time I told Phillip, who was in his senior years at school, that if he wanted to experiment, he should do so at home. My children both knew that they could rely on me to protect them, in whatever circumstance.

That was probably why Josie asked me to help Sally Anne Krivoshaw, who had been at school with Phillip, and an occasional visitor at the Darling Point apartment, next to Zdenek's, which Phillip and Josie shared while I was still in Europe. One day Josie phoned me at work and asked me to come to the children's court. »Josie, what did you do?« I asked. She replied, »Oh no, Mama, it's not for me. You have to help Sally Anne because I told them that you will.«

Sally Anne was then about 16, and looked like an angel, with the loveliest blonde hair. Her parents, who were Russian, had separated. She had a grandmother who adored her, but who couldn't cope with her. I doubt that this was the first time she'd been in court, though I can't remember. The judge was intending to send her to the Parramatta Girls Home unless someone could vouch for her, and give her a place to live. Josie had put her hand up, and said, »Yes, my mother will.« When I arrived, and the judge asked me why I would do this, I told him how, when I was about Sally Anne's age, and completely alone in the world, somebody took me in and helped me. I thought she deserved a chance. So he let me take her home, with the proviso that a probation officer would come regularly to check on her, and me.

I explained to Sally Anne why I was helping her. My conditions for doing so were that she go back to school and get a part-time job. There were not many rules in my house, I told her. I trusted my children, and I wanted to trust her. If we agreed that she was to be home by a certain time, I expected her home by then, or to telephone me. For a few weeks, she complied, and then it all went horribly wrong. There were apologies and tears, and we adjusted the terms. She told me she wasn't used to so much protection and surveillance. So I allowed her to move into a little house I owned in Redfern, again on certain conditions. Once again, it went well for a few weeks, and then one weekend she didn't turn up at the penthouse. Phillip and I went to Redfern and broke into the house. There were comatose bodies all over the floor. We gave her 24 hours to clean up and get out, or I would call the police.

She was already using drugs, but I didn't know what or how much. I told the probation officer I couldn't manage. Over the years I would meet her occasionally in the street and sometimes she would pop in to see me, bringing little gifts. She had such potential, but the drugs got her in the end. In 1987, she was found strangled and floating in a pond in Centennial Park. History remembers her as the prostitute and heroin addict Sally Anne Huckstep. I was desolate when I heard about her murder.

My relationship with Adrian started to become complicated. Part of that was to do with pot, and part of it to do with money. Adrian was almost always high and although I'd agreed once to try pot when he cooked it in a cheesecake, I didn't like it. Also, he liked to drink and I drank very little. Adrian interpreted this as a sign of my disapproval of him, which it wasn't. I never acquired a taste for alcohol. Then there was the even more difficult question of his financial dependence on me, which as time went on took on an unpleasant undertone. Adrian began to see me less as a lover and more as a supporter. I didn't mind investing in his projects, but I didn't like the way Adrian thought of me as the lady with the money.

I didn't think of myself as a businesswoman. Zdenek had always complained about my lack of focus on the business and my obsession with books and paintings. In that marriage, I was the ›arty‹ one. In my relationship with Adrian, however, the tables were turned. Adrian was comfortable with his role – he loved living in the penthouse and driving around in the grey Mustang convertible we'd brought back from Europe – but I wasn't. He produced a lot, but struggled to get much published. Probably his most successful venture was the hippie love-rock musical Grass, composed by Sven Libaek, for which he wrote the libretto. But relatively little of his work saw the light of day, and he was easily discouraged.

I knew I had to be self-reliant. There was no-one else. I set up various partnerships, but the one I remember most fondly was a property development company with Vera King. Vera was an architect by training, though she had a day job with the Water Board. She and I had complementary skills. I'd look at a house and have visions of what we could do, and she, with her practical knowledge, would pour cold water over my enthusiasm. We worked extremely well together.

I've mentioned that I always like to be doing more than one thing at a time, so after a while, I wanted to open my own interior decorating business. There was too much competition in Double Bay so I went looking in Paddington, a working-class suburb undergoing gentrification, and Woollahra, which had a gentler pace. Woollahra's Queen Street was just beginning to be transformed into the classy shopping strip it is today. I saw an isolated pair of shops on the south side of the street, just up from the post office, one of which had been used as a laundry. The building was a bit neglected, but I wanted it. It had just been passed in at auction. I went to the seller and made him an offer, which he accepted, and a date for exchange of contracts was agreed upon. Then about two days before exchange, the agent contacted me and said, »Sabina, I'm terribly sorry but the building has been sold.« The highest bidder at the auction had made a better offer to the seller. I'd been gazumped. I was terribly upset. »This is my building«, I protested. »I can see myself in it. It's written all over the building, Sabina's building.« He laughed, but said there was nothing he could do. I asked if he could do me a favour and tell me the name of the buyer. It's not normally done, but I'd given his agency a lot of business. He told me the name. The man was an investor. I rang him and said I'd like to meet with him. When he asked why, I said I couldn't tell him over the phone. I asked him to come to the penthouse.

There was no-one else at that meeting. I told him that I'd found what he'd done most unethical. He laughed at me. »Ethical, schmethical«, he quipped. »This is business.« Yes, I agreed, but even in business people should still behave ethically.

Now he was upset. I told him I hadn't invited him over to criticise him, that I had a proposition. He raised his eyebrows. »Not that kind of a proposition«, I said. I offered him a certain amount of cash, all the cash I could lay my hands on to tear up the contract. Not a bad profit to make in one week, I said.

I got my building. I still own it. I didn't have much left to live on, but that didn't worry me. I opened an interior decorating store, which I called *Sabini Design Profiles*, and after a short time I began travelling twice a year to Europe and bringing back container loads of objects and furniture. Whatever the Swedes and the Finns were making suited me very well. I was never comfortable with antiques. I didn't know enough about them, and I didn't have time to study and learn. I loved the cleanness of Scandinavian design, and their quality was wonderful. I brought in tubular furniture, which didn't exist at that time in Australia. I also bought from certain manufacturers in Italy and Britain. My commercial relationships always had a personal component. I couldn't buy products just because I thought they would sell. I had to like something. It had to be an extension of my taste. Similarly, if I didn't have anything in common with a manufacturer, I couldn't represent them. We had to connect.

I discovered I could run a business well. It allowed me to combine my enjoyment of people with a liking for design. And it gave me a standard of living I appreciated. I've always respected what money can buy, but I'm not materialistic in the sense that I want to have more and more. If I liked something beautiful, for example, a painting in an auction room, or a nice car, I would buy it. I became a contented person, enjoying life, free in a way I had never felt before.

But before that happened, I had to let Adrian go.

The beginning of the end came when Adrian met a charming American who was also, as it happened, a conman. Adrian was mesmerised by him. They were going to do great things together. Meanwhile, nothing was really happening with Adrian's various ventures. Then, when I came back from one of my buying trips to Europe, I found out he'd had an affair. It was a fling more than an affair, but I couldn't cope. I told him I wanted to end the relationship. We lasted a week apart, and then he came back. But deep in me, I need to respect the person who is closest to me, and I couldn't respect Adrian when I stopped trusting him. I wasn't going to mother Adrian. I believe people have to be responsible for themselves.

It finally ended when in 1972 I went away on another buying trip, and Adrian followed me to Europe because he said he wanted to meet me. I said I would meet him in London, but in the end, he didn't show. When I came back to Sydney, he wasn't there either. He never came back to Australia. He walked away from our life leaving loans I'd guaranteed, unpaid tax, bills and more bills. Adrian fulfilled me as a woman, but he crossed lines that I couldn't tolerate. I was strong, but not strong enough to survive if I allowed Adrian to scramble the moral compass my mother had fixed in me and which, for better or for worse, has guided me all my life. So I separated from Adrian. He occupied my life for four years and, yes, it ended in tears. But no regrets. I was disappointed when my marriage to Zdenek ended, but I knew from the beginning that Adrian was unreliable, that he drew his charm from an addictive personality, that his brilliant mind was nearly always high and his creative soul clouded. I went into our romance with my eyes wide open. I adored Adrian. I needed him. Every woman needs an Adrian at some time in her life.

I didn't see him again for many years, though we corresponded. At one point he was living in Iran where he became, ironically, a businessman. We saw each other again only once more before he died of a heart attack in 1993, aged 57. Adrian left a wife and two daughters. And me.

XXIV. KJELD

The year Adrian and I separated – 1972 – turned out to be a watershed year in Australia's political history. After 23 years of continuous conservative rule, Australians heeded the Labor Party's campaign slogan *It's time* and, at the federal election on 2 December 1972, gave Gough Whitlam the go ahead to form a new government. In their first year, the charismatic Labor Prime Minister Whitlam and his crew rolled out a heady programme of reforms in health, education and welfare. They could afford to. In 1973 the Australian economy expanded by six per cent, with the private sector growing even faster.

The housing industry was booming. I threw myself into building my interiors business and developing properties, working like a woman possessed. I wasn't just chasing the dollars. Keeping moving is my usual strategy for coping when tragedy strikes, as I've mentioned. At this end of my life, people like to call me a strong woman, but it's a particular kind of strength I possess. I'm not a stoic. I don't soldier on with grim determination. I shed the tears, I fall in a heap. But then I get up again. I'm what psychologists call resilient. I like to compare myself to a willow tree. However much of a beating it takes from the wind and the rain, it always springs up when the sun comes out.

The way I looked at it, Adrian was part of my life, but not all of it. I had other commitments. Phillip was still living with me. For all my busyness, I was an attentive mother. I made a point, for example, of responding to a circular letter sent home in this period by Phillip's school principal, which informed parents of the school's option of using corporal punishment by caning in the manner laid down by the Department of Education. The tone and content of the letter disturbed me deeply, and I advised the principal, and the Department of Education, accordingly. I wrote: »I consider violence as one of the most destructive forces which breeds nothing but violence, that hate breeds hate, prejudice breeds prejudice and so on. I believe that blind obedience to rules imposed on them by whatever form of authority (Nazism, Stalinism, Fascism etc) creates a nation of mentally and emotionally frustrated people, not capable of performing to their best in any field ... I believe that love and care, that respect and understanding of the needs of our children is the main factor in their upbringing and not forcefully imposed rules and fear of punishment. Finally I believe that the best way by which we can teach is by the example we give.« I had never been shy, but the confidence I was gaining through my dealings in the business world filtered down to deeper levels. I was growing strong enough to stand up and be counted.

In a wider sense, Australians were transforming themselves too. The Whitlam government upturned laws and institutions and gave birth to new ones at a frenetic pace. It was a time unlike any other Australia had known, and even today, many remember it with great nostalgia. The whole place seemed to come alive. It felt more spirited, more assertive, more ... interesting. Just as I had needed my romance with Adrian, it seemed Australia needed this great rush of blood to the head. But it too ended in tears.

Everyone had become used to the stability and prosperity of the postwar years, but by the time Cyclone *Tracy* flattened Darwin on Christmas Eve 1974, the good times were over for Australia. The trouble began in October 1973 when the oil producers' cartel, OPEC, doubled the price of oil, tipping Western economies into recession with inflation worldwide shooting into double digits. The savagery of the economic slump took six months to register in Australia, but by July 1974, businesses had begun laying off workers in their thousands, and by November unemployment had doubled to four per cent. Wages and prices soared out of control, industrial action escalated, profits collapsed, and the housing boom gave way to the steepest bust on record. The Whitlam government staggered on, spending as if money grew on trees, until it was famously and abruptly dismissed on 11 November 1975, by which time Vera and I, along with just about everyone else in the building industry, were on our last legs.

We owned several properties when the banks started calling in their loans. I didn't want to sell, because they were not yet developed, and I would have lost everything I had worked so hard for. So I rang around all the suppliers I owed money to, and asked them to extend credit to me for three to six months. All but one obliged. I had a good record. I always paid on time. So we finished all the buildings, sold them at a loss, and paid back all the creditors except for the bank, which forced me to sell the penthouse. That left me with the Queen Street building, and two mortgages, but I was still trading. I was not going to go bankrupt. It was important to me to keep my name clean and not to disappoint anybody.

Another interior decorator, Leslie Walford, bought my penthouse and I moved into a hotel in Elizabeth Bay until I could find a house to rent. I had fallen hard, but I wasn't desperately unhappy. I didn't dwell on what might have been. That's not how I am. If I reach a stage when I find it's impossible to continue with something, it's finished. I don't make that decision quickly, but when I do, I'm as incisive as a surgeon. I cut out whatever it is that's causing me pain, and I don't look back.

I'm afraid of pain, but I'm even more afraid of not knowing what's going to happen next. During the war, every day was agony, continuing agony. I never knew at what moment I might be discovered, or denounced, or shot. The way I managed my fear then was to think, well, that's tomorrow, and today I am here. I want to spend it as a decent human being. It was probably instinctive, but when I was locked up under the police station, expecting to be shot the next morning, I concentrated on what was in front of me, the filth that I wanted to remove in order to lie down and sleep. I have this ability to live in the present. It's not that I deny past experience. I try to extract something from it, to learn, so I don't make the same mistake again.

So I closed the door on the penthouse in which so much had happened to me during the most radical years both of my life and in Australia's post-war history, and I came back down to earth. I kept trading at Sabini, my interiors business, and I kept travelling and buying. To satisfy the European manufacturers from whom I had gained exclusive Australian rights, I needed to sell more than I could channel through one shop. There was a Danish man supplying me, whose tastes and mine lined up, so in 1975 we started a wholesale import company called *Dansab*. Dan for Danish, Sab for Sabina. This time my lawyer wouldn't allow me to go into a fifty-fifty partnership. He insisted I have a majority, so it was 51:49.

A few months after we had combined our stock, I started getting letters from Denmark demanding payment. I had started the company with all my stock clean and paid for, but unfortunately my partner hadn't. We started with a problem, and it went on that way. I continued travelling and buying, and he sold the stock, but we were going backwards. He didn't seem worried about the prospect of going bankrupt, but I was. I had guaranteed our loans with Queen Street. He had nothing to lose. Eventually, I called a friend, Frans Krijnen, whom I had met through Adrian. I had developed some property for him, and asked him to help me out. He lent *Dansab* money on the basis that my partner sold him half his share in the company. When it became obvious that I was being robbed left, right and centre, we called a meeting and put it plainly to my Danish connection: »Resign or we will press criminal charges.« He did, in December 1977. By that time, however, there was another Dane in my life, a young man named Kjeld Hansen.

I met Kjeld on the water towards the end of 1976. It was one of those glorious sunny days that I had come to expect after more than 25 years in Sydney. The poster in the Paris Métro hadn't lied after all. Some friends invited me to go sailing, and I was looking forward to a peaceful day with them on the harbour. To my surprise, there was another guest on board, a young man with unkempt, long blond hair wearing torn jeans and not much else. Looks can be deceiving though, and the Viking turned out to be articulate, witty and entertaining. I enjoyed his company until, when evening came and I was about to step ashore, he cheekily suggested that I stay with him on the boat. I wasn't impressed.

Two or three weeks later, he called, and said he was in the neighbourhood. I had moved to a rented house in Paddington by then. Could he come to visit? I opened the door to a neatly dressed, longish-haired, rather attractive young man, the same Viking in a different package. He stayed a while, and then he came back, and he stayed longer. And eventually he moved in with me and Phillip.

A few months later, Kjeld had a birthday. I asked him how old he was turning. »Twenty-eight«, he said. I choked. »What did you say? Twenty-eight?« He looked at me strangely. »Yes, 28. What's wrong with that?« Silence. And then I said faintly, »Nothing. Do you know how old I am?« He said he didn't, and when I asked him if he wanted to know, he said he couldn't care less. I don't know when he found out that I was so much older than him, but it obviously didn't derail our relationship. We're still together. In February 2007 we hosted a party to celebrate 30 years of unwedded bliss. We are, as I said on that evening, ideally suited. My children Phillip and Josie put it beautifully when they said that I was the colour in Kjeld's life, and he was my rock. It's true. That's how it works between us. I have the ideas, and Kjeld helps me make them happen. I am impulsive, while he is analytic. I am impatient, while he is prepared to wait. Our difference in age is the least of our differences, and it's what we have in common that gives us the greatest pleasure. I didn't expect it to last, but it has. I never expected to fall in love with anyone after Adrian, and I was lucky to meet such a supportive decent human being at that stage in my life.

Kjeld trained as an architect in Denmark, and in our first year together had a job with an architectural firm in Bondi Junction. When things started to come unstuck at *Dansab* in the week before Christmas 1977, and I was left on my own, our few other staff having resigned for completely unrelated reasons, Kjeld handed in his notice. He came home one day and said he was going to come and help me. I was unnerved. I asked him why he'd want to do that. My experience with Zdenek had made me wary of emotional complications in the workplace. Kjeld calmly repeated his offer. »Sabina, I don't know if you heard me properly«, he said. »I want to come in and help you. I don't want to make life more difficult for you. It's your business. If it doesn't work out, I can always go back to my work.«

Kjeld became my business manager, my backroom man. I did the talking to the banks (there was always a lot of that), and the travelling and buying. He made the numbers work. By the time he came in, *Dansab* had already shifted its focus away from furniture and towards smaller design items such as lighting, glass and tableware. The market for our furniture had always been limited, given that my taste was so selective and the products I imported were ahead of their time. When the architectural firms and innovative developers who had been our main clients folded during the building industry collapse, *Dansab* suffered badly, and I realised we had to diversify as an import company.

Sometime in 1975 I went to San Francisco to visit my cousin Helen, Adolf's daughter. I wanted to buy her a gift for the house, and we went together to I. Magnin, the luxury department store once considered among the most elegant in the United States. I saw a beautiful square glass plate there. Today, square plates are common, but in those days, plates were round. I hadn't seen anything like it in Europe or Australia. Helen liked it, and we bought it. On the box was a tiny label, *Sasaki*. I thought it sounded Japanese. There was some trade with Japan then, but mostly at the cheap, mass-produced end of the market.

When I returned to Sydney, I phoned the Japanese consul general and found out that *Sasaki* was one of the biggest glass manufacturers in Japan. I knew nothing about Japan, but I wrote to *Sasaki* to find out about its product. After I'd had no reply to three letters, I assumed they weren't interested. I was in Europe on a buying trip early in 1976 when I got a telex saying that the export manager from *Sasaki* would be in Sydney to see me on such and such a date. I made sure I was back in time, but in fact, Mr. Nagamine didn't come to Sydney that year. In April 1977, when I finally met Tom-san, as I learned to call him, I had already placed my first order with *Sasaki*. I asked him for an exclusive agency. He told me that *Sasaki* already had an agent with whom they had been working for years. I didn't know anything about working with the Japanese then. I didn't know how ethical and principled they are in their business dealings. Tom-san wouldn't break with his agent, but agreed to sell different product to me, on an exclusive basis.

The market's first reaction to Japanese crystal and glass wasn't good. Not only did I have to introduce the brand, but I also had to convince people that it was top quality. I had two things working in my favour – price (the exchange rate of the Australian dollar was still fixed, and the yen was weak) and design (there was nothing like *Sasaki* in Australia then). But business was slow.

In February 1978 I made my first trip to Japan. I remember arriving at Tokyo airport, and being greeted by a delegation from *Sasaki*. And then waiting. I didn't know what we were waiting for. After a while I realised that they thought the chairman of *Dansab* was still to come, and that I was probably his secretary. The name Sabina Van Der Linden was as foreign to them as their names were to me. They weren't expecting a woman.

My friend Elizabeth Kata had given me some notes about how to behave in Japan. I met Elizabeth in the late '60s through Adrian. By then she was already a well-known writer. Her novel *Be Ready with Bells and Drums* made a huge impact when it was published in 1961. Its readership was extended when it was made into a film, A Patch of Blue, starring Sidney Poitier and Shelley Winters. Elizabeth was never a creature of Hollywood though. Born in Sydney, she had fallen in love with a visiting Japanese pianist, Shinshuro Katayama, in the 1930s. She was given permission to go to Japan where they married, with due ceremony, in 1937. A few years of newly married bliss were changed forever when the Japanese bombed Pearl Harbor. Elizabeth, who was loved and protected by her husband's family, spent the Pacific war in the Japanese Alps under the close and suspicious eyes of the Japanese authorities. Her son, David, was born three weeks before the first atom bomb was dropped on Hiroshima.

A few years after the war ended, the Katayamas separated, though they never divorced. Elizabeth needed special government permission to re-enter Australia with her son. Her understanding of the essence of humanity, love without prejudice, resonated strongly with me, and was the basis of our friendship, but in this instance, what Elizabeth furnished me with was something few people at the time possessed – a working knowledge of Japanese etiquette.

I followed her instructions. Be polite, be patient, wait, say a few nice things, have a cup of tea, ask how business is … and then ask if it's all right to have a look around. For me, excitable and gregarious as I am, doing business in Japan was an ordeal, but an ordeal I gradually learned to make sense of. Actually, in some respects, the Japanese way of doing things suited me well. I liked their punctuality. I liked the security in knowing that what was agreed upon was firm. It wasn't easy to get an agreement out of them – the Japanese do not think it polite to say no, even when that's their intention – but once arrived at, a decision was always reliable. It seemed to take forever, but when *Sasaki* eventually did offer me their agency in Australia and I, instinctively, briefed my solicitor to prepare a contract, the Japanese looked puzzled. What contract? They said they didn't need a contract, but if I wanted a contract, I should write one. Slowly and gently Tom-san taught me that in Japan, the wheels of business are oiled by trust, and that friendship, once earned, is a vital and enduring part of the mix.

I put a lot of energy into *Sasaki*. I advertised heavily and worked closely with the glossy magazines and architectural journals. The business grew, and even more so after *Sasaki* opened its own branch in New York, and I could piggyback on the large orders of the New Yorkers, whose taste was so similar to mine.

In 1983, I took another large leap of faith. I decided to buy a commercial building. We had been renting space over three floors in Pyrmont, but by that time we were importing by the container load, had a large distribution network, and were selling to the department stores, which eventually offered us in-store *Sasaki* shops. I thought it would be more efficient if we could be on one floor, plus I wanted to computerise the business.

The building I found to buy was an old four-storey warehouse with timber floors and a nice roofline in Chippendale, not far from Sydney's Central Railway Station. Of course, I didn't have the money to buy it, so I was fully extended with interest-only payments on a loan of about one million dollars.

We repaired and renovated the building, which was renamed *Dansab* House. We set ourselves up on the first floor, putting in a large new showroom for *Sasaki*, which then made up about 70 per cent of our import business. The rest of the building was leased to other like-minded tenants to create a sort of design hub. In September 1985, when the Lord Mayor of Sydney Doug Sutherland opened the building, in the presence of Shinji Sasaki and his wife, everything was going splendidly. At the party, we served caviar with sour cream in miniature tartlets, oysters, king prawns, Danish smoked salmon on rye, fried stuffed mushrooms – I like to look after my guests. This was the 1980s. We were flying high, and I was enjoying myself.

And then, boom, we got hit by the foreign exchange crisis.

I need to go back a bit. In December 1983, the then Prime Minister and Treasurer, Bob Hawke and Paul Keating respectively, floated the Australian dollar, a move which set off a cascade of financial deregulation – the licensing of foreign banks, the freeing up of lending, lowering of trade barriers and the abolition of import quotas, the shift away from centralised wage-fixing, and so on.

When the dollar was set loose, its value fell sharply, and kept falling. In fact, it didn't start to rise again until the late 1980s. In order to avoid high Australian interest rates in 1983, I had taken my loan offshore. By 1986, with the dollar showing no sign of improvement, the bank was pressing me to bring my loan back onshore and, to my horror, I found I now owed more than double the amount I had borrowed. By that time, I was living in a new Japanese-influenced house that I had built behind my Queen Street property. I didn't want to sell it. Nor did I want to sell *Dansab* House at a loss. The bank kept off my back as long as I could meet my interest payments. It was just a question of hanging in there. Zdenek and I had started seeing each other occasionally for family celebrations. We were friends again, and he lent me some money. All the same, they were difficult years. I was travelling a lot, up to four times a year to Japan and Europe buying stock. Kjeld could never come with me. One of us needed to stay with the business. I was worried about Josie who by then was bringing up a child on her own and who, between 1987 and 1990, was hit with two separate, and serious, health problems.

When I collapsed after a difficult meeting in Tokyo and was diagnosed with dangerously high blood pressure, I knew I had to face some unpalatable truths. I made diary notes only sporadically in those years. But on 25 October 1988, when I found myself in hospital, exhausted and suffering from blackouts and palpitations of the heart, I wrote:

»So here I am on enforced rest. It will do me good no doubt... I've had many many tests, rather unpleasant, thinking about life, priorities, direction ... How quickly the time has gone by.

I have become more aware of every day of my life. I ought to contribute more, to give more of myself to others. There is so much pain and suffering around us. I have to make some plans for the future, and try to follow them.

Shall I sell the business? What will I do if I sell the business? Do I really like being so busy all the time or has it become second nature to me?

By the way, what about the results of the tests?«

I was keeping my head above water as far as the bank was concerned, but I had no money to run the business. I had to open letters of credit to buy product to sell. In Japan, interest rates were around four per cent, as compared to up to 18 per cent in Australia, and *Sasaki* helped me borrow money in Japan at the lower rates to pay for its stock. I was surviving, but at a cost.

The doctors were telling me that I was heading for trouble with my heart. Their advice was that I work much less. I knew I couldn't run the business and work less. I either ran it, or walked away. There wasn't much interest in buying an import business with the dollar the way it was, so I arranged to sell the stock, and on 14 September 1990, I announced that I was closing down. A month later, I threw another party at *Dansab* House – *Sabina and Kjeld's Time to take things easier party*. We went out in style, and with a lot of goodwill. *Sasaki* was generous to the end. I found it hard to pull back. I knew I had to for the sake of my health, but it's not in my nature to take things easy. I am not the meditating type. However, life has a way of forcing its lessons on you.

On 25 February 1991, my son Phillip and his wife Suzy had their third child, a son called Zachariah Joseph. I was as wonderstruck by this first grandson as I had been at the arrival of each of my granddaughters. By then, Josie had a daughter, Poppy, and Phillip and Suzy had two daughters, Pia and Sophie, each little girl a miracle to my mind. I hadn't expected to survive my own girlhood, let alone become a grandmother. Of course, I wished that my mother could have seen them.

Five months later, on 6 August, Zac died in his sleep. Phillip and Suzy were inconsolable, and for me his death was as incomprehensible as my brother Josek's death 45 years before. When little Sophie stayed overnight with Kjeld and me, and asked, »Meme, why did Zac have to die?« I had no answer for her, other than to say that sometimes things happen, and that wherever he was, he was happy and well. There are some things a child cannot be told. I felt so inadequate. »But I miss him, and I can't see him«, Sophie said. I knew. I turned to Swiss-born psychiatrist Elisabeth Kübler-Ross's books on death and dying for help. They helped with this new grief cycle I was entering.

And then, in February 1992, Zdenek learned that he had cancer of the lungs and liver. His diagnosis shocked me deeply. The bitterness of our divorce was long past. Zdenek had never liked Adrian, but it had been 20 years since Adrian and I parted. Zdenek was fond of Kjeld, and I, in my own way, never stopped loving Zdenek. I spent almost every day with Zdenek for the last two months of his life. He died seven months after his diagnosis. I wrote in my diary:

»Zdenek passed away on Tuesday, 15 September. I was not there, I left him at 6 p.m. saying I shall see you tomorrow, darling. He embraced me, kissed me on my lips twice, squeezed my hand, and nodded. I'm devastated and somehow surprised at my reaction. Those last few weeks were so tragic and sad, and especially the last few days. He stopped eating. There was nothing but skin and bone left, most of the time dozing off, other times so uncomfortable suffering in silence. I prayed that the end should come soon. I thought I was prepared for it, but I wasn't. I feel such a dreadful loss. A large part of my life has come to an end.«

On 1 December 1992, Suzy gave birth to a baby boy, whom she and Phillip called Remy Dennis (Zdenek had Anglicised his name to Dennis many decades earlier), and shortly after the New Year, with Kjeld back in Denmark visiting his parents, I wrote in my diary: »A peaceful serene day. It's early afternoon. Music fills the house with the genius of Mozart. I'm grateful to be alive.«

XXV. REMEMBERING

My children, Josie and Phillip, were well into adulthood with children of their own before I said much to them about my wartime experiences in Poland. It wasn't something I wanted complicating their lives when they were young. I had seen the damage caused when Holocaust survivors allowed their unutterable pain and bitterness to seep into the deep tissue of their family life. I wanted my children's growing up to be bathed in light. I thought the time would come when they would want to know about the Dark Ages I had lived through.

As it happened, the first children to whom I told my story in detail were somebody else's. In late September 1992, a week after Zdenek's death, I kept an appointment with a group of 15 year olds at a Jewish college in Sydney's eastern suburbs. I was feeling fragile. I had a dreadful cold. But I had given my word to a friend, Ruth Wilson, that I would help her with a project to educate young people about racism and prejudice. At first I was reluctant, but then, on impulse, I agreed to be interviewed about my experiences. Several years later, Ruth published a short story about that morning when I came to speak at Emanuel School, titled *Sabina, My Friend*. »She almost didn't come that morning ... [but] Sabina is gentle, so her heart rules her head. Perhaps that is the secret of her survival. That day her heart triumphed over her aching body.« She was right. Of course, I was getting older and my perspective on my wartime experiences, and their place in history, was shifting. But mostly, I felt like it was time. I felt responsible towards those who hadn't survived to do the hard work of remembering.

I was fortunate with that first group of students. They listened intently, appalled and enthralled in turn, as Ruth wrote. When we finished the sessions at the school, a small group of students came home with me and we continued there. I experienced a sense of catharsis, as I had when Adrian had first probed into my past, but more importantly, I saw how directly my experiences connected with the powerful drive in young people to make sense of life. My nightmares returned, but I was prepared to pay that price to persuade young people that if they closed their eyes and pretended it was raining when someone was spitting in their face, they were condoning the insult. I tried to give them the courage to speak out rather than remaining silent when they encountered racism or prejudice or discrimination.

Once I started speaking, I felt compelled to do it again, and again. I began speaking in other schools, as I was invited. It was always emotionally demanding, but I felt as if I were contributing in a small way by bearing witness to the horrors I'd experienced. I promised myself at the outset that I would tell the truth and that if I didn't know something I would say so. Several years later, I joined the speaker list of the NSW Jewish Board of Deputies, and expanded my audience beyond schools to include service clubs, and university and professional forums. But I never shifted from this basic principle of telling only what I knew.

Towards the end of January 1993, I went to Melbourne to a conference for child Holocaust survivors, or Hidden children, as people with wartime experiences like mine were just beginning to be known. The first international meeting of Hidden children had been held in 1991 in New York. I didn't go, but I had heard about it, and when a Sydney group of child Holocaust survivors was formed that year, I went to an early meeting, which is where I met Ruth. It was there, in the company of strangers who, like me, had buried their childhood memories for 50 years, that I began to gingerly reopen my past.

So few Jewish children survived the war. The Nazis deliberately targeted the new generation of Jews for early deportation and death. Of the six million Jews who were murdered, around one and a half million were boys and girls. For many years, we lucky ones who had survived our childhood either in hiding or in the camps, were thought to have been too young to have been affected by the horrors of Nazi rule. If we thought differently, we didn't say so. We locked down our nightmares as we grew into our adult skins, which the Nazis never intended us to have. Many of us left Europe and built new homes, new families and new ambitions in places where there was nothing to jog our memories. But as our lucky lives began to reach their natural conclusion, many of us, including me, felt an urge to speak of what had happened to us during the war. We child survivors of the Holocaust understood that not only were our testimonies the last direct link to Hitler's attempt to consummate 2000 years of European anti-Semitism, but also that there was no hierarchy of victims. In the face of death and torture, our youth had not protected us from suffering.

After the child survivors' conference in Melbourne, I decided to go to the second Hidden Children international gathering in Jerusalem in July 1993. Before I left, I had a letter from the Heiligs, the couple who had introduced Zdenek to me over coffee and cake at their home in

Wałbrzych all those years ago. They had lived in Israel for many years. They asked me if I would be interested in going with them to Poland, and then on to Borysław, after the conference. Some Americans who came from our town were organising the trip, they said. It was to be a kind of reunion of Borysław survivors.

Some people I know never want to go back. Rita doesn't, nor does Róża. But I agreed to join the Heiligs. I had to see the place again. I felt this intense desire to retrace the early years of my life, to see the places where I'd lived with my parents and my brother, to see where my childhood and my family had been so violently destroyed, to come face to face with the physical reality of Borysław so I could try to make sense of what had happened there.

Neither Phillip nor Josie had been to Poland, and until then we had spoken very little together about my experiences during the war. I didn't ask them to come with me. They offered. They said they wouldn't let me go back alone. They would be my protectors, my guardians.

I have a photograph of Josie and me, standing inside the barracks at the spot where, I was told, my brother and my father and Mendzio were executed. Josie, my lovely and free-spirited daughter, is holding me tight. It had rained that day, and in the photograph there are muddy puddles on the broken-up concrete ground. The sky is low, and dull. I remember standing there, in my daughter's embrace, wondering how they had felt, what their last moments were like. My heart was breaking, again. I hadn't been there with my brother. I could only imagine how much he had wanted to live just before the bullets hit him.

The camp was derelict, but the structures I remembered – the men's and women's quarters, the White House where the chemists and so on lived, and the gatehouse where I stayed with the Eisensteins – were still intact. The dead were commemorated by a small plaque on the wall near the front gates, which are just as they were in the years when Hildebrand's order to murder was called the rule of law. The plaque read: *In memory of the Jews murdered by the Germans in the Borysław ghetto 1941–1944.* That's it.

I visited the place at Łoziny where I'd last lived with my mother. The house had never been much to speak of, but like most of what we found in Borysław, the area was neglected, dilapidated. The Jewish cemetery in which I had arranged for the remains of my brother, my father and Mendzio to be buried when they were accidentally exhumed in 1945 no longer existed. The Russians had dug it up and built a car park over it. Our group organised for a memorial plaque to be laid on the site, but there were no Jews left in the town to keep the memorial tidy and clean. So high were the levels of anxiety and mistrust raised by our visit that the local police gave us protection as we made our way around the town, paying homage to the destruction of the Jews of Borysław at sites of both shared and personal tragedy. In each place, we felt the eyes following us.

I found the Staniszewskis' house, where I'd spent the terrible night of 21 July 1944, and the park bench on which I'd sat and watched the last transport of Jews being driven by the SS and their dogs towards a train destined for Auschwitz. I sat on that bench with Josie and Phillip, whose existence helps me to make sense of my survival, and told them how I had waited to be recognised and called to join the deportation. And how the column of doomed Jews passed on without me. Then I told them how grateful I was for the gift of life, for them, and for their children, my grandchildren – Poppy, Pia, Sophie and Remy. Josie and Phillip had been born in Australia, such a free country. Before they came with me to Borysław, it had been impossible for them to understand what I had lived through as a girl. After that visit, they saw me differently, I think. We were closer.

In Poland, we went to the concentration camps, to Auschwitz and to Majdanek. I'd never seen them before. And we went to Belzec. It was overgrown with weeds and bereft of a single Jewish emblem. There was no memorial for the one in ten victims of the Holocaust who met their deaths in the first place in human history to use permanent gas chambers. We lit some candles for my mother, her parents, her brother and her sister and their families, and wept for the abandonment of our dead.

In July 1995 I was approached to do a taped interview, as were many others, for the *Shoah Foundation*. The foundation was established in 1994 by Steven Spielberg, a year after he had filmed *Schindler's List*, originally to record testimonies of all remaining survivors of the Holocaust. When Spielberg's interviewers came to Sydney, they asked permission to copy and catalogue my photographs and letters and diaries for the archives of the United States Holocaust Memorial Museum (USHMM), which had opened in Washington in April 1993. Kjeld and I visited the museum in 1995. It was a shattering experience.

During that same trip in 1995 I went to another conference for Hidden children, this one in Los Angeles, hoping against hope that I would find someone, maybe a cousin whose name I had forgotten, maybe someone from my father's family whose name I never knew. I was buoyed by having made contact with a cousin in Buenos Aires shortly before, Ana Natalia, daughter of my mother's brother Jacob. Kjeld and I visited her en route to Los Angeles. She was a theatre and costume designer, a woman three years younger than me with similar interests and tastes. We were grateful to know each other, we Kulawicz girls who had spent a lifetime apart. In LA, there were no other relatives that I could find, but I met people to whom I could talk about the appalling conditions of the death camp site at Belzec. In March 1996 I wrote to Alan Elsner, who was the chief US political correspondent for Reuters at the time, and who had visited Belzec the previous year with his father and written about its neglect. He told me he had persuaded the USHMM to adopt the project, and that the USHMM and the Polish government had agreed to build a memorial and museum there. He referred me to Jacek Nowakowski, the USHMM's director of collections and acquisitions, and over the next few years, Mr Nowakowski kept me informed of the project's fitful progress. I wanted to be of help but in the end, there was nothing I could do, and when the Belzec memorial was finally inaugurated on 3 June 2004 I applauded from a distance.

I had a few problems closer to home during these years. In April 1997 I was admitted to hospital for a quadruple heart bypass operation. If I was worried, I didn't show it, but I also remember thinking as I was wheeled into the operating theatre that I was not ready to go yet. I had more I wanted to do, including a new property development to complete. Kjeld and I had lived since 1982 in our exquisite black-and-white townhouse in the eastern suburbs, but I had decided it was too small. I wanted more room for house guests, more room to entertain, and I wanted a swimming pool in which to exercise. So, in November 1996 I bought an old carpet warehouse nearby with the intention of converting it into two large townhouses, one to sell and one to keep, and asked architect Alex Tzannes to design the project.

The bypass operation renewed the urgency I had to live, and live well. I'd always read a lot, but when I felt my energy returning, I read more. I'd always loved paintings, and so I boosted my collection. I went to the theatre more often, made new friends, mended old bridges. I gave more time to Courage to Care, an organisation which educates Australians about racial tolerance, and stresses that each individual can make a difference. I was enjoying the present and thought I was gradually coming to terms with my past.

Even so, when in April 2003 I received a letter from Berlin, addressed to Mrs. Haberman van der Linden, it stopped me in my tracks. No-one had called me Haberman since 1943. And now somebody was writing to me, Sabina Haberman, from Berlin?

XXVI. BERLIN

The letter writer introduced himself as a young German researcher named Dr. Ulrich Baumann who was preparing documentation for an information centre to be linked to the planned Memorial to the Murdered Jews of Europe in Berlin. He had been working in the photo archives of the USHMM in Washington the month before, and had seen the photographs and documents I'd submitted to the collection. He wanted to know if I could imagine that pictures and documents telling the story [of the Haberman family] could be a part of an exhibition [in Berlin]. He was, he wrote, impressed by the photos of my brother and his friends in the ghetto, and wanted to express how sad he felt reading of his tragic death by German murderers. He wondered if I had saved other pictures of my family and our daily life in Borysław.

I cried for two days after the letter arrived. Something burst in me. After the tears had run their course, I wrote back agreeing to help. I hadn't heard of the memorial in Berlin until then, but once I'd done some research I knew that this was something I wanted to be involved in. The path I'd been following over the past few years – meeting other child survivors, speaking publicly about my war experiences, travelling back to Borysław, going to Belzec, seemed to have led me to this point. I understood that while anti-Semitism had been my particular burden to bear, prejudice and hatred in any form, whether it be against blacks, or Asians, or Muslims, or women, demeaned humanity and contained within it the seeds of evil. I understood, and wanted future generations to understand, that those who remained silent in the face of prejudice and hatred gave prejudice and hatred permission not only to exist but to flourish. This memorial was an acknowledgment by the German nation, for centuries considered one of the most civilised people in Europe, that in addition to its great accomplishments, it would always be identified as the nation that had launched the deadliest genocide in history. It was an acknowledgment that many German citizens had stood by as the Nazis stripped other German citizens, who happened to be Jewish, first of their political rights and then of their human rights, and an acknowledgment of their responsibility for the consequences of staying silent in the face of this monstrous prejudice and hatred – the mass murder of six million European Jews. Of course I wanted to be involved with an initiative that gave the Holocaust memory a central place in Berlin. Why me? Yes, I asked that question, too, but I didn't dwell on it.

In July 2004, after many months of correspondence, I went to Berlin to see the progress on the memorial. By then I knew that the memorial was controversial. The idea for a monument dedicated to the Jewish victims of the Holocaust was mooted in 1988 by a small group of private citizens, led by television journalist Lea Rosh and historian Eberhard Jäckel, neither of whom is Jewish. The German public argued and complained furiously for years about who such a memorial was for, whether it should be built, and if so, what was the right way to do it and what it should look like. There were two design competitions with hundreds of entries. The breakthrough came on 25 June 1999 when the German parliament (Bundestag), in one of its last decisions taken in Bonn before relocating to Berlin, finally approved the memorial's construction on five acres of land freed up by the tearing down of the Berlin Wall. Even while it was being built »on the ruins of the centre of Nazi power«, as Lea Rosh put it, the arguments continued. In October 2003 a row broke out when it was discovered that the parent company of the contractor providing anti-graffiti spray for the concrete pillars had supplied *Zyklon B* gas pellets to the Nazis for their extermination camps. If this monument was to be built, then which resources could be used, it was asked, and who could take part in its construction?

The Germans pushed on and finished the job, and like many others, I was impressed by the way they handled the whole process. For example, one design submission had suggested blowing up the Brandenburg Gate, grinding it down and sprinkling the dust over its former site before covering the entire memorial area with granite plates. How better to remember a people murdered in the name of the German nation, the artist Horst Hoheisel suggested, than by destroying Germany's national monument and carving out an empty space on prime real estate at the heart of the reunified German capital?

Of course, Hoheisel's proposal was never seriously considered. The design eventually selected was by an American Jewish architect Peter Eisenman. It's a sea of stone blocks, which Eisenman calls stelae, arranged in a grid pattern on gently and irregularly sloping ground. I liked the Eisenman design from the outset, but I was aware that there was dissatisfaction, both within and outside Germany, with the form the memorial took, the fact that it represented only Jews, that it represented Jews as victims, and that it avoided asking the question Why? and making pronouncements about the guilty and about the causes and reasons behind Hitler's war.

If I had any lingering doubts about being involved with the memorial, they were banished on that first visit to Berlin. I'd arranged to meet Dr. Ulrich Baumann, as he signed himself, at the hotel café which, in warm weather, spills its tables out onto the pavement of the Kurfürstendamm. West Berlin's most fashionable avenue was seething with sightseers and shoppers. I spotted a slender young man, slightly balding, arriving on a bicycle. For some reason, I knew this was *my* Dr. Baumann. I was completely at ease with Uli, as I now know him, from the start. He took me to meet his colleagues, who were all in their late twenties or thirties, young Germans trying so hard to make their contribution. I had long since stopped being anxious about hearing the German language. I had visited Cologne and Dusseldorf many times for trade fairs in my import business days. Uli and I spoke openly of my feelings about Germany, past and present, about racism and hatred and the notion of collective guilt.

At that stage I wasn't yet sure if my family would be one of the 15 European Jewish families featured in the information centre's Room of Family Histories. Uli had sifted through several thousand documents and photographs at both Yad Vashem, the memorial to the Holocaust in Jerusalem, and at the Washington museum. He had specific requirements for each family selected, not the least of which were photographs not only of pre-war daily life, but also diaries, letters and photographs of family members from the war years. Think of the enormity of this task. In Poland, as in other occupied countries, the Nazis used slave labour to gut Jewish houses of their belongings once their inhabitants were disposed of. So much evidence of Jewish life was destroyed. I have mentioned that Marek gave me a rare photograph of our discovery in the bunker under the rabbit hutch, and that Rita's Polish uncle saved the photograph of my brother's birthday party in the ghetto. I had other photographs. There was one of my brother posing in 1941 in front of an oil drilling derrick with other members of the youth group of the Zionist movement *Hashomer Hatzair* (Guardians of Zion). And another of myself, my brother, my mother and her friend Mrs Herzfeld, dressed in our best winter coats, walking down Pańska Street in Borysław. (When I made my first visit to the new memorial at Belzec in 2005, I saw a huge print of that photograph displayed in the entrance to the museum. I was astonished. It had been selected by the museum's historians for hanging without my knowledge.) I also had photographs of my grandparents sent to me after the war by my cousins in America. I was lucky. I had letters from Josek and my diaries which, as I have said often, I still do not understand how I managed to preserve. Because of this comparative wealth of documentation, and also because the story of our town is somewhat unusual, my family, the Haberman family from Borysław, was eventually among those included in the information centre display.

Then, in January 2005, the president of the Bundestag, Wolfgang Thierse, invited me to speak at the 10 May opening of the memorial on behalf of all Jewish victims and survivors of the Holocaust. I was bewildered by the honour, nervous about its implications, and aware of the enormous responsibility placed on me. I was aware by then that some people felt that no memorial would ever be up to the task, that the crimes perpetrated in Germany's name could not be remembered without redeeming them in some way, that their causes and effects could not be grasped without justifying them. Others felt that the memorial was incomplete because it focused only on the murdered Jews and not the Nazis' other victims, among them murdered members of the Sinti and Roma peoples, homosexuals and Jehovah's Witnesses, and innocents who died among the German civilian population, all victims of war and tyranny. I was also aware that some people felt the memorial brushed too lightly over the guilt of the perpetrators, that it avoided making any judgment on the causes of a war launched by Germany, which eventually killed 50 million people and which was used as a screen for genocide, and failed to ponder what would have become of Germany if the Nazis had been victorious.

I never considered turning down Herr Thierse's offer. I thought if the Germans had asked me to do this, they must have their reasons. But when it came to thinking about what I would say, the main responsibility I felt was to other survivors. I chose not to talk about my speech, or the event itself, with a lot of people. I didn't want to dissipate my energy, nor did I want to be influenced by the opinions of too many others. I sought out the opinions of those I respected. I read a lot, as I always have done. I let my thoughts percolate. I still hadn't written my speech when, on 22 April 2005, I collapsed with serious internal bleeding. I was taken by ambulance to hospital and given an emergency blood transfusion. Another two blood transfusions, and a week later, I was allowed to go home. Of course, my doctors didn't want me to travel, so there was a back-up plan involving Phillip acting as my proxy at the opening ceremony. But nothing was going to stop me from going to Berlin, and certainly not an ulcer. I wrote my speech in three days, during which time Kjeld was consumed with finalising paperwork for the sale of *Dansab* House, which was to be settled while we were away. I didn't know how to use a word processing programme, so he instructed me in the basics over the phone from the office. And then we got on a plane for Berlin.

Peter Eisenman says: »The context of the Memorial to the Murdered Jews of Europe is the enormity of the banal. The project manifests the instability inherent in what seems to be a system, here a rational grid, and its potential for dissolution in time. It suggests that when a supposedly rational and ordered system grows too large and out of proportion to its intended purpose, it in fact loses touch with human reason. It then begins to reveal the innate disturbances and potential for chaos in all systems of seeming order, the idea that all closed systems of a closed order are bound to fail.«

As I stood before the thousand-plus crowd gathered to dedicate the memorial, I understood that I and my children and grandchildren who had come with me from Australia were evidence of the futility of closed systems. We were not meant to exist. The central goal of the Nazis' genocide policy was the destruction of Jewry. A girl born Jewish in Poland in 1927, even a girl with a vivid imagination like mine, could never have seen herself in the surreal surroundings of a formal dinner in the Reichstag at which she was the guest of honour, rubbing shoulders with the German chancellor, his ministers and his ambassadors. Yet, as I said in my speech, our oppressors have perished and we have survived. Closed systems, like closed minds, are doomed to failure.

I had complete freedom to say what I wanted. Nobody asked to see my speech before I delivered it, except the translator. I didn't want to make anyone uncomfortable on this important day. I was conscious of the conflicted feelings that Holocaust survivors around the world had about this memorial. I knew I couldn't represent how everyone felt. I still don't know, for example, what Róża, whose approval I've sought all my life, thinks about what I said, nor my ex-brother-in-law and sister-in-law. They've never mentioned it. In the end I decided I had to say what I myself believed. There was no other way.

I asked the 1,300 dignitaries to see me not as I stood before them, an elderly woman, but as a young girl from the small Polish town of Borysław. I asked them to put themselves in her shoes as I took them through the insane cruelty which began the day the German army occupied our town on 1 July 1941. And then I told them what I had learned from that bitter experience. I spoke slowly. I was determined not to break down. Actually, I had very little recollection of what I did until I watched the video sometime after. People said to me, you seemed so composed.

I know I had eyes only for my family, not just those who were there with me in Berlin, protecting me with their love and support, but also for the dead, for my parents and my brother, and my grandparents, those lovely simple country people. I wanted so much for them to be proud of their little Binka who could barely believe where she found herself.

When I finished, people were standing, they were crying and clapping, and when I returned to my seat they opened their arms and I was passed around to be hugged and kissed. Their recognition and approval of what I thought was important to me. I had tried to work through these problems of guilt for years.

I thought it was tremendous that this memorial was built in Berlin, and I said so. Maybe there are some who choose to think I offered absolution to the German nation. But I'm not a religious person. I'm just one person who happens to think that way. If other people are comfortable with it, and it helps them, that's great. For some it would be of some help, for others probably not. I don't aspire to absolve everybody or everything. It would be conceited of me to think in that way.

On the plane from Australia, I had thought to myself, ›perhaps this is why I survived‹. I'm not saying that I was saved so that one day I would go to Berlin, that I was the chosen one, selected especially for that task. I don't think in those terms. I did think it might give meaning to my survival to be able to say what I wanted to say. It would justify my survival. That's something most of us survivors question all the time. Why was I spared? What does it mean to survive?

I'm still asking that question. I think I've turned out to be a reasonably decent human being. Somehow, with the help of other decent people, I rebuilt my hopes for the future. I married and raised children who are themselves decent human beings. I made money – and I lost money – and, depending on the moment, I either spent it or gave it away. Both give me great pleasure, but I've never worried about my ability to pay my way. I've been doing that for a long time. What I need more than anything else is to be loved. I'm always looking for love, even now. I don't think I ever really got over the loss of my mother.

Eighty per cent of Polish Jews were deported to Nazi concentration camps and died there. Twenty per cent tried to survive, and of those only half were successful. I was among the 10 per cent of Polish Jews who survived the Holocaust. I survived because ...?

To that question, there is no answer. Nor are there answers to the other questions I've carried with me for most of my life. I have stopped asking those questions that were once such a burden to me. What does it mean to be Jewish? Why do things happen to Jews that don't happen to other people? What is it that causes anti-Semitism? Why did the Holocaust happen? Why were six million Jews killed? Why did my mother, my father, my brother, my grandparents, my uncles and aunts and cousins die? Why did I survive? There are no answers, and the questions don't help me or help anyone else to live better. And living well is what's important. What I do, I do now because I am here, and not because I want to be rewarded in the afterlife. We don't know what comes after death.

Several years ago Phillip, ever protective, asked me, »Mama, when are you going to make peace with God?« It may have been after the birth of his first child, Pia. Phillip identifies as Jewish more strongly than I do. His father did too. There's a synagogue near where I live, so I went to talk about my stand-off with God with the rabbi, Jeffrey Kamins. I even took a few evening classes to learn more about Judaism, but then I stopped. I had learned all I wanted to know about religion. But I joined the synagogue and I go there to celebrate the High Holy Days, and also to say prayers in memory of my family killed during the war, and of my grandson Zac. Why do I say those prayers? The Jewish tradition has endured thousands of years, and though I am not religious, I want to, and do belong to that enduring tradition. I am proud to be Jewish.

I have my causes and a philanthropic fund named for my parents, my brother and my grandparents. I am my mother's daughter. I believe in giving to those less fortunate than me and in telling the truth. I believe in love and in beauty. I believe in a kind of cosmic consciousness and in the possibility of changing the world for the better. But I am not, as a rabbi would understand it, a believer. How could I be? There is no peace on earth, and there can be no understanding of what took place in my lifetime; the attempt by a nation at the heart of civilised Europe to annihilate a people not because of what they had done, but because of who they were. The Holocaust was, and remains, beyond the limits of my comprehension. But perhaps I've reached a certain level of acceptance. My life hasn't been wasted. In Berlin, I looked out over the throng of dignitaries, and saw my children and my grandchildren, and a good man whom I call my husband. If I could put it in a nutshell, that's the victory. Whilst I was so nervous, I glowed because they were there. I have always needed to love and be loved. Mama, I took Berlin, but you taught me that the heart is the site of our greatest triumphs.

XXVII. SABINA'S SPEECH ON 10 MAY 2005

Excellencies,
Chairman of Yad Vashem, my dear Holocaust survivors,
Ladies and Gentlemen!

Not even in my wildest dreams could I have dreamed of this extraordinary day. Here, in this very place, after many years of controversies, public disputes, debates that have taken place and the Bundestag Resolution of the 25th June 1999, the vision of Lea Rosh and the people around her has come true. And today I am standing here before you at the inauguration of this magnificent Memorial to the Murdered Jews of Europe, and I thank you for it. I am humbled by the honour bestowed on me and overwhelmed by the responsibility. For I am the voice of the six million tortured and murdered Jews of which one and a half million were children, and I am also the voice of the lucky few – the voice of the survivors.

I am the only one of my whole family who survived. I am a witness to unbearable crimes against humanity. Try not to see the elderly woman standing before you, but [a young] girl from Borysław, a small town in former Poland. The date is the 1st of July 1941, a significant date – the German army occupies our town. Three days later: a pogrom lasting two days, the first taste of what our life was going to be under the rule of Nazi Germany. German authorities have given a free hand to the Ukrainians and Poles who attacked their unprotected Jewish neighbours. I, [a 14-year-old girl], witness indescribable cruelty, murders, rape and torture. Bewilderment, total incomprehension – why? Why is this happening? How can people, ordinary people be so heartless and cruel? Why is it happening to us? We did not do anything wrong. Weeks pass.

I have to wear an armband with the Jewish star – why? I am not allowed to keep my beloved dog and cat – why? My friends are not allowed to play with me any more; I am not allowed to go to school – why?

The time passes and the killings and deportations continue. The despair, degradations, hunger, humiliations – and still I'm desperately trying to cling to the last shreds of dignity. This has become our daily life. On the 6th of August 1941 an *Aktion* lasting three days begins. My mother and I are in hiding, but our place is discovered and we are taken to a place where a selection is made. I am hanging desperately to my mother's hand but I am brutally separated from her and taken out to work to a different place from where I am released after a few days. I never see my mother again. It was not until many months later that the rumours reached us about the Belzec death camp, and this is where she and the five thousand other Jewish victims from the same transport were put to death by gassing.

And again the daily life, if one could call it life, devoid of any hope continued. From *Aktion* to *Aktion*, trying to hide, building bunkers in the forest, escaping deportation – the struggle to survive, the mean desperate struggle. And the fear, paralysing fear ...

My father and my brother, Josek, were looking for a safe haven for me. So they approached some of our Christian friends asking if they would shelter me. And those decent, brave people have taken me into their home, risking their own lives because hiding a Jew was punishable by death. And so I lived controlling my emotions, hiding my identity, in constant fear of discovery. And when it became too dangerous for our friends to protect me any longer my brother took me to the bunker in the forest, which he and his friends have built. Whilst I was hiding in the forest, my father, my brother and my brother's best friend were in the labour camp. They tried to escape but they were caught and as a warning to other Jews who were still in the camp they were killed on the order of the inspector of the camp. It was in the morning on the 19th of July 1944. Seventeen days later, on the 6th of August, the Soviet Army liberated our small town, Borysław.

It happened such a long time ago, 60 years ago. Memories fade slightly but are never forgotten. And what are my thoughts and my feelings as I stand here before you gazing at my family, my son and daughter, their partners, my grandchildren and my husband who all travelled from far-away Australia to be with me, to protect me with their love and support? What have I learned from my bitter experience? I have learned that hatred begets hatred. I have learned that we must not remain silent and that each of us as an individual must fight the evil of racism, discrimination, prejudice, inhumanity. I have repeatedly said that I do not believe in the collective guilt. And if I may paraphrase the great writer and an exceptional man Elie Wiesel: »The children of the killers are not killers. We must never blame them for what their elders did. But we can hold them responsible for what they do with the memory of their elders' crime.«

It has been the lot of our people to confront the worst manifestation of evil in human history, and yet our oppressors have perished and we have survived. And from this perspective we face our future, confident in the ultimate triumph of the human spirit over brute force. A victory not only for Jewish people, but a victory for all decent people over evil.

Ladies and gentlemen, thank you.

LIVING AND SURVIVING IN CENTRAL EUROPE FROM 1939 TO 1948: A HISTORICAL AFTERWORD

The memoirs of the Polish Holocaust survivor Sabina van der Linden-Wolanski begin with her fulfilling a childhood dream of living in Paris after arriving in the French capital from Silesia in 1948. However, this new life was not at all what she had hoped for. She was orphaned, a refugee, and did not stay for long in the city. Reading her memoirs leads one to wonder how her life would have turned out had she had a peaceful childhood and had she not lost her parents, her brother, practically all of her Jewish friends and neighbours, the family property and ultimately her homeland. Would she have remained in Borysław, the oilfield town where she was born? Would she have studied in Lwów or Crakow? Would she have moved to Berlin or America like her relatives before her or emigrated to Palestine? Would she have ended up living in Paris under completely different circumstances?

Sabina was born Sabina Haberman in 1927 and had a brother, Josef (›Josek‹), who was three years older. Her parents had grown up in the Kingdom of Galicia, a province of the Austro-Hungarian Empire, but Sabina and her brother only knew about this period of Polish partition from what they had been told. They were born during the second Polish Republic. Sabina was devastated when its founder, Marshal Józef Piłsudski, died in 1935, when she was eight years old. The younger generation of Jews born after World War One began to transform the face of Polish Jewry, at least in linguistic terms. It seemed likely that Yiddish, which had been preserved for centuries, would cease to be the dominant language. At the time of the 1931 census, 79.9 per cent of respondents (3.2 million people) gave Yiddish as their mother tongue and only twelve per cent Polish. However, the cultural unification of the territories formerly partitioned by Prussia, Russia and Austria into one Polish state along with the cultural policy implemented by the government in Warsaw paved the way for a rapid process of acculturation. By the mid-1930s, the majority (almost two thirds) of Jewish children, Sabina included, went to a primary school where teaching was exclusively in Polish. Sabina's parents were among those at the forefront of this development. They only spoke Polish with their children at home and when they wanted to discuss something between themselves, they switched to German – the lingua franca of the Habsburg Monarchy.

The Polish language is a recurring theme, almost a leitmotif, in *Destined to Live*. Sabina emphasises the importance of her proficiency in Polish for her own struggle to survive and ultimately her rescue. Like Sabina, many European Jews found it crucial to be fluent in the language of their country of residence. From summer 1942, the only hope for Jews in occupied Europe was to go into hiding. In most cases, this required them to assume a non-Jewish identity and to keep moving from place to place. Some took the risk of pretending to be Catholics, Protestants or Orthodox Christians. This required considerable cultural and linguistic expertise and knowledge of the respective religious customs. Language at least did not pose a particular problem for the mostly assimilated Jews in Germany, the Netherlands and also parts of Hungary. The situation was different in regions where the Jewish community had a markedly different minority culture and its own linguistic traditions. In occupied Poland, even those who had learnt fluent Polish at school were usually from a Yiddish-speaking background. They had to do all that they could not to betray their roots in everyday discourse. Certain turns of phrase or a distinct way of speaking were often enough to attract suspicion. The fear of betrayal gave rise to a high degree of self-discipline, which in turn lent a sinister new meaning to the notion of ›mastering a language‹.

Various families took the young Sabina in between February 1943 and spring 1944. One of these was the Blums, a Jewish family living under the false name ›Machnicki‹, who also led Sabina to believe that they were not Jewish. During this period, Sabina used the Polish-sounding surname of her Jewish Orthodox maternal grandparents, Kulawicz. This new identity, or the fear at its heart, permeated her consciousness to such an extent that even after liberation she did not go back to her original surname, Haberman, and in an official document from 1946 she was still describing herself as Catholic. Sabina considered that her native speaker proficiency in Polish was a deciding factor in Polish families agreeing to take her in.

What was life like for Sabina after she went into hiding in February 1943? Around a month previously her diary entry following her brother's birthday party in the ghetto referred to: »[...] the pain of this horrible life, living like animals from day to day, from ›Aktion‹ [raid or operation] to ›Aktion‹«. By this time, she had already spent one and a half years under the German occupation. She had documented this period in Polish in her diaries, especially the traumatic loss of her mother in August 1942. Eastern Galicia, the region where Borysław was located, had the densest population of Jews in Europe (530,000) at the start of World War Two. When the Red Army arrived in summer 1944 there were around 5,000 Holocaust survivors in this region, including Sabina, who was now 17 years old.

With the German invasion of Poland on 1 September 1939 and the arrival of Red Army troops in the country on 17 September of the same year, Poland was again erased from the map of Europe after just 21 years as a newly independent state. The National Socialist and Soviet occupying forces both established reigns of terror, each with distinct features. The one goal they initially shared was that of targeting the (Catholic and Jewish) elites in the country. The National Socialist persecution of Poles and Jews was racially motivated, whilst the Soviets sought to eliminate allegedly ›bourgeois elements‹ in society. Sabina writes in detail about the brutal impact of the regime on her family's formerly middle-class existence in Borysław. Other families were hit even harder. Everyday life under the occupation was marked by torture and shootings carried out by the Soviet secret police (NKVD). Around ten per cent of the male population was arrested arbitrarily, leading to overcrowded prisons. Mass deportations to the East, mainly to Siberia and south-west Asia, began in February 1940. At the end of September 1939, German diplomats failed to persuade the Soviet Union to relinquish the oil fields in Borysław and Drohobycz to Germany. However, in practice Stalin gave Germany access to the region's entire oil production in return for coal supplies. This was one of the reasons why the Wehrmacht was able to conquer France so rapidly. Ironically, tankers were crossing the demarcation line between German and Soviet occupied territories right up to the day of the German invasion of the Soviet Union on 22 June 1941.

In summer 1941 the Wehrmacht took just a few days to advance deep into eastern Galicia. The German leadership had long planned this campaign against its former ally as a war of annihilation, with the Jewish population its prime target. The National Socialists accused the Jews of ›spreading Bolshevism‹. The occupying forces adopted a number of strategies. On the one hand, they gave anti-semitic and nationalist groups from the region itself carte blanche, on the other hand they implemented a programme of mass murder that extended from the Baltic Sea to the Black Sea. In Borysław – as in the rest of eastern Galicia – the Ukrainians carried out pogroms, such as those described so vividly by Sabina. At the same time, the SS and police units carried out the first mass shootings of Jews. As in the rest of occupied Eastern Europe, Jews living in the territory between Lwów and the Carpathian Mountains were systematically stripped of their assets and their means of making a living and made to work as forced labourers. The Jews were soon impoverished and hunger and epidemics were widespread. The German administration responded to this crisis of its own making with increased violence. A heightened wave of murder began in eastern Galicia with the massacre of up to 12,000 Jews who were shot dead by members of the SS and police at the Jewish cemetery in Stanisławów on 12 October 1941. In November 1941, so-called Aktionen also started in the area close to where Sabina was living. The German Labour Office (Arbeitsamt) was instrumental in preparing the programme of murder in the Drohobycz district as well as in the neighbouring districts of Sambor and Stryj. In Drohobycz, the town next to Borysław, the official in charge of ›Jewish labour‹ summoned around 350 to 400 unemployed Jews to appear on 22 November. Around 250 of these turned up, along with an unknown number of children. They were murdered in the nearby Bronica forest. Some of the victims were still alive after being shot by the commando and screamed as soil was shovelled over them. Security police officials then shot them again. One of those involved in carrying out the crime had a nervous breakdown and was treated in a psychiatric clinic in Hamburg. This ›Labour Office Operation‹ (Arbeitsamtaktion) was followed on 29 November by the ›Invalid Operation‹ (Invalidenaktion) in Borysław. Several hundred Jews classed as ill or unfit for work were shot dead in the surrounding forests. By the New Year of 1941-42, 3,000 of Borysław's 14,000 Jews had already met a violent death.

The mass murder in occupied Poland reached new heights in late 1941. On 8 December 1941 the SS began to systematically murder Jews with exhaust fumes released into sealed vans in Chełmno nad Nerem, part of the western Polish territory annexed by the Third Reich in 1939 to form the ›Warthegau‹ province. Up to this point the SS had mainly used this method to killed disabled people. In early November 1941 the SS started planning the construction of an extermination camp in the General Government, the region including eastern Galicia. They installed several gas chambers in wooden buildings near Belzec in the Lublin district. Jews were later killed here using fumes from the engines of captured Soviet tanks. Whilst preparations were underway for the mass deportation and murder of Jews, further Jewish communities were forced to move into segregated residential districts in their towns (Judenbezirke). However, there was a delay in establishing a ghetto in Borysław: Dr. Wilhelm Dopheide, the district's medical officer, advised against it on account of a typhus epidemic. In March 1942 the SS began to carry out mass murders in Belzec. On 25 March 1942 the first deportation train left Drohobycz for Belzec, possibly also carrying Jews from Borysław. Several weeks later the deportations to the extermination camp were halted for a few weeks while the SS had new gas chambers installed in Belzec. The building works were finished by mid-July 1942. Around the same time, on 19 July 1942, Reichsführer-SS Heinrich Himmler decreed that the ›Final Solution‹ (Endlösung), the murder of the entire Jewish population in the General Government, was to be completed by 31 December that year. Two additional extermination camps in Sobibor and Treblinka were constructed for this purpose under the codename *Operation Reinhardt*.

Sabina saw her mother Sala for the last time on 6 August 1942. This day marked the start of an extensive and systematic hunt for Jews in Borysław, with the aim of deporting them to Belzec. However, many had heard about similar ›Aktionen‹ in the neighbouring district of Sambor, where the Security Police and Gestapo had been wreaking devastation since 4 August, and had therefore gone into hiding in the surrounding area. Those behind the ›Aktion‹ in Borysław pretended to call it off, only to resume it the same evening after many had returned home. Sala Haberman was deported to Belzec with around 4,000 Jews from Borysław on that day and murdered on arrival.

Following the first wave of deportations in spring 1942, members of the Jewish community did all that they could to find steady employment with German firms. By this point the main oil industry was in the hands of two German manufacturing companies, *Beskid Crude Oil Plc* (Beskiden-Erdöl-Gewinnungs GmbH) and *Beskid Oil Refining Plc* (Beskiden-Erdöl-Verarbeitungs GmbH). Directly after the German invasion in 1941, Wehrmacht General Wilhelm Schubert sacked all Jewish oil industry workers in eastern Galicia. He mistakenly thought that oil production could continue to operate on an entirely ›Jew free‹ basis, even though Jewish engineers had been instrumental in building up the ›Polish Texas‹. Jews were therefore re-employed in Borysław from autumn 1941 and Berthold Beitz, the business manager of *Beskid Crude Oil*, which later became the *Carpathian Oil Company* (Karpathen-Öl AG), also employed Jews in administrative roles from February 1942. Beitz, aged 28 at the time, was one of the young industrial experts who welcomed the chance to expand their career portfolios in the occupied territories. He arrived in Borysław just a few days after the German invasion and was horrified by the pogrom there that he witnessed firsthand. Almost exactly 13 months later Beitz used his position and status to save lives. In the early morning of 8 August 1942 he managed to release around 150 Jews, including women and children, from the clutches of the police just before they were due to be deported to Belzec. The murders committed in the town and at the station, but above all the cynical remarks made to the victims, such as ›they need doctors in heaven too‹, led Beitz to conclude that the Jews were going to be killed. From this point onwards he and his wife acted to save the lives of Jews in Borysław.

In mid-August, the deportations from eastern Galicia were halted for a fortnight. At the end of July 1942, Fritz Katzmann, the SS general and police commander of the Galicia district, began to plan the murder of the majority of the approximately 100,000 Jews remaining in Lwów. All work permits were declared void and only a small number of new permits were issued. On 10 August, members of the Gestapo, the Ukrainian police and the Jewish militia sealed off the roads in the Lwów ghetto. The Jews were hunted down for the next two weeks, by the end of which 40,000 Jews from Lwów had been murdered in Belzec.

Any Jews remaining in the General Government soon faced a new threat. On 5 September 1942, General Field Marshal Wilhelm Keitel, the chief of the Supreme Command of the Wehrmacht, issued an order to sack all Jews from Wehrmacht and armaments firms in the General Government. This order fitted in with Himmler's timetable. From the late summer of 1942, the programme of murders implemented in Borysław and the surrounding area resulted from the interplay between the *Carpathian Oil Company*, the Wehrmacht and the SS, in other words between exploitation and murder, the wartime priorities of the military and the desire of the National Socialist leadership to annihilate the Jews.

By 11 September 1942, there were just 1,760 Jews still working at *Beskid Crude Oil* in Borysław. As the SS was clearly unconcerned by the staffing needs of the company, *Beskid Crude Oil* contacted the Wehrmacht armaments commando on 11 September 1942 and proposed sacking all unskilled workers. At the same time it agreed to house its Jewish workers ›in a designated residential district‹ in Borysław guarded by Ukrainian ›protection units‹. In return, the company asked the Wehrmacht armaments commando to instruct the SS and SS Security Service to exempt company workers from the scheduled deportations. This did nothing to prevent the ›sudden cull‹ of Jewish workers that ensued. The company then approached the National Socialist administration in Berlin. Adolf Eichmann, the official in charge of ›Jewish affairs‹ in the Reich Security Main Office, ultimately contacted the Security Police on 17 September 1942 with Himmler's order that Jews should only be ›removed‹ from *Beskid Crude Oil* in numbers that could be replaced by non-Jewish workers. On 22 September Adolf Hitler then took the personal decision to retain specialist Jewish workers in the armaments industry in the General Government. Himmler finally confirmed that ›Arbeitsjuden‹ (›working Jews‹, those deemed fit for forced labour) could continue working in these companies, but only as temporary staff leased out by the SS. The historian Thomas Sandkühler considers that there may have been a macabre reason behind Himmler's decision of 17 September: Odilo Globocnik, who was responsible for the three *Operation Reinhardt* extermination camps, needed more fuel for the gas chambers.

In order to carry out these orders from Berlin, the SS and Wehrmacht in the General Government, along with SS and police commander Fritz Katzmann, came to an initial agreement with the armaments inspectorate in Lwów regarding the procedure for ›removing‹ Jewish workers from companies. The next day, Katzmann sent the *Carpathian Oil Company* a list of 700 employees to be deported to Belzec and the forced labour camp at Janowska near Lwów. The company immediately set about recruiting non-Jewish replacement staff. By 19 October 1942, 4,860 of a former population of 14,000 Jews were still living in Borysław. They had been confined to ghettos six days before. In the meantime, the SS had started additional deportations from the surrounding areas. The renewed hunt for Jews in Borysław began on 23 October 1942. Around 1,500 people were deported as a result. On 6 November, Katzmann sent out additional instructions along with the ›R‹ badges, which Sabina refers to in her memoirs [the R stood for Rüstungsarbeiter or armaments worker]. This coincided with the most horrendous wave of persecution in Borysław since summer 1941. Those rounded up during this ›major Aktion‹, were taken to the auditorium of the Colosseum cinema and locked in there for weeks in cramped conditions. At the end of November, the approximately 2,000 detainees were taken by train to Belzec.

Sabina had a document from this period that illustrated the shift in occupation policy described above. On 9 November 1942, after the start of the ›major Aktion‹, the *Carpathian Oil Company* attested that it employed a Sabina Haberman, who was also »housed in company barracks«. However, Sabina was not employed by the oil industry, at least not directly, and unlike her father and brother she had not moved into the company accommodation but lived by herself in the ghetto. On 20 January 1943 there was a birthday party in Sabina's room in the ghetto, which she writes about in her diary. A surviving photo of the party is featured on the front cover of *Destined to Live*. Those Borysław Jews not living in the ghetto (or in hiding) were housed in three ›barracks‹ belonging to the *Carpathian Oil Company*: the Mraźnica forced labour camp, the ›Carpathian block‹ and a housing block nicknamed the ›White House‹. Beitz had already housed Jews who worked for him in the latter in autumn 1942 and he succeeded in keeping the German Security Police and the Ukrainian militia away from the building. When ›Aktionen‹ were taking place, Beitz applied to the head of the municipal police (Schutzpolizei) in Vienna for personnel to guard the ›White House‹.

In February 1943, SS and police commander Katzmann ordered another ›resettlement‹. Intoxicated members of the municipal police force and a member of the Security Police shot dead around 600 Jews at a pit dug out in advance outside an abattoir seven kilometres from Borysław. Beitz was able to rescue a woman from a truck near the site where the murders were committed by claiming she was his secretary. It was at this time that Sabina was taken to her first hiding place. Her brother and father were living in the oil company ›barracks‹. Sabina probably also lived here for a while as she moved between various hiding places. It is possible that Bernard Eisenstein, the head of the Jewish police, helped her as his son Imek was Sabina's boyfriend.

In August 1943, SS-Obersturmführer Friedrich Hildebrand, Katzmann's former ›expert for Jewish affairs‹ became commandant of the forced labour camp in Borysław. Beitz did not rate Hildebrand's intelligence and saw this appointment as a chance to extend his own influence. In 1943, the *Carpathian Oil Company* had a workforce of up to 1,300. In November 1943 the company's head office instructed its managers to draw up new lists of all employees. The *Carpathian Oil Company* was again willing to hand over employees to the murder squads in order to retain its specialist staff. Beitz would have faced consequences had he refused the order to specify ›dispensable Jews‹. However, the 384 people who he ultimately named as such were initially spared from murder.

The forced labourers were both physically and mentally exhausted and in a state of despair – most could only think one day at a time. This makes it all the more remarkable that Sabina's brother and his friends dedicated such courage and energy to constructing hideouts in the forest to help people escape the impending ›Aktionen‹. Sabina went into hiding there in the spring of 1944. Life in Borysław had completely changed by this point. Berthold Beitz was now serving with the Wehrmacht elsewhere. The Red Army was advancing relentlessly. The prisoners of the two forced labour camps in Drohobycz and Borysław were moved to the Plaszow concentration camp near Crakow in April 1944. However, many had heeded Beitz's advice: ›My children, get out of here!‹ and fled. Hildebrand implemented a cunning plan. He had a number of Borysław Jews, including Bernard Eisenstein, brought back from Plaszow. They were initially allowed to move around unsupervised and had the task of persuading those in hiding to return of their own free will. Unlike Sabina, many did come back as they were short of food. They were also under threat from the right-wing forces of the Ukrainian Insurgent Army, which killed any Jews that they came across. Hildebrand then changed tack. The new strategy was for members of the Security Police, Ordnungspolizei (regular uniformed police force) and Wehrmacht to comb through the forests in search of Jews. Numbers in the forced labour camp increased again and a second transport was sent to Plaszow. The hunt for Jews continued. Sabina's brother and father were captured in unexplained circumstances. Hildebrand had Fischel and Josek Haberman executed on 19 July 1944. Two days later, the third train carrying prisoners left Borysław for Auschwitz.

Sabina emerged from her final hiding place in August 1944 following the arrival of the Red Army. She was completely alone. Her cousin Benio was the one other member of her family still alive. The end of the German reign of terror in no way heralded the end of the war in this region, which was far away from the borders of the Third Reich. The Soviets, who had occupied eastern Poland from 1939 to 1941, were now back in control; »the same lot who, not so very long ago, we had called oppressors«, as Sabina puts it. Months before the capitulation of the Wehrmacht, which was still occupying western Poland and half of France at the time, Stalin presented Eastern Europe with a fait accompli. The ›Great Leader‹ from the Kremlin and members of the Communist ›Polish National Liberation Committee‹ in Lublin had already held talks on the demarcation of the future border between the Soviet Union and Poland and agreed to ›evacuate‹ Poles from eastern Poland, which was to be ceded to the Soviet Union. Stalin not only again ensured that he would win the spoils of the German-Soviet non-aggression pact (Molotov-Ribbentrop pact) of 23 August 1939, but he also deliberately humiliated the Poles in forcing Poland to conclude the accompanying treaty with the Ukrainian, Lithuanian and Belarusian Soviet Republics rather than with Moscow. Poland lost its eastern borderland territories (the ›Kresy‹) forever, including the cultural heartlands of Wilno and Lwów. It gained considerable territory in eastern Germany as ›compensation‹ and its borders were thus moved westwards. The signing of the Soviet-

Polish border agreement led to a fairly organised process of resettlement, known as ›repatriation‹, particularly between spring 1945 and summer 1946. Yet this was not about returning people to their homes; instead it uprooted them. Polish Jews who had fled or been deported to Soviet territory after 1939 or 1941, were also selected for ›repatriation‹. Sabina was among those waiting to leave for the West.

These ›repatriation‹ transports took people to the German districts in Eastern Europe now under Polish ›administration‹: Silesia, East Brandenburg, Pomerania and south-east Prussia. Residents of these districts were themselves ›resettled‹. At the end of 1944, around seven million Germans were living to the east of the Oder-Neisse line. From the arrival of the Red Army up to spring 1946, this was more or less a lawless territory owing to the fledgling status of the Polish administration and disputes with the Soviet leadership over areas of responsibility. The German population fell victim to attacks, looting and ›wild‹ expulsions. The Potsdam Agreement of summer 1945 gave the Polish state the responsibility for the »orderly transfer of German populations« out of these territories. However, the transports to the West organised by the Polish authorities after 1946 were chaotic and sometimes incurred fatalities. Instructions from the Polish authorities on how Germans were to be treated prior to their expulsion also bore the hallmarks of revenge following almost six years of German occupation. On top of this, food was extremely scarce.

Despite these conditions, Polish-Jewish survivors considered Poland's new ›wild West‹ to provide a safer haven than their home towns within the country. They were not welcome there and in most cases the planned move back was incredibly traumatic as relatives had been murdered, property was now in the hands of non-Jewish neighbours, and anti-semitism was rife. By contrast, Jews and Poles in the former German territories in the East completely rebuilt their lives from scratch. They were presented with financial opportunities to make a new start by taking over German property. In June 1945, around 7,000 survivors in Silesian towns such as Wrocław, Wałbrych, Dzierżoniów, Bielawa and Świdnica began to re-establish a Jewish community. In the same month, the Polish Minister for Public Administration lent his support to the »re-establishment of a new community in this territory«. Warsaw wanted to make Lower Silesia a ›region of Jewish resettlers‹. By the end of December 1945, 16,000 Jews were living here. The number increased to 40,000 by April 1946 after the start of regular transfers from the Soviet Union. It is possible that Sabina was among these new residents of Lower Silesia, having left Borysław with her first husband and her cousin Benio in spring 1946. By summer 1946 around 90,000 Polish Jews were living in Lower Silesia. Outside this region, a fairly large Polish-Jewish community established itself in the port of Szczecin in Pomerania, counting around 20,000 residents by this time.

Between 1946 and 1949 Silesia was a transient and non-synchronous place. Jews inhabited a world that existed alongside the Christian Poles who had moved to the area and the Germans who still resided there, a world in which traumatised Holocaust survivors sought to revive the interwar culture that had been destroyed. Yiddish posters went up in the streets of Wrocław, the ›Lower Silesian Jewish Theatre‹ rehearsed plays, and the Jewish community published its own books and newspapers. The Jewish voivodeship committee was keen to establish a Jewish school system as soon as possible. This posed a major challenge to those responsible. The children of those ›repatriated‹ from the Soviet Union had Russian as their main language, whereas other children only spoke Polish or Yiddish, the latter being the intended language of instruction. It was clear that ›Polonisation‹, one of the principles of national educational policy before 1939, now suddenly counted for nothing. This approach to the linguistic identity of the younger generation raises fundamental questions about the emotional status and aspirations of the new arrivals in the region. The historian Katharina Friedla, one of the first to research Jewish resettlement in Silesia after 1945, points out that it was not attitudes towards religion or Marxism that divided the Jewish population. »Holocaust survivors in particular«, she writes, »were spurred on by the desire to establish a new existence, and above all a safe future. Some of these Jews saw their future in a socialist Poland with an autonomous or assimilated status in society. However, a smaller number strove from the start to establish an independent Jewish state, which would guarantee them protection and equality.« This attempt to establish a new Jewish life was overshadowed by the ominous events in Kielce in central Poland in July 1946. Incited by the crowds, a Catholic mob carried out a pogrom of Polish Jews, murdering over forty and injuring about eighty.

How did the young Sabina Kulawicz fit into this new Silesian world? At the time, she continued to conceal her Jewish identity, although she did associate with people ›repatriated‹ from Borysław. After the breakdown of her first marriage to a Catholic Pole, it was here that she met Zdenek Wolanski, a Jew who was to become her second husband. In her heart she had long made the decision to emigrate – not to Israel but to the United States, as she had received a letter in July 1946 from an uncle living there. Many did the same. After 1949, the newly-established Jewish community in Lower Silesia gradually fell apart under pressure from the Communist regime and by 1968 it had almost entirely disappeared as a result of the anti-semitic campaigns conducted by the leadership in Warsaw.

In the end Sabina found a new life in Australia. It was here that she was able to be herself, far away from the places where she had been persecuted and lost friends and family. These invaluable memoirs were made possible by her courageous decision to revisit and confront her European, Jewish and Polish past, a difficult and painful process.

This book was launched on 11 May 2010 in the Australian Embassy in Berlin. Sabina and Kjeld travelled to Berlin from Sydney and Phillip was able to join them for two days. Dagmar Manzel was Sabina's voice in German. Shortly afterwards Sabina went to Essen to meet the now 97 year-old Berthold Beitz, the man who had saved her life. She was already in very poor health by this point. On 6 June 2011 – two days before her 84th birthday – the TV channel ABC broadcast *The Girl from Borysław* as part of its series »Australian Story«, and people across Australia were thus able to hear Sabina's story. We learnt of Sabina's death on 23 June that year. Beitz died on 30 July 2013.

Sabina, Binka, »our other Grandma«, Field Marshal! We, your »Berlin Family«, will ensure that you are never forgotten!

Ulrich Baumann · Uwe Neumärker

ACKNOWLEDGMENTS

When I was asked by *HarperCollins Publishers* to write my memoirs, I was astonished, apprehensive and feeling inadequate to the task. I needed help. It was Shona Martyn and Amruta Slee who introduced me to my co-author, Diana Bagnall. The process of remembering the past, especially a past such as mine, is difficult and very painful. I wish to thank Diana for her perception, compassion and for caring so much. Without Diana this book might not have been written.

My thanks to Shona and Amruta for taking on my book and for trusting me, and to Lydia Papandrea for her admirable editing.

I am indebted to Kathryn Everett for her counsel, and Freehills for their extraordinary generosity, Martin Indyk and Jeffrey Kamins for their wisdom, John Landerer for his advice and friendship, and Peter Wertheim for his inspiration for the Berlin speech.

Very special thanks to my cherished friends Rita Harmelin, Jo Kalowski and Ruth Wilson for their support and encouragement. Thank you also to Krystyna Duszniak for her search of my family data, and to Lewis Morley for his magnanimity. To my wonderful friends overseas, thank you to Henrietta Braun in Sao Paolo for helping me to put together the missing parts; Renate Reinke, my kindred soul in Germany, for crossing the bridge with me; Claudia and Hartwig Bierhoff for their help and affection; and the Staff at the Foundation Memorial to the Murdered Jews of Europe, in Berlin, for their support and commitment. In Poland, my thanks to Magdalena Abakanowicz, Jan Kosmowski and Artur Starewicz for their hospitality; Adam Garlej, our driver, for taking us on a very exacting trip around Borysław and the places of my childhood (now part of the Ukraine); Robert Kuwałek, for his compassion when guiding me through an abyss of grief in the Belzec Memorial Museum; and Tadeusz Wróbel, it was through him that I found Henrietta after 62 years.

Extra special thanks to Kjeld Hansen, my husband, for putting up with me during this emotionally demanding time and for sustaining Diana and me with delicious food and innumerable cups of coffee. To Josephine and Phillip, my children, and Poppy, Pia, Sophie and Remy, my grandchildren, for their love. Writing my memoirs has been a great intrusion into their life and I am grateful to them for being so gracious about it.

Finally, to Andrea Stretton, a very special and beautiful human being. She encouraged, inspired, nurtured and believed in me. I was devastated by her untimely death, but I will treasure forever having her as my friend.

ACKNOWLEDGMENTS FOR THE GERMAN EDITION

Five years have passed since the Memorial to the Murdered Jews of Europe was inaugurated on 10th of May 2005, where I delivered my speech on behalf of all Jewish survivors of the Holocaust.

It was an extraordinary day, which I will remember as long as I live. A day that marked the beginning of an incredible journey for me, rich in many wonderful learning experiences, and that ultimately brought about the publication of this book.

In 2006 I was asked by publishers Shona Martyn and Amruta Slee of *HarperCollins Publishers Australia* to write my memoirs, and with the help of my co-author Diana Bagnall, the English edition was published in 2008.

Now I am thrilled to be published in this German translation and am deeply indebted to *Harper Collins* for their generosity and co-operation in making this possible.

I would like to thank many people, even though thanks seem hardly adequate to express my feelings.

I am honored and immensely grateful to: The Bundespräsident Prof. Dr. Horst Köhler for his thoughtful, generous and supportive words, and the Australian Prime Minister the Honorable Kevin Rudd for his perceptive, emotive and compassionate Foreword.

My deepest gratitude to the then President of the Bundestag, Wolfgang Thierse, who invited me to speak at the inauguration; the German Minister for Cultural Affairs, Mr. Bernd Neumann; the former Australian Ambassador to Germany, H. E. Ian Kemish; and the Australian Ambassador to Germany, H. E. Peter Tesch.

Thanks to Dagmar Manzel who generously agreed to read pages from my book at the book launch.

I am forever grateful to Uwe Neumärker for this amazing determination, commitment and dedication to have the book published, and to

Uli Baumann for the extraordinary care taken in reading, reviewing and researching the English edition. Uwe´s and Uli´s professional attention to detail is remarkable.

Special thanks to my husband, Kjeld, for perusing, sorting and scanning all my diaries, photos and letters, and for putting up with my impatience.

My appreciation goes to the many members of the Staff at the Foundation Memorial to the Murdered Jews of Europe, who worked so diligently to make this German edition possible.

Thank you also to Barbara Kurowska, for translating Polish diaries, and to Katarzyna Friedla, Leonie Mechelhoff, Felizitas Borzym, Jana Mechelhoff-Herezi, and Doron Oberhand, and Anja Sauter.

Sydney, 25th February 2010

BIBLIOGRAPHY

Browning, Christopher R., Ordinary Men: Reserve Police Battalion 101 and the Final Solution in Poland, New York: HarperCollins Publishers, 1992.

Fogelman, Eva, Conscience and Courage: Rescuers of Jews during the Holocaust, New York: Doubleday, a division of Random House Inc., 1994.

Foundation Memorial to the Murdered Jews of Europe (ed.): Materials on the Memorial to the Murdered Jews of Europe, Berlin: Nicolaische Verlagsbuchhandlung, 2005.

Frankl, Viktor E., Man's Search for Meaning, New York: Simon & Schuster Inc., 1962.

Gilbert, Martin, Atlas of the Holocaust, London: Michael Joseph, 1982.

Hertz, Aleksander, The Jews in Polish Culture, Illinois: Northwestern University Press, 1988.

Kola, Andrzej, Belzec: The Nazi Camp for Jews in the Light of Archaelogical Sources, Warsaw-Washington, Council for the Protection of Memory of Combat and Martyrdom and US Holocaust Memorial Museum, 2000.

Kübler-Ross, Elisabeth, Death: The Final Stage of Growth, New York: Simon & Schuster Inc., 1975.

Reder, Rudolf, Belzec, Krakow: Judaica Foundation Auschwitz-Birkenau State Museum, 1999.

Reinke, Renate, Antworte, Mensch!, Bremen: Schwiefert, 1968.

Sacher, Howard M., A History of Jews in the Modern World, New York: Alfred A. Knopf, 2005.

Schmalhausen, Bernd, A Man of Courage in an Inhuman Time: Berthold Beitz in the Third Reich, Jerusalem: Yad Vashem, 2006.

Schwarz, Chris, Photographing Traces of Memory: A Contemporary View of the Jewish Past in Polish Galicia, Krakow: Galicia Jewish Museum, 2005.

Wiesel, Elie, And the Sea Is Never Full: Memoirs 1969 – New York: Alfred A. Knopf, 1999.

PERMISSIONS' ACKNOWLEDGMENTS

The authors would like to acknowledge and thank the following:

Extract on p. 40 from Ordinary Men: Reserve Police Battalion 101 and the Final Solution in Poland by Christopher R. Browning, Copyright © 1992, 1998, reproduced by kind permission of HarperCollins Publishers, New York.

Extract on pp. 42 from The Righteous Among the Nations – Berthold Beitz, published by Yad Vashem (http://yad-vashem.org.il/ righteous/bycountry/germany/beitz_berthold.html), reproduced by permission of Yad Vashem.

Extract on p. 46 from Belzec by Rudolf Reder, Krakow: Judaica Foundation Auschwitz-Birkenau State Museum, 1999.

Extract on p. 64 from Lokomotywa by Julian Tuwim as translated by Walter Whipple, reproduced by kind permission of Walter Whipple.

Extract on p. 80 from ›The Final Report by Katzmann, Commander of the SS and Police in the District of Galicia, On »The Solution of the Jewish Problem« in Galicia, 30 June 1943‹, published by Yad Vashem (http://yad-vashem.org.il/about_holocaust/documents/ part2/doc159.html), reproduced by permission of Yad Vashem.

Extract on p. 86 from Conscience and Courage by Dr Eva Fogelman, published by Doubleday, a division of Random House, Inc., Copyright © 1994, reproduced by kind permission of Random House, Inc.

Extracts on pp. 153–154 from Antworte, Mensch! [Answer, People!] by Renate Reinke, reproduced by kind permission of Renate Reinke.

Extract on p. 180 from Sabina, My Friend by Ruth Wilson, reproduced by kind permission of Ruth Wilson.

Extract on p. 277 from Memorial to the Murdered Jews of Europe by Peter Eisenman, published by Nicolaische Verlagsbuchhandlung GmbH, Copyright © 2005, reproduced by kind permission of Peter Eisenman.

PICTURE CREDITS

Archiv Dr. Bernd Schmalhausen: 4
Archiv für Philatelie der Museumsstiftung Post und Telekommunikation, Bonn: 23
Howard Moffat, AUSTIC: 2
Berthold Beitz: 22
Rita Braun: 24
Deutscher Bundestag, Berlin: 50
Wojciech Kryński: 46
Boris Mehl: 1, 49
MMCD NEW MEDIA GmbH, Düsseldorf: 54, 55, 56, 57
Muzeum Regionalne im. dr Janusza Petera w Tomaszowie Lubelskim: 43, 44
Helmut Schiffmann: 45
Staatsarchiv Bremen: 14
Stiftung Denkmal: 52, 54, 55
Peter Wieler: 56
Tomasz Wiśniewski Coll.: 3
United States Holocaust Memorial Museum, Washington D. C.: 10, 12,16,18
Sabina van der Linden-Wolanski: .... all others
Żydowski Instytut Historyczny im.
Emanuela Ringelbluma w Warszawie: .... 30 (sygn. 1325 AJDC, Nr. 63), 32

3 and 4: Borysław, around 1930: wooden oil rigs dominated the town's skyline and the countryside on the edge of the Carpathian Mountains. This part of eastern Galicia became known as the Polish ›Texas‹.

5: Sabina's grandparents Chana and Joel Kulawicz, around 1930

6: Sabina's father, Fischel (›Filip‹) Haberman, around 1920

7: Sabina's mother Sala Haberman and her brother Josef (›Josek‹), around 1927

8: Borysław, around 1932: Sabina with her nanny Katarzyna (›Kasia‹)

9: Borysław, around 1932: the siblings Sabina and Josef

10: Borysław, around 1936: Sala Haberman (centre) with Sabina, Josef and a friend, Frau Herzfeld, in their ›Sunday best‹

11: Borysław, around 1935: Sabina (back, third from left) and classmates in traditional folk costumes standing under a banner featuring the slogan: »The more schools we have, the better citizens we have.«

12: Borysław, around 1941: Josef Haberman (third from right) and his friend Imek Eisenstein (squatting) with members of the Zionist youth organisation *Hashomer Hatzair* (Guardians of Zion)

13: Certificate for Sabina Haberman, signed by Berthold Beitz (1913–2013) and dated 9 November 1942. This faked proof of her employment and residence afforded her a certain degree of protection from the SS.

14: The Borysław oilfields, 1943

15: Borysław ghetto, 20 January 1943: Josef Haberman (far right) celebrates his 19th birthday. From left to right: Rolek Harmelin, Ducek Egit, Sabina, Imek Eisenstein

16: Borysław ghetto, 20 January 1943: Josef Haberman (front) with his friends. Imek Eisenstein (far right) was Sabina's boyfriend at the time.

17: Sabina's diary entry on the day of Josef's birthday party. She described the mood as »very forced« in view of the loss of their mother a few months previously.

18: Borysław, 1943: Sabina (back left, head turned away) and other Jews arrested after their hiding place was discovered.

19: The hiding place located under a rabbit hutch with a pile of clothes, bedding, some bread and crockery visible. It was cleared out by members of the Ukrainian militia and the Viennese municipal police force.

20: Note from Mendzio Doerfler to his friends (»Dear ones«), probably written in June 1944, informing them of the death of Lonek Hoffman

21: Lonek Hoffman, a friend of Josef Haberman and Mendzio Doerfler. He played a major role in constructing camouflaged hiding places in the area around Borysław.

22: Galicia, January 1943: Berthold Beitz, business manager of the *Carpathian Oil Company* in Borysław

23: Colour sample of a stamp for the Government General featuring an oil refinery. The stamp was probably due for issue at the end of 1944 but never went into circulation.

24: During the German occupation Edmund Blum assumed a non-Jewish identity under the surname ›Machnicki‹ and hid other Jews, including Sabina.

25: Borysław, 2 September 1945: Róża, the cousin of Sabina's first boyfriend Imek, remained one of Sabina's closest friends right up until Sabina's death in 2011.

26: Borysław, 1944: Sabina at the age of 17, following her liberation

27: Borysław, 1944-45: Sabina (right), Nina and Luka Fleischer with Red Army soldiers

28: Poland, late 1946: Sabina's ›first proper boyfriend‹, Janek (left), an officer with the Polish People's Army

29: Wałbrzych, around 1948: Sabina with her friend Anda Katz, who had been in hiding with her in the ›Machnickis‹ cellar in Borysław

Wojewódzki Komitet Żydów w Polsce
　　na Dolny Śląsk
Wrocław, ul. Włodkowica 5.
Wydział E"id i Ziomkowstw

Wrocław, 22.IV.1947.　63

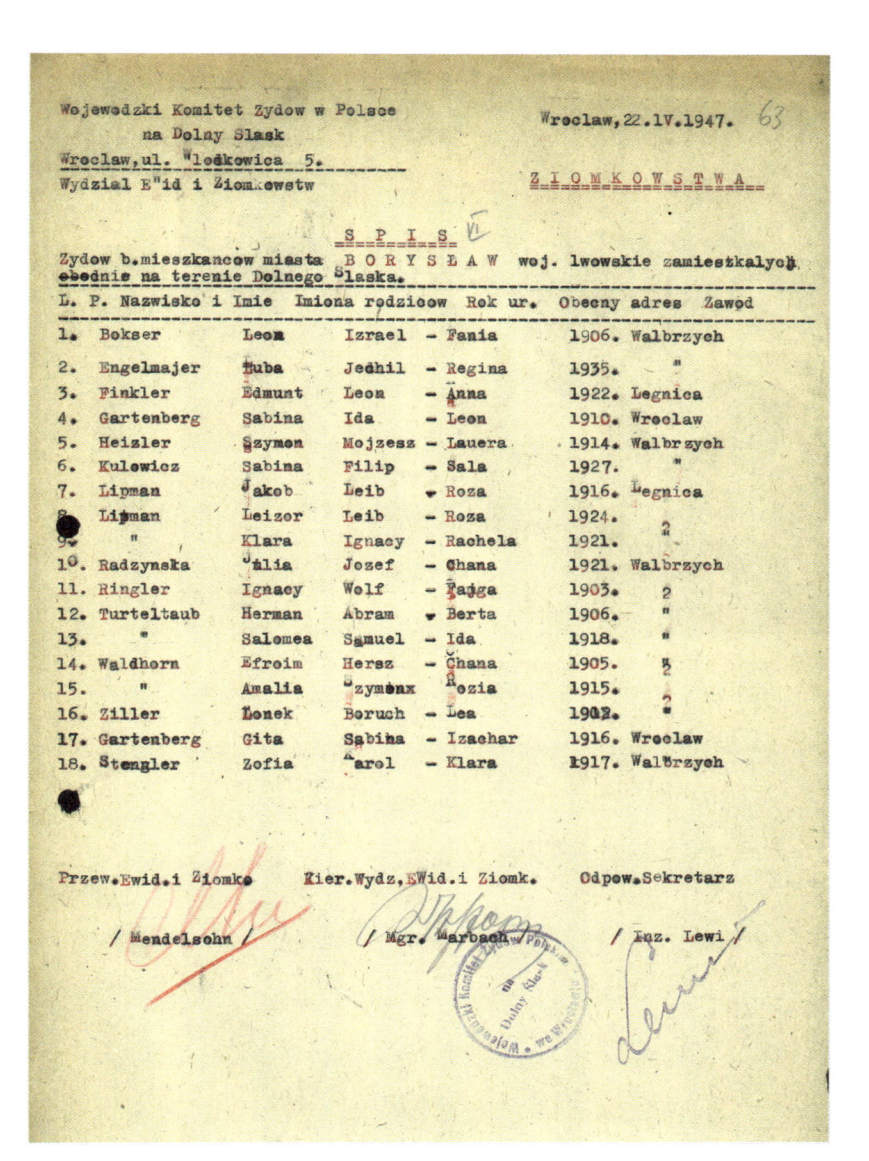

ZIOMKOWSTWA

S P I S VI

Żydów b. mieszkańców miasta BORYSŁAW woj. lwowskie zamieszkałych obednie na terenie Dolnego Śląska.

L.P.	Nazwisko i Imie	Imiona rodziców		Rok ur.	Obecny adres	Zawód
1.	Bokser Leon	Izrael	– Fania	1906.	Wałbrzych	
2.	Engelmajer Huba	Jechil	– Regina	1935.	"	
3.	Finkler Edmunt	Leon	– Anna	1922.	Legnica	
4.	Gartenberg Sabina	Ida	– Leon	1910.	Wrocław	
5.	Heizler Szymon	Mojżesz	– Laura	1914.	Wałbrzych	
6.	Kulewicz Sabina	Filip	– Sala	1927.	"	
7.	Lipman Jakob	Leib	– Roza	1916.	Legnica	
8.	Lipman Leizer	Leib	– Roza	1924.	"	
9.	" Klara	Ignacy	– Rachela	1921.	"	
10.	Radzynska Ulia	Jozef	– Chana	1921.	Wałbrzych	
11.	Ringler Ignacy	Wolf	– Fajga	1903.	"	
12.	Turteltaub Herman	Abram	– Berta	1906.	"	
13.	" Salomea	Samuel	– Ida	1918.	"	
14.	Waldhorn Efroim	Hersz	– Chana	1905.	"	
15.	" Amalia	Szymon	– Rozia	1915.	"	
16.	Ziller Lonek	Boruch	– Lea	1902.	"	
17.	Gartenberg Gita	Sabina	– Izachar	1916.	Wrocław	
18.	Stengler Zofia	Karol	– Klara	1917.	Wałbrzych	

Przew. Ewid. i Ziomko　　　Kier. Wydz. Ewid. i Ziomk.　　　Odpow. Sekretarz

/ Mendelsohn /　　　/ Mgr. Harbach /　　　/ Inz. Lewi /

30: List of Jews from Borysław belonging to the ›Jewish voivodeship committee in Lower Silesia‹ in Wrocław, 22 April 1947. Sabina is number 6 on the list, with an address in Wałbrzych.

31: Wrocław, 1947: sale of Jewish and Yiddish newspapers

30: Dzierżoniów (Lower Silesia), around 1946: Jewish people ›repatriated‹ from the Soviet Union

33: Sabina with her Alsatian, Dolma, in Wałbrzych

34: Sabina (dressed in a trouser suit) with colleagues at the wood factory in Kłodzko

35: Nina Heilig, Sabina and her husband Zdenek in Lower Silesia, around 1948

36: Paris, 1949: Sabina Wolanski and her husband Zdenek (wearing a scarf). She is dressed in ›that season's sensation‹, a bikini.

37: Sydney during the 1950s: Sabina and Zdenek in the showroom of their first business venture, a company selling clip-on ties

38: Sabina with her third husband, Adrian van der Linden, 1968

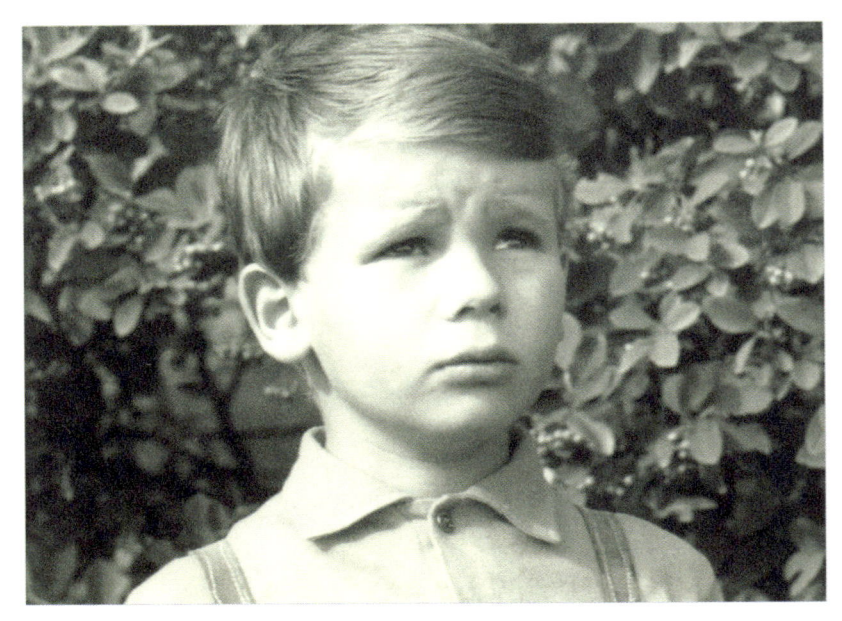

39: Phillip Wolanski, Sabina's son, at the age of seven

40: Sabina with her daughter Josephine, around 1960

2× 14jährige verlor Vater und Bruder

„Hildebrand ließ sie töten" — Auch Mutter wurde erschossen

Die erschütternde Leidensgeschichte der heute 36jährigen Sabina Wolanski aus Sydney in Australien stand gestern im Mittelpunkt des Judenmord-Prozesses gegen den 64jährigen ehemaligen SS-Obersturmführer Fritz Hildebrand. Vater und Bruder der Zeugin, der 46jährige Kaufmann Fischl Habermann und sein 20jähriger Sohn Josef, waren am 19. Juli 1944 angeblich auf Befehl des Angeklagten im Zwangsarbeitslager Boryslaw von drei SS-Männern nach einem Fluchtversuch erschossen worden. Mit ihnen zusammen wurde auch der jüdische Lagerinsasse Immanuel Derfler getötet.

Die damals 14jährige Zeugin hatte nach ihren Angaben von der Ermordung ihres Vaters und ihres Bruders aus dem Munde anderer Leidensgenossen erfahren, als sie von der Arbeit ins Lager zurückgekehrt war. „Zuerst wollte man mir davon überhaupt nichts erzählen, aber ich las aus den Gesichtern meiner Freunde, daß etwas Furchtbares geschehen sein mußte. Dann erfuhr ich die Wahrheit. Ich wollte zu Hildebrand gehen und ihn auffordern, mich ebenfalls erschießen zu lassen — mein Leben schien sinnlos geworden zu sein", berichtete Sabina Wolanski unter Tränen. Man habe sie jedoch davon abgehalten.

Die ihr gegebene Schilderung von der Erschießung deckte sich genau mit den Angaben anderer Überlebender, die Zeugen der Exekution geworden waren.

Zuvor hatte Sabina Wolanski von der Festnahme ihrer Mutter im Getto von Boryslaw berichtet. Sie sei damals elf Jahre alt gewesen und habe sich angsterfüllt an den Rock ihrer Mutter geklammert. SS-Leute hätten sie jedoch zurückgestoßen und die Mutter mit etwa 600 Juden in das Kino „Collosseum" gebracht. Von dort aus sei ihre Mutter zur Erschießung abtransportiert worden. Sie selbst sei später ins Lager Boryslaw gekommen.

„Als Hildebrand 1943 Kommandant wurde, da wußten wir, was uns erwartet. Er hatte in Mensinger einen furchtbaren Adjutanten gefunden, der jede Gelegenheit nutzte, um Juden zu erschießen oder zu mißhandeln", sagte die Zeugin. Ihr sei es unverständlich, wie Hildebrand diese ganzen Taten vor seinem Gewissen verantworten könne. Die Zeugin war nach der Ermordung ihres Vaters und ihres Bruders aus dem Lager geflüchtet.

M. H.

41: Newspaper article on the evidence given by Sabina at Bremen regional court on 20 February 1967

42: Bremen, 13 May 1967: Friedrich Hildebrand on the final day of the trial. He was sentenced to life in prison.

43 and 44: Belzec after 1944: the grounds of the former camp following the arrival of the Red Army. The SS had attempted to erase all traces of the extermination camp.

45 and 46: Belzec, June 2002 and summer 2005: the memorial site before and after the construction of the new memorial and museum

47: Borysław-Mraźnica, 1993: Sabina at the gates of the former forced labour camp of the Carpathian Oil Company

48 Borysław, 1993: Sabina with her children at the site where she witnessed the final deportation of Jews from Borysław to Auschwitz in 1944

49: Berlin, 10 May 2005: Sabina standing next to the Federal President, the President of the Federal Constitutional Court and the President of the Bundestag

50: Berlin, 10 May 2005: speaking at the inauguration of the Memorial to the Murdered Jews of Europe

51: Sabina with her daughter Josephine, her son Phillip (hidden) and her grandson Remy Dennis in front of the section on her family in the Information Centre of the Memorial to the Murdered Jews of Europe, May 2005

52: Berlin, 13 September 2006: Sabina Wolanski on another visit to the Memorial to the Murdered Jews of Europe while preparing her autobiography

53: Sydney, 2007: Sabina and her family celebrating the 30th anniversary of her ›unwedded bliss‹ with Kjeld Hansen

54: Sabina holding the German edition of her memoirs in front of the section telling her family's story in the Information Centre, May 2010

55: Book launch and reading with Dagmar Manzel in the Australian Embassy in Wallstrasse, Berlin, 11 May 2010

56: Villa Hügel, Essen, 17 May 2010: Sabina meeting the then 97 year-old Berthold Beitz, who had saved her life

Abb. 57: Poland following the Potsdam Agreement (1945). The dotted line shows the Polish border in August 1939.

Stiftung
Denkmal für die
ermordeten Juden
Europas